Christopher O'Donnell OCarm

Love in the
Heart of the Church

VERITAS

First published 1997 by
Veritas Publications
7-8 Lower Abbey Street
Dublin 1

Copyright © 1997 Christopher O'Donnell OCarm

ISBN 1 85390 391 4

British Library Cataloguing
in Publication Data.
A catalogue record for
this book is available
from the British Library.

Cover design by Bill Bolger
Printed in the Republic of Ireland by Betaprint Ltd, Dublin

Contents

Dedicated in thanksgiving to Thérèse of Lisieux
with gratitude to the Carmels of
Firhouse, Kilmacud and Knock
who taught me much about Thérèse
and with special thanks to
John Madden OCarm, an astute reader,
and to Fiona Biggs, a patient editor.

Abbreviations

LastConv   *Her Last Conversations.* Trans. J. Clarke (Washington: ICS, 1977). Day, month, entry are given from critical edition followed by page in Clarke translation as well as reference to *Oeuvres complètes.*

Letters   *Letters of Saint Thérèse of Lisieux.* Trans. J. Clarke. 2 vols. (Washington: Institute of Carmelite Studies, 1982, 1988). The date of the letter is given followed by the enumeration LT 1-266 of the critical edition, the volume and page from the Clarke edition and the *Oeuvres complètes.*

PO and PA   *Procès de béatification et canonisation de sainte Thérèse de l'Enfant-Jesus et de la Sainte-Face.* Vol. 1 – *Procès informatif ordinaire;* Vol. 2 – *Procès apostolique* (Rome: Teresianum, 1973, 1976).

OeuvC   *Oeuvres complètes. Textes et dernières paroles* (Paris: Cerf-Desclée de Brouwer, 1992). Texts of critical editions.

PN   *The Poetry of Saint Thérèse of Lisieux.* Trans D. Kinney (Washington: Institute of Carmelite Studies, 1995). The poem number, PN 1-54/PS 1-8 from critical edition and stanza is given followed by reference to Kinney translation and *Oeuvres complètes.*

Pri *Prayers of Thérèse.* The number Pri 1-21 is given from critical edition, followed by reference to *Oeuvres complètes.* An English translation is forthcoming.

RP *Recréations pieuses.* Eight playets written by Thérèse for community recreation. English translation forthcoming.

SSoul *Story of a Soul: The Autobiography of St Thérèse of Lisieux.* Trans. J. Clarke (Washington: Institute of Carmelite Studies, 1976). The manuscript reference is given first, followed by the pages in Clarke and *Oeuvres complètes.*

Thérèse, O'Mahony C. O'Mahony, ed. *St Thérèse of Lisieux by Those Who Knew Her* (Dublin: Veritas, 1975). Mostly texts from the diocesan inquiry (PO above).

Translations from PO, PA, Pri and RP are by author.

Thérèse was very fond of capitalisation, underlining, ellipsis points (...) and exclamation marks. These are reproduced in quotations, with underlinings being replaced by italics.

PART ONE

THE CHURCH AND THÉRÈSE

Chapter One

The Faces of Thérèse

St Thérèse of Lisieux, the Little Flower, is one of the most popular saints of our time. Yet there is no agreement about the 'real' Thérèse.[1] There are many images in art and literature; there are many presentations of her authentic spirituality. Some reject her as a pious figure with no relevance for today and its problems; others, like the American social activist, Dorothy Day, found Thérèse to be a profound inspiration for a dynamic life. Whilst some people are turned off by the pious and rather effusive style of her writings, many bishops and serious theologians have advocated that she be added to the ranks of the Doctors of the Church – an élite group of thirty-two saints who are venerated by the Church as its major teachers.

Pictures and images
There have been many faces of Thérèse.[2] We find her portrayed in statues and pictures, in a variety of styles from contemporary abstract depictions to pietistic kitsch in dreadful taste. Indeed, we had to wait until 1961 before two annotated volumes of authentic undoctored photographs were published.[3] Then we saw a different visage of Thérèse: for some not as attractive, perhaps, as the pictures of the Little Flower: she had a rather plain face but with a strong jaw that conveyed a force of character hitherto not conveyed in portraits or art.

The autobiography
But there are also many faces in biographies and studies which show enormous variation. There are also the faces to be seen in

the various editions of her writings. She had written three accounts of the graces which the Lord had bestowed on her; these comprise what is known as her autobiography, commonly called *[The] Story of a Soul*. She did not undertake this work on her own initiative. The first part, now usually called Manuscript A, was written at the command of her older sister Pauline, then prioress, with the Carmelite name of Mother Agnes. The second part, Manuscript B, consists of two letters to her eldest sister Marie, called Sister Marie of the Sacred Heart. When she was no longer superior Mother Agnes got round her successor, the formidable Mother Gongazue, to have Thérèse complete her biography. Thérèse worked on this part, Manuscript C, only for a month as her strength rapidly gave out. She left this third part uncompleted when she was moved to the infirmary on 8 July 1897; she died about eleven weeks later on 30 September.

Thérèse herself became gradually aware that her writings would have some importance. She told her sister Mother Agnes two months before she died to be careful in speaking about it, lest its publication be hindered.[4] It is also clear that Thérèse appointed Mother Agnes to take care of the text after her death. The latter affirmed this under oath at the beatification process. Mother Agnes stated that one day, commenting on the number of interruptions she had from well-wishing sisters, Thérèse said:

> I am writing about charity, but I have not been able to do it as well as I would have liked to; in fact, I couldn't have done it worse if I'd tried. Still I have said what I think. But you must touch it up, for I assure you it is quite a jumble… Mother, whatever you see fit to delete or add to the copybook of my life, it is I who have added or deleted it. Remember that later on, and have no scruples about it.[5]

It is also clear that the inspiration to publish the three manuscripts also came initially from Mother Agnes.[6] But it must be admitted that she carried out her editorial duties somewhat too lavishly. She claimed before the beatification process in 1910 that

> There were some changes, but of little importance *(mais de peu d'importance)* and which do not change the general and substantial sense of the narrative.[7]

In fact there were seven thousand changes and what amounted in places to a rewriting of the text. Mother Agnes worked quickly and the volume was published as *The Story of a Soul* in a limited edition of two thousand copies a year and a day after Thérèse's death.

Many people have judged Mother Agnes over-harshly. She did have the commission from her late sister to correct the text. She herself was a simple contemplative with little formal education or sophistication who was taking the very unusual step of having family and community memoirs published. Her sense of what it would be inappropriate to release to the world about her own Martin family and about the Lisieux community was conditioned by the religious and bourgeois culture into which she was born and in which she lived. The editor of the critical edition of the manuscripts, Father François de Saint-Marie, was undoubtedly right in stating that the writings of Thérèse could not have been published at that time in their original form.

There was, moreover, another irregularity. Mother Gonzague, then prioress, insisted that the text of the first part be altered so that it would appear that all three parts of the *Story of a Soul* were addressed to her rather than to Thérèse's sister Pauline, or Mother Agnes, who was the original recipient of the first part. We can understand why she would have judged that it would be better not to have the published work as a family memoir. There may have been some less admirable motivation also involved: Mother Marie de Gonzague surely found four sisters and a cousin in the one community somewhat threatening; she seems on occasion to have given way to some simple jealousy along with a touch of vanity. What is now the second part of the autobiography, the letters to her sister Marie (Ms B), appeared as an appendix. At the process for beatification it was agreed that an authentic copy of the life be sent to Rome, which was done in 1911.

For most of her life Mother Agnes continued to peruse the manuscripts of her sister and for several decades made stylistic changes, modified the orthography and the punctuation, which in some places affected the meaning of the text. Indeed it was she who introduced the phrase 'way of spiritual childhood' into Thérèse's works in 1907. Even though Thérèse may not have used the expression, most scholars will agree that it is a legitimate way of presenting her doctrine; at any rate it is not original, as it is found a few centuries earlier in the French school of spirituality.[8] But the exposition of Thérèse is quite original.

Scholars became increasingly dissatisfied about not being in possession of a fully authentic text. In 1947 the Superior General of the Discalced Carmelites wrote to Mother Agnes demanding the original text. Then aged eighty-six she could not face the task. It went against the convictions of her lifetime as guardian and in some sense interpreter of the text; moreover, she feared that many who had come to love *The Story of a Soul* would be disturbed. She left the task to her younger sister Céline, Sister Geneviève. A facsimile of the restored manuscript was published in 1956 and a transcription the following year. We now have a reasonably critical or authentic text of Thérèse's own writing.

In this history of the text we see the family of Thérèse and the Carmelite community of Lisieux at work in presenting their vision of Thérèse. The publication of the original text and of the untouched photographs gave rise to much criticism and some quite harsh judgement on those involved. A rather unpleasant example of this genre was the overly sensational *Two Portraits* by Etienne Robo.[9] He makes no allowance for the fact that the community of Lisieux was quite ill-prepared for having one of its members beatified within twenty-six years of her death, and canonised two years later in 1925. They did what they thought was best for the honour of Thérèse. With hindsight we can indeed be critical of their manipulation of her image and of the faces they portrayed; but the Lisieux Carmel was at most misguided rather than dishonest.

Early enthusiasm

The Story of a Soul was to prove enormously popular. Within a year the initial edition was sold out and a second edition of four thousand copies was issued in 1899. Within seven years it had appeared in English, Polish, Dutch, Italian and Portuguese. In one year alone (1910), the Carmel received 9,741 letters. By 1914 it was getting two hundred letters daily, and the autobiography was now available in Spanish and Japanese.

The local bishops of Bayeux were well disposed towards the Lisieux Carmel: they permitted the publication of the autobiography and allowed the introduction of Thérèse's cause. The first major statement on Thérèse from a Church authority was by Benedict XV who signed the formal decree about Thérèse's heroic virtue and spoke on her spirituality in August 1921. In the twenty-four years since her death, there had been an explosion of interest, veneration and prayer at the grassroots level of the Church.

This movement of popular enthusiasm would lead to her beatification and canonisation, to Pius XI naming her Patroness of the Missions equal in rank with St Francis Xavier (1927), to the blessing of the huge basilica at Lisieux (1937), to Pius XII naming her secondary patron of France on a par with St Joan of Arc (1944). Another sign of papal approval as well as of popular esteem is the fact that by 1976 the title of basilica was given by the Holy See to five churches dedicated to her, including one at Lisieux (1937).[10] To this can be added innumerable churches named in her honour throughout the world, and the presence of statues and shrines in countless other churches. All this is a reflection of the devotion of the entire Church, so many of whose members felt a deep empathy with a young contemplative Carmelite and sought her confidently as an intercessor.

The shower of roses

To an extent that is hard to judge, Thérèse herself had some inkling of her future destiny. We have already seen her care about her autobiography. In her last words which began to be recorded from the April before her death we have two of her most famous statements. When her eldest sister, Marie of the Sacred Heart, spoke of the sorrow they would have when she died, she replied: 'Oh, no, you will see; it will be like a shower of roses,' and then she added, 'After my death you will go to the mail-box and you will find many consolations.'[11] A few weeks later she said to Céline: 'I want to spend my heaven doing good on earth.'[12] On the same day writing her last letter to her courageous but deeply damaged sister, Léonie, she said: 'You want me to pray in heaven to the Sacred Heart for you. Be sure that I shall not forget to deliver your messages to Him and to ask all that will be necessary for you to become *a great saint*.'[13] We know that within two years Léonie had entered the Visitation Convent at Caen and in this, her fourth attempt to be a religious, she came into mature holiness.[14]

On the Feast of the Holy Cross just a fortnight before she died Thérèse was given a rose. She removed the petals one by one and pressed each to the wounds on a crucifix. When she noticed that the petals were slipping from her bed to the floor Mother Agnes states that she said quite seriously *(très sérieusement)*: 'Gather up these petals, little sisters, they will help you to perform favours *(faire des plaisirs)* later on... Don't lose any of them.'[15] The huge number of letters received by the Lisieux convent gave ample evidence that the shower of roses foreseen by Thérèse became a reality. In the early years they began to publish *Pluie de roses* (Shower of Roses, 1907-1925) – seven volumes testifying to favours received.

Lives and early studies

From very early on she became known as 'The Little Flower.' It distinguished her from the outset from the then better known St Teresa of Avila. But it has a basis in her own self-identity. She gives a formal title to the autobiography: 'Springtime Story of a Little White Flower Written By Herself and Dedicated to the Reverend Mother Agnes of Jesus.'[16] We know too that in all her writings flowers were one of her favourite images.

But this name is but one of the sources for the saccharine image that was soon to seize the public imagination. The activities of the Carmel and especially her own blood relatives inside and outside the cloister only continued what could be described as an anticipated canonisation by a group from within the Lisieux community. The existence of the volume called *The Last Conversations* seems to owe something to a conviction of the holiness of Thérèse and something to a family desire on the part of her sisters to recall her last sayings. This book, first issued as *Novissima Verba/Derniers Entretiens* in 1927, appeared in a satisfactory edition, that is full and undoctored, only in 1971.[17] The earlier editions were heavily censored and edited by Mother Agnes, and comprised only about half of Thérèse's last conversations with her three sisters Mother Agnes (Pauline), Sister Geneviève (Céline) and Sister Marie of the Sacred Heart (Marie) plus a few testimonies of other witnesses and some quotations from letters of Thérèse written during her last illness. In *The Last Conversations* the material recorded by Mother Agnes in the so-called 'Yellow Notebook' *(Le Carnet Jaune)* is more than half of the contents.

We can detect two attitudes in testimonies about Thérèse. One is that exemplified by one of her former novices, Sister Marie of the Trinity, who testified at the process for beatification in 1911:

During her life in Carmel, the Servant of God passed by

unnoticed in the community. Only four or five of the nuns, including myself, got close enough to her to realise the perfection hidden under the humility and simplicity of her exterior. For most of the nuns she was a very regular religious, always above reproach.[18]

A comparable comment was made by another of her novices, Sister Mary Magdalene:

> Generally speaking, the Servant of God was unknown and even misunderstood in the convent. Apart from some novices who were close to her, no one noticed the heroism of her life.[19]

Indeed it was only when her sister Pauline got round to reading the first part of *The Story of a Soul,* which she had commissioned whilst prioress, that she realised that there was something wholly exceptional about her youngest sister. It was then that she became determined to record Thérèse's sayings,[20] primarily for the family, including Léonie who was recovering from her third rejection in religious life (July 1895). It is unlikely that she had any premonition of the future of her sister, even though she now greatly admired her virtue.[21] She began the Yellow Notebook on 2 June 1897, but included some entries dating from April and May.

But it would seem that as Thérèse's death approached what we have called an attitude of anticipated canonisation began to take root among some in the community. In *The Last Conversations* we have many compliments paid her, and many references to her holiness and imminent entry to Heaven. Thérèse brushed these off, sometimes with a serious comment that deflected attention away from herself, sometimes with the gentle, wry humour that was characteristic of her attitude to herself. The changing stance of her own blood sisters, of her family outside as well of as members of the community was quite significant for the face of Thérèse that was soon to emerge from the Lisieux Carmel.

Later studies

After her death an enormous number of books and articles began to appear. Many of them portrayed a sugary figure evidencing a style of piety no longer attractive to many people in the late twentieth century. Nevertheless many of the earlier studies are not without value, even though they may be hard to read today. They allow us to grasp the feelings of the time of Thérèse's beatification, and they recall details and events that might otherwise have been forgotten. A recent study of Thérèse by A. Wolbold gives a useful outline of the kinds of literature that appeared on the saint in this century.[22]

Earlier biographies and other studies are unsatisfactory from several points of view. Some present the syrupy images that represented something of the 'official' version of the saint from the Lisieux Carmel. More seriously, others projected on to Thérèse their own psychological, spiritual and theological prejudices. But already, soon after her canonisation, serious studies were beginning to appear, most notably by two Dominicans, Fathers H. Petitot[23] and M.M. Philipon.[24]

The period after the Second World War was notable for several reasons. It saw the first publication of the remaining major document concerning Thérèse, the notes taken mostly during her novitiate by Thérèse's novice and older blood-sister Céline (Geneviève of the Holy Face).[25] From Lisieux also we have two journals, one popular – *Les annales de Sainte Thérèse,*[26] the other, a later supplement, being more theological and scholarly – *Vie thérésienne.*[27]

At the popular level we have the writings of Mgr Vernon Johnson, formerly an Anglican priest, who attributed his conversion to Catholicism to a chance reading of St Thérèse. He wrote much for a popular magazine, *Sicut Parvuli,*[28] the quarterly of the English branch of the Association of Priests of St Teresa of Lisieux, a pious union of priests established in Lisieux by the Holy See in 1933; many of these and other articles were gathered in various volumes.[29] These sound spiritual reflections of perhaps the best-known exponent of Thérèse's spirituality in the English-speaking world are characteristic of a new wave of more solid devotional writing that emerged after the War. There were many other such writings, often part biography, part reflection.[30]

On quite a different level we have the French theologian lecturing at the Lateran University in Rome, Father and later Mgr André Combes. We do not have complete information about the perplexing relations between him and the Lisieux Carmel, and we only know one side of the story. Nonetheless, what we can learn gives valuable insight into the problems and hesitations surrounding the image of Thérèse in the middle of this century.

Combes gave a theological course on Thérèse to the French faculties of Paris in 1947 on the occasion of the fiftieth anniversary of her death. At the same time he began to study her letters. Despite some initial apparent enthusiasm on the part of the Carmel, he was soon conscious of being fobbed off with incomplete letters and of being denied the possibility of adequate examination of the originals. He began to demand strenuously that the authentic writings be released. Relations between him and the Lisieux Carmel became more and more strained;[31] eventually he was denounced to Rome and commanded by an apostolic visitator to leave Lisieux as his presence there was disturbing the community. Combes has had, nonetheless, a most important place in Thérèsian studies. He was one of the first to use critical methods in dealing with her text, not unlike what scripture scholars were beginning to do in the Catholic Church at the time. He was careful to see the meaning of passages in their proper context and to examine carefully questions of vocabulary, style and possible influences.

We can understand how this new approach would have

seemed very threatening to Thérèse's sisters; it would have been destructive of the face of Thérèse which they felt to be the authentic one, the one of which they were the privileged guardians. His writings were more austere than the devotional ones to which they were accustomed; his theological acumen brought a new tone of scholarship into Thérèsian writings, one that at first sight did not give as much sustenance to piety as traditional presentations of the saint; his incessant demands for the full texts which the Lisieux Carmel did not want released seems to have led to some coolness in the relationship between influential figures in the convent and the scholar, and to much frustration on the part of the latter. Though pioneering work in need of occasional nuancing, the Combes' writings[32] are still valuable for an understanding of Thérèse, especially his *Introduction to the Spirituality of St Thérèse* which became two volumes in English when translated from French,[33] as well as other significant studies.[34]

More trusted apparently by the Lisieux Carmel was the Franciscan Father S.J. Piat who made a speciality of studying the family of Thérèse.[35] A most significant study of Thérèse in this period was the profound exploration in 1950 by the Swiss theologian, Hans Urs von Balthasar.[36] He revised it twenty years later, but did not substantially modify his views, even though some of them had been seriously questioned.[37] Balthasar was not only the most eminent theologian to have investigated Thérèse, but one who made a contribution whose importance can scarcely be exaggerated. He was among the first to see the life and teaching of Thérèse as a major source for theology and as a profound theological message for, and mission in, the Church. Thérèse exemplified one of the great themes of Balthasar's theology, one he shared with Karl Rahner, viz. the need to unite spirituality and theology. He had long regarded the split between the two, which occurred at the end of the thirteenth century, as disastrous for both theology and spirituality.

The next period was marked by the appearance of the original text of *The Story of a Soul,* which gave rise to many new studies. A very important work, originating in 1944, whose later editions took into consideration the newly available texts, was *The Hidden Face: A Study of St Thérèse of Lisieux,* by the German lay woman Ida Görres.[38] This set a new standard for biographies of Thérèse. Görres got behind the pietistic faces of the previous fifty years and, with the aid of German personalist psychology, she cut through the language and conventional interpretations. She did not suggest that any of the acts of Thérèse were in themselves necessarily great or heroic, but she showed with total clarity the genuine heroism of a life made up of utter fidelity in every little thing. New standards were also set by the astonishingly mature doctoral thesis of the Discalced Conrad de Meester which studied the evolution of Thérèse's Little Way, with great critical attention to the differing stages of her thought and to the specific chronology of her texts.[39]

From that time there have been many serious studies of every aspect of the life and thought of Thérèse. But there is still no critical biography, even though there are valuable books on her life. Four more recent studies should be noted. Firstly, a splendid pictorial study which was translated into English for the centenary.[40] Secondly, the article on Thérèse in the authoritative French dictionary of spirituality in 1991. This last is a good summary of her spirituality, its origins and influence. It has a fine selective bibliography of French sources and studies.[41] Thirdly, a fine popular biography by the Discalced Bishop of Lisieux, Guy Gaucher, who had long been a student of Thérèse, was reissued in paperback.[42] Fourthly, a magnificent corcordance of Thérèse's writings, published in 1996, which will be of inestimable value to future scholars.[43]

The centenary
As we celebrate the centenary of Thérèse's death it is appropriate

to look at her contribution to the life of the Church. Her discovery of her vocation as being 'love in the heart of the Church' is well known.[44] But what is not so well appreciated is the rich teaching about the Church that is to be found in her life and her writings. It is not, however, enough to study the great text which tells of her discovery. We need also to appreciate how she viewed the Church of her time, and then to see how she lived out her breakthrough. It will be obvious that even before she was able to articulate her sense of being 'love in the heart of the Church,' she already had this calling and lived it to an intense degree.

We therefore look at the Church of her time before considering her rich doctrine of love and of the Communion of Saints. These provide the necessary backdrop for investigating her rich ecclesiology, or understanding of the Church, which she located in the most ordinary circumstances of daily life. Such a study should show in a clearer light the profound theological genius of Thérèse, even though at all times we have to be aware of the need to interpret her thought carefully.

Chapter Two

The Church of St Thérèse

When we approach the writings of St Thérèse of Lisieux, we enter a world which is in many ways alien to us. Whilst we can recognise it as the modern world, and not the Middle Ages, the language and atmosphere nevertheless seem quite unfamiliar a century later. We continually encounter adjectives like 'sweet' and 'little', and Thérèse's favourite images such as flowers and a little bird. Her manuscripts are conspicuous for exclamation marks, capital letters and underlining (reproduced as italics in printed versions), as well as ellipsis points (...).* The cultural values of her family are quite bourgeois. Above all, her vision of the Church is one that we seem largely to have left aside since Vatican II. It is therefore important that we identify the Church of Thérèse so that we can see what in it is time-conditioned and possibly a needless barrier to approaching the saint. In this chapter we examine the Church of her time and ask if, and how, we might expect to find an ecclesiology, or theology of the Church, in her life and writings.

Background

In any presentation of the Church in France in the latter part of the nineteenth century it is not easy to find a starting-point. The identity of the French Church at that time had roots quite deep in the past. In Thérèse's writings we can find traces of hundreds of years of secular and Church history. She would scarcely have

---

* These are faithfully reproduced in the quotations cited in this volume.

been aware of them explicitly, except for her beloved St Joan of Arc (d. 1431), but they formed the culture in which she lived. In secular history we could go back to the time of Louis XIII (d. 1642) or even earlier. There was for nearly two centuries an attempt to strengthen France, and especially the monarchy. But from the point of view of the Church there were several ambiguous aspects. There was a tendency to emphasise the independence of the French Church and to strengthen the bishops against the papacy which gave rise to Gallicanism. Gallicanism thrived on an anti-Italian spirit aroused by the fact that important posts in the French Church were held by Italians. The tension between the bishops and the pope was finally resolved at Vatican I (1869-1870) with the definition of papal primacy and infallibility. There are echoes of this strand of French history in Thérèse's writings. She is strongly papalist and shares in a simple way the enthusiasm for the person of the pope which began under Pius IX (1846-1876)[1] and continued under Leo XIII (1878-1903) to whom she went on pilgrimage in 1887.

The contemporary history of France can be seen to have impinged quite substantially though indirectly on the Lisieux Carmel and the Martin family. The Third Republic came into existence in 1875. Almost immediately it showed itself hostile to the Church. For about fourteen years (1878-1892) there was an attempt at reconciliation between the Church and secularist aims of the Republic. The defeat of moderates of the Catholic party in the 1893 elections led to a hardening of attitudes, and even greater hostility from the State. Religious, the lower clergy and the middle classes at the time tended to see things from a rather black and white perspective; their views could be found in the newly founded national paper, *La Croix*. Faced with an unfriendly civil administration soon to be an active persecuting power, they adopted a citadel mentality.

In addition to general Church and secular history, several currents of spirituality were very significant for an understanding of Thérèse. The first was the French or Bérullian School of spirituality which can be seen to originate with Cardinal Bérulle (d. 1629).[2] This approach to the spiritual life laid great stress on the divine persons of the Trinity, the centrality of Christ, deep devotion to Mary and a profound concern for the spiritual and pastoral renewal of the priesthood. These four themes are dominant characteristics of all Thérèse's writings, even though her language and images are somewhat different.

The second current was Jansenism, called after Cornelius Jansen whose ideas were propagated after his death (1638).[3] A heretical movement grew up which was rigorist about morals and deeply pessimistic, stressing the unworthiness and sinfulness of the human condition. People were crushed by the difficulty of achieving salvation; reception of the Eucharist was discouraged. Apparitions of the Sacred Heart to St Margaret Mary Alacoque (1673-1675) were a significant counterforce to Jansenism. But the fact that daily Communion was not allowed until 1905 is reflected in Thérèse's joy at being allowed to communicate more frequently than was the norm of her time. During Thérèse's lifetime there were the first eucharistic congresses beginning with one in France at Lille in 1874; they became international at the same venue in 1881, this time with the formal blessing of Leo XIII.[4] Traces of the Jansenistic mentality were still around in the time of Thérèse, but her spirituality was far removed from it; she stressed love, the simplicity of the way to God and unbounded confidence in his mercy.

Another spiritual current was Quietism which had followers in France from the 1690s. This movement was a reaction against the over-organised and intellectual disciplines in the spiritual life which had been imported from the preceding century. It emphasised resignation and the pure love of God, but was excessive in its playing down of the human cooperation that must accompany the bestowal and reception of grace. One result of Quietism was to bring contemplation into disrepute. Once again, we can see

Thérèse's complete distancing of herself from an unhealthy approach to God. She tended to avoid the word 'contemplation.' She showed no interest in the analysis of the mystical states or even the classical descriptions of spiritual growth. But she took what is of value in the Quietist view, namely surrender or, in her word, 'abandonment'; she integrated it with a spirituality of practical love of God and others, and with a profound emphasis on the humanity as well as the divinity of Christ.

A fourth spiritual current was Pietism. When the whole notion of revelation and of the Christian religion was attacked firstly in the name of reason by the Enlightenment, and later by agnostic Liberalism, the Church was seriously lacking in a credible response. Its reaction was to retreat from science, philosophy and politics, concentrating on piety and devotions. It was not a good time for theology in France. We need also to take account of the French Revolutions of 1789 and 1830 which became progressively anti-clerical and antagonistic to the Church. The response was a withdrawal from the world to a certain glorying in the spiritual goodness of the Church.

This pietistic answer to the challenge of the world finds echoes in Thérèse's culture of the late nineteenth century and is indeed one of its weaknesses. From reading her works we would scarcely suspect that there were controversies raging outside the Church, or that the issues involved were important. Her Church was largely a closed system; she managed, however, to avoid the worst limitations of Pietism. Thus we note that she was not attracted to prayer-books or many devotions, preferring the scriptures. She shows, however, quite a number of the externals of spirituality which marked her age.

It would be easy to exaggerate this sense of the Church turned inward on itself. We must not forget the strong missionary movement of the nineteenth century which accompanied or preceded French colonial expansion. Thérèse was enormously concerned with the missions. Indeed, at one time before her health collapsed, it was proposed that she go to the Carmel in Saigon. Her missionary brothers were of great importance in her eyes.

The Church of Thérèse
The family of Thérèse showed some of the narrow traits of the contemporary French Church. Despite being middle class and comfortable, the Martins were marked by a certain aloofness from the world, though Thérèse's uncle, Isidore Guérin, became quite involved in politics, supporting Catholic and monarchist positions. For Thérèse's circle the Church was the secure refuge from an evil world. The Vatican I statement on the Church (1870) well reflects the atmosphere of her family:

> The Church by herself, with her marvellous propagation, eminent holiness and inexhaustible fruitfulness in everything that is good, with her Catholic unity and invincible stability, is a great and perpetual motive of credibility and an irrefutable testimony of her divine mission.[5]

This view of the Church accords with the French pilgrimage which Thérèse, her father, Louis Martin, and her sister Céline, made to Rome in 1887. Its occasion was the priestly jubilee of Leo XIII, but for the episcopal organisers, whatever about the pilgrims, it was intended much more as a gesture of solidarity with, and homage to, the pope, 'the prisoner at the Vatican'. The pilgrimage was clearly a modern rather than a penitential, medieval one: it had comfortable travel arrangements and sightseeing of religious and secular monuments. The 180 pilgrims, Thérèse tells us, were mostly nobility,[6] though there were seventy-four clergy. One senses that both Thérèse and her father would have preferred a more spiritual atmosphere for the four-week trip, as well as more religious behaviour on the part of the pilgrims. It was her only major exposure to laity and clergy outside her family circle, but she did not find those values which were natural and self-evident for the Martins. Even though this pilgrimage was quite Christian when compared with the harsh secular society that was emerging in France, for Thérèse it was a startling glimpse of 'the world'. In her autobiography we can see her mentality through the things she recalled as having seen; they are practically all religious. Her comment about Rome is most revealing: 'Six days were spent visiting the principal attractions of Rome; it was on the seventh I saw the greatest of them all, namely, Leo XIII.'[7]

The life of the Church at the time of Thérèse was rather devotional. There is no doubt about the high esteem in which the Mass was held, but the Church also laid a great deal of emphasis on novenas, shrines, pilgrimages, pious associations and acts of piety. The faith and institutions of the Church were accepted without question; the laity, whilst devout, was largely passive – obedience and submission were cardinal virtues at the time. We can find echoes of the late nineteenth century everywhere in the writings of Thérèse. Though she was formed by a particular religious culture, she overcame its limitations to a large extent. She never opposed her milieu; she did not have the necessary intellectual training to do so. But she transcended it: she did not allow the more superficial concerns of her time to be central. We can read her writings and be aware of course of their late nineteenth-century qualities. The core of her message nevertheless comes through, and it has a solid, perennial character that can enrich the Church in other places and times.

Thérèse and the Church of today
If we ask whether Thérèse has a message for the Church today, we immediately encounter a problem. We are living in what many would call a post-Christian age, or at any rate in a Church which has seen Vatican II and its aftermath. Our world is very different from that of a contemplative religious in a French provincial

27

town at the end of the last century. There is a serious danger of distorting Thérèse's thought, of reading into it what she did not intend, or of drawing conclusions from her work which are not apposite for our time. If we are to be faithful both to Thérèse and to the Church of our time, we have to be concerned with hermeneutics even though we might never use the word. Hermeneutics is the science of interpretation; it provides guidelines for contemporary readers about the way to approach a classical text and grasp its meaning.

There are three steps that we must take if we are to grasp the relevance of Thérèse's doctrine on the Church for today.[8] We need to perceive what she says and we need to explain it. These first two steps go hand in hand and can be taken together, even though they are distinct. The third step is to ask then the significance of this teaching for our time. We have several advantages over people of other decades. Since Vatican II we have a much richer idea of the Church than had previous readers of Thérèse, a much more profound understanding, indeed, than she herself could have had. Our interests in reading her writings will be different from those of people living at the time of her canonisation. Furthermore, we now have authentic texts and the benefit of a huge number of studies on the saint, her life and times, and her teaching.

But is it legitimate to search in Thérèse for teaching on the Church? Several writers on the topic of her ecclesiology have quoted the remark of the great ecclesiologist of the mid-twentieth century, Cardinal Journet: 'St Thérèse of Lisieux did not write anything explicitly about the Church.' However, he went on immediately to say:

> (S)he had a living knowledge of what the Church is – a knowledge underlying her writings, a vision of the Mystical Body, before whose splendour the theologian can but remain in silent adoration.[9]

These sentiments would encourage one to examine the vision of the Church in Thérèse and to test its validity for our time.

The difficulties of such an investigation should not be minimised. We have to keep in mind what we have seen of Thérèse's background and that of the French Church. It is, however, even more important to grasp the nature of her writings. They make up about a thousand pages in the one-volume French edition. But apart from her autobiography, which consists of three manuscripts addressed to three different Carmelite sisters, our legacy from her consists of fifty-four poems, 266 letters, eight playlets for community recreation and twenty-one prayers; there are also nearly two hundred pages containing her last conversations, recorded and annotated mostly by her sister, Pauline.

Just as the literary form of the various books of scripture has to be kept in mind for a correct exegesis, so too we cannot approach all of Thérèse's works in the same way. We must take account of the different types of writing and, as her spiritual development was so rapid, it can often be important to know the exact period in her short life to which a particular extract is assigned.

We might ask if there is room for yet another study of Thérèse and the Church. There seem to be so many. Yet the position noted by the Abbé Combes in a major study over twenty-five years ago still exists.[10] He noted that despite several studies which investigated her ecclesiology, very few got to its essence; most have still been content to repeat without much further reflection the saint's profound discovery of her vocation to be 'love in the heart of the Church'.

In studying Thérèse's vision of the Church and its relevance for us, we are engaged in a special kind of theology. If we want a systematic or organised theology of the Church, we should go to the theologians who have specialised in this area. We would also need to examine their sources, especially scripture, the councils and particularly Vatican II, the patristic writers, and various statements of the magisterium or teaching office of the Church. Such a search will give some kind of overall theology of the Church; it will have a certain completeness. But Thérèse, as Journet and many others have pointed out, never set out to write a theology of the Church. Indeed, Journet's remark (quoted above) alerts us to the specific kind of writing on the Church we can expect to find in Thérèse: it will be a vision of the Church from the point of view of spirituality.

We can broadly distinguish systematic or dogmatic from spiritual theology: the former is concerned with an expression and understanding of the truths of the faith; the latter considers these truths from the point of view of the journey to God and holiness. It is this second that we find in Thérèse. Though we do not obtain from her a comprehensive vision of the Church, we find partial statements about the mystery of the Church, insights that enriched her and are still important, perhaps even more important for the Church today. We seek what Journet called her 'living knowledge' of the Church. It is not the intellectual knowledge of the theologian.

In a different context we find a similar procedure operating in St John of the Cross. He wrote his *Spiritual Canticle* for a Carmelite prioress, Mother Ana de Jesús. He tells her in the prologue that the verses 'were obviously composed with a certain burning love of God' and asks:

> Who can describe in writing the understanding he gives to loving souls in whom he dwells? And who can express with words the experience he imparts to them? Who, finally, can explain the desires he gives them?[11]

He explains the difference between academic theology and what he calls 'mystical theology':

> Even though Your Reverence lacks training in scholastic theology, through which the divine truths are understood, you are not wanting in mystical theology, which is known through love and by which these truths are not only known but at the same time enjoyed.[12]

What St John calls 'mystical theology' has two characteristics. It is not the result of theological education or human endeavour, but a gift of God which comes about through love. Again it is experiential and not merely intellectual; it flows into the person's life.

Thérèse's position is similar. She did not study books on the Church, but through her love and prayer she received deep insights into the meaning of the Church. However, although systematic theology and spirituality are two distinct ways of coming to knowledge, they are not independent: it is the one mystery of the Church which theologians study and which Thérèse grasped through prayer and love. It is therefore legitimate for us to bring to her writings the insights that we receive from Church teachings or theology; neither will contradict the other.

Seeking the teaching of St Thérèse on the Church
An obvious starting-point would seem to be the places where Thérèse uses the word 'Church'. These are, however, surprisingly few. There are in total only fifty-seven occurrences of the word: of these nineteen are found in her autobiography, nine in her letters. In addition there are seven occurrences in the *Last Conversations*. Quite remarkable also is the fact that the majority of these usages belongs to the final eighteen months of her life (1896-1897). Indeed, fifteen of them are found in that intimate part of her autobiography called Manuscript B, the letter requested by her sister Marie, which is chapter nine in modern translations. It is, of course, in this section that she recounts her vocation as 'love in the heart of the Church'. We could compare

this frugal use of the word Church with the similarly surprising absence of the name 'Christ' – nineteen times only – and contrast it with the free use of 'Jesus' and 'God' – found 1,616 and 895 times respectively.

The Abbé Combes has rightly noted that Thérèse's ecclesiology is to be sought not only where she uses the word 'Church,' but also where she speaks about 'souls'; in her autobiography alone this latter word is found 326 times. But there are also other places in which we can seize her notion of the Church. We need to examine her missionary vocation and the letters to her missionary brothers, because these are intimately related to her sense of Church. There are also texts in which she speaks about what we would today call 'apostolate'; these too contain insights. Again, her statements on the Communion of Saints, on intercession and on martyrdom also reveal an implicit ecclesiology. There are other concepts too that we shall examine in due course.

But theology is not about names and words. It is above all concerned with a reality, in the case of the Church with a mystery. Our current understanding of the Church today is based largely on the Vatican II Constitution on the Church, *Lumen gentium.* We can note the main ecclesiological themes of this central document of the Council: Trinity, images of the Church, Body (chapter 1); people, priesthood, sacraments, charisms and communion (chapter 2), hierarchy (chapter 3), laity (chapter. 4); the nature of holiness (chapter 5); religious in the Church (chapter 6); the Church as pilgrim and its heavenly destiny (chapter 7); Mary as Mother and model of the Church (chapter 8). It is by studying these themes in Thérèse that we can obtain a rich grasp of her sense of the Church, one which has contemporary relevance. Thus, for example, the sixth chapter of the Constitution speaks of religious life in the Church. This teaching will alert us to take careful note of what Thérèse says about her contemplative vocation and how she understands it in relation to God and to others. Again, the contemporary theology of charism will allow us to see in Thérèse an exceptional gifting by the Holy Spirit, even though she never used the word. She clearly had the charisms which we might call discernment, knowledge, wisdom, prophecy, faith, as well as a Spirit-given ability to penetrate the scriptures.

An approach

If St Thérèse's literary output is to be examined for such themes, then the question arises about how the results might be ordered; it would not perhaps be satisfactory to present chronologically some five hundred texts with a note on the ecclesiological significance of each. But any ordering will be personal on the part of an individual and it risks a distortion of Thérèse's thought or at least of the internal balance of her ideas. Given, however, the necessity of some arrangement or classification of her doctrine, it is appropriate to try to avoid in so far as possible any misrepresentation. It would seem wise to present first her lived experience of the Church, the central vision found in Manuscript B, addressed to Marie. This has the advantage of being a late text, written just over a year before Thérèse died. If we keep this doctrine in mind, we will be less open to misinterpretation of other sayings. We will also see that this blinding insight merely articulated her commitment to living in the Church.

A further corrective against deformation of her thought will be the teaching that has emerged in and after Vatican II, especially what has been taught authoritatively. In this period the notion of communion has been presented by the Congregation for the Doctrine of the Faith as 'the core of the mystery of the Church and...a key for the renewal of Catholic ecclesiology.'[13] This truth will most easily be illustrated through drawing out the implications of Thérèse's living deeply the doctrine of the Communion of Saints. In turn this central doctrine about the Church is lived by Thérèse according to her teaching on merciful love and her Little Way.

Chapter Three

Love in Thérèse's Final Years

There are two paragraphs on the Church written in the 1970s by Hans Urs von Balthasar which have since become famous. In the first he speaks of the consequences of the imbalance of the male principle in the Church so that the Church has

> to a large extent put off its mystical characteristics, it has become a Church of permanent conversations, organisations, advisory commissions, congresses, synods, commissions, academies, parties, pressure groups, functions, structures and restructurings, sociological experiments, statistics, that is to say more than ever a male Church, if perhaps one should not say a sexless entity.[1]

In the second he warns:

> Christianity threatens imperceptibly to become inhuman. The Church becomes functionalistic, soulless, a hectic enterprise without any point of rest, estranged from its true nature by the planner. And because, in this masculine world, all that we have is one ideology replacing another, everything becomes polemical, critical, bitter, humourless, and ultimately boring, and people in their masses run away from such a Church.[2]

As is well known, Balthasar's solution was to look to the Marian principle of the Church. Whilst accepting the validity of this answer, it could also be suggested that we could look to the life, mission and writings of St Thérèse of Lisieux to seek a response to some of the problems facing the Church today.

It would be generally agreed that in some sense the core of Thérèse's message about the Church is to be found in Manuscript B, the account of God's graces to her that her sister Marie requested when she went on retreat in September 1896. But though the text is frequently cited, its meaning is not nearly so self-evident as people might suggest. It has been carefully studied by A. Combes who has shown that it is a profound and complex passage that needs quite an amount of teasing out and explanation.[3] Before engaging in some further analysis of this text which recounts Thérèse's discovery of her vocation to be love in the heart of the Church, we need to place it in the context of her life and concerns.

The final two years

The final two years of Thérèse's life were a time of special grace and of ever deeper intuition into her vocation and into love. An impression is given of accelerated spiritual insight and of a remarkable phase of interior growth. It is a period which surely gives the lie to the commonly presented picture of Thérèse as one who lived the Little Way, a totally ordinary existence devoid of any remarkable religious experiences.

After a long and very disturbing illness her father died on 29 July 1894. As her autobiography makes clear, Thérèse had no doubt about the sanctity of her father,[4] whom she called God's 'incomparable servant'.[5] She asked for, and received a sign which she specified: if opposition from one of the community to her sister Céline's entry were to cease, she would know that he had immediately gone to God. As Thérèse left the chapel the sister in question indicated her agreement to Céline's entry.[6] In August of that year Thérèse composed a poem, *Prière de l'Enfant d'un Saint* (Prayer of the Child of a Saint).[7]

During the autumn of the same year she discovered in a

scripture notebook which Céline had brought into the convent with her the two Old Testament texts on which she based her 'little way' (Pr 9:4; Is 66:13.12). She recounted this discovery twice in her autobiography.[8] Shortly afterwards, in January 1895, she did in fact begin part one of her life-story Manuscript A at the request of another sister, Mother Agnes, then prioress. We know from the testimony of Sister Teresa of St Augustine that as early as April of this momentous year, 1895, she had a presentiment of dying soon.[9]

On 6 June 1895, Trinity Sunday she made her Offering to Merciful Love, and some days later she received a mystical wound as she did the stations of the cross. In October of that year the first of her missionary brothers, Maurice Bellière, was confided to her; he was then a seminarian to whom she would write eleven letters. On 30 May 1896 she was given her second missionary brother, Adolphe Roulland. He was ordained a month later and visited the Carmel on 3 July before his departure to China. Thérèse afterwards sent him seven letters.

On the night before Good Friday of the same year, 1896, she had her first haemoptysis, which was an early sign of the tuberculosis which would eventually ravage her whole body. That Easter she entered into a dark night, the profound trial of faith that would last until her death eighteen months later.

During a private retreat in September 1896 she wrote the second part of her autobiography (Manuscript B), in which she recounted her discovery a month or two earlier of her role of being love in the heart of the Church. After that breakthrough she was led ever more deeply into the mystery of loving others, especially her sisters in the community. In April the following year she became gravely ill. On 3 June she was asked by the prioress to continue her life-story, but she was able to write for less than five weeks before weakness forced her to leave the text (Manuscript C) unfinished. Mother Agnes began to write down her various sayings from April 1897 until her death on 30 September 1897.

These two years of remarkable insights and graces are the context in which we see her mature vision of the Church. Her most profound account of her place in the Church needs to be seen against two intense experiences of love: the *Offering to Merciful Love* and her subsequent discoveries of the meaning of the love that is expressed in daily fidelity. These two occurrences are also ecclesial and have their own contribution to our understanding of her view of the Church and of her place in it.

The offering to merciful love

The most important experience of Thérèse in 1896 undoubtedly occurred on Trinity Sunday, when, as she wrote, 'I received the grace to understand more than ever how much Jesus desires to be loved.'[10] But in the manuscript, rather surprisingly, she then immediately began to write not about any active love on her part, but about allowing herself to be a victim of merciful Love. She carefully distinguished her approach from the 'victim spirituality' that was current in nineteenth-century France:[11] she stated that whilst she recognised the greatness and generosity of those who offered themselves 'as victims of God's justice in order to turn away the punishments reserved to sinners, drawing them upon themselves', she was not attracted to making such an offering. She felt that divine Love needed victims too: 'O my Jesus, let me be this happy victim; consume Your holocaust with the fire of Your Divine Love.'[12] She stated that from the time she made this offering, 'rivers or rather oceans of graces flooded my soul.'[13] She went on to describe the love which penetrated and transformed her.

She seemed for the moment to have forgotten her earlier statement that her experience was to realise how much Jesus wished to be loved. But she returned to it:

> Oh! how sweet is the way of Love! How I want to apply myself to doing the will of God always with the greatest self-surrender.[14]

Here Thérèse touches almost accidentally on a most profound truth that is rarely noted with such clarity elsewhere in the history of spirituality: the most intense love for God consists in letting him fully love us.

A study of the offering confirms this remarkable insight into divine love. It begins with her desire to love:

> O my God! Most Blessed Trinity, I desire to *love* You and make you *Loved,* to work for the glory (Fr. *glorification*) of Holy Church by saving souls on earth and liberating those suffering in purgatory. I desire to accomplish Your will perfectly and to reach the degree of glory You have prepared for me in Your Kingdom. I desire, in a word to be a saint, but I feel my helplessness and I beg you, O my God! to be Yourself my *Sanctity.*[15]

This complex statement shows Thérèse's love unfolding in various directions: to love God and make him loved; love for the Church in its members on earth and in purgatory. These desires are both the will of God and will lead to the glory for which she was predestined. She summarises it as a desire not just to be holy, but to be a saint (*je désire être Sainte*).

Her desires for holiness arose from her early youth, but was not always encouraged. She met a Jesuit, Fr Blino, perhaps in May 1890, her second year in Carmel, and confided to him: 'Father, I want to become a saint; I want to love God as much as St Teresa.' He, however, replied: 'What pride and what presumption. Confine yourself to correcting your faults, to offending God no longer, to making a little progress in virtue each day, and temper your rash desires.' She protested: 'I don't think they are rash desires,' but the father was not convinced.[16] In fact she held it as a spiritual axiom that God does not give us desires that cannot be fulfilled: this principle would lead her to her discovery of the Little Way,[17] and of her place in the

Church.[18] A year later, in October 1891, a community retreat was preached by a Franciscan, Fr Alexis Prou. Of the Lisieux community only Thérèse seems to have appreciated him; he set her free on the path of confidence and love to which she had felt attracted, but on which she had not dared advance.[19] Here in the *Offering to Merciful Love,* which we are considering, she understood that embarking on becoming a saint is the supreme way of loving God, of making him loved and of loving others in the Church.

In this oblation she proceeds in traditional language and sentiments to offer up the merits of Christ to the Father; the Son is seen as both Saviour and spouse. She then opens her vision to the merits of the saints in heaven and earth, especially the Virgin Mary. We note once again the vivid sense of the Communion of Saints which is such a feature of Thérèse's spirituality. She then again refers to her desires and her confidence that they cannot be in vain: 'I am certain, then, that You will grant my desires; I know, O my God! that *the more You want to give, the more You make us desire.*'[20]

She alludes only very briefly to the theme of reparation so current at her time: 'I want to console You for the ingratitude of the wicked.' She does not develop the point here. Within the wider context of her spirituality one can safely point to the way in which she would thus seek to console God, that is by saving the souls of those who have gone astray.

Then follows the important note of her thanksgiving for all the graces she has received, 'especially the grace of making me pass through the crucible of suffering.' This theme is found elsewhere, for example in one of her poems from February of that year (1895).[21] What is surprising perhaps is the fact that the intense suffering caused by the collapse of her health would not begin until ten months later, although she had begun to have persistent throat problems the previous spring. The suffering she refers to here and in the poem is almost certainly the pain of her father's illness, which she elsewhere describes as being inexpressible.[22]

A significant passage follows in which she looks to heaven, but also disclaims the mere acquisition of merits which was so much part of the accountancy type spirituality that was prevalent at her time:

> After earth's Exile, I hope to go and enjoy You in the Fatherland, but I do not want to lay up merits for heaven. I want to work for Your Love alone with the one purpose of pleasing You, consoling Your Sacred Heart, and saving souls that will love You eternally. In the evening of this life, I shall appear before You with empty hands, for I do not ask You, Lord, to count my works. All our justice is stained in Your eyes.[23]

Later in her short life even this vision is transcended as she looks to heaven itself as the opportunity of doing good on earth, a theme we shall examine in the next chapter on the Communion of Saints. It is difficult for us to grasp the radical nature of Thérèse's ecclesial vision, even if it is still not the way that most Christians would think. The spirituality of religious and laity at the time of Thérèse was individualistic, not to say rather selfish. There was enormous interest in storing up merits for one's future blessedness. Allied to this was a concern to accumulate indulgences and good works to shorten one's stay in purgatory. Thérèse has a sovereign disdain for such considerations and, as we shall see later, she declares herself uninterested in whatever purgatory might await her. She was, however, very concerned to help those who might be in purgatory. In the beginning of the *Act of Oblation* we saw that she expressed the desire 'to work for the glory of Holy Church... by liberating those suffering in purgatory'.[24] About her profession day she said, 'I wanted to deliver all the souls from purgatory and convert all sinners.'[25]

The *Act of Oblation* concludes with three main statements: the formal offering of herself as a victim, the highlights of which she stresses even in the way she writes the text; a vision of this offering as martyrdom; a sense of her offering being renewed throughout her life and into eternity:

> In order to live in one single act of perfect Love, I OFFER MYSELF AS A VICTIM OF HOLOCAUST TO YOUR MERCIFUL LOVE, asking You to consume me incessantly, allowing the waves of *infinite tenderness* shut up within You to overflow into my soul, and that thus I may become a martyr of your Love, O my God! May this martyrdom, after having prepared me to appear before you, finally cause me to die and may my soul take its flight without any delay into the eternal embrace of *Your Merciful Love.* I want, O my *Beloved,* at each beat of my heart to renew this offering to You an infinite number of times, until the shadows having disappeared I may be able to tell You of my *Love* in an *Eternal face to Face!* [26]

Her desire here 'to live in one single act of perfect Love,' recalls the first sentence of the *Offering* quoted earlier which states her desire 'to Love you and make you Loved'. Her way of loving God totally is to allow him to love her totally, 'to consume me incessantly'. She sees this as a martyrdom which will result in her dying from love. We will take up in a later chapter the theme of martyrdom which had so fascinated Thérèse from early youth. It is in this offering that she resolves its tensions and sees how her desire for martyrdom can indeed be fulfilled in love.

Thérèse's Act of Oblation was total and radical. Her sister Céline made it with her on 11 June. Another sister, her godmother, Marie (Sister Marie of the Sacred Heart) was disturbed by its implications.[27] Thérèse wrote a brief but important letter to her, emphasising that the act is for those who know their littleness, that one needs only confidence and love.[28]

Years later Marie recalled a conversation with Thérèse who

asked her whilst tedding the hay if she wanted to offer herself as a victim to the Merciful Love of God and that she answered:

> 'Certainly not. I am not going to offer myself as a victim; God would take me at my word, and suffering frightens me very much. In the first place, this word victim displeases me very much.' Then little Thérèse answered that she understood me, but that to offer oneself as a victim to God's love was not all the same thing as offering oneself to His justice, that I would not suffer more, that it was in order to love God better for those who did not want to love Him. She was so eloquent that I allowed her to win me over, and I am not sorry either.[29]

Here surely is a reversal of roles. Marie was the strong and wise guide when she acted as mother and spiritual director for Thérèse, especially in the latter's trial of scrupulosity. Now Thérèse is the mentor. Moreover, her explanation of the Act draws out significant ecclesial implications. The conversation may have taken place some months after Thérèse discovered the Act of Oblation. However, we cannot be sure of the exact phrasing of Thérèse, as our record is from a conversation which took place in 1934 between Marie and the infirmarian, Sister Marie of the Incarnation, and recounted by the latter.

The Act of Oblation was no mere devotional action. It summarised Thérèse's spiritual journey to date, and it was also a new point of departure. She noted its date as one of the great days of grace given by the Lord on the coat of arms which she had designed probably in the following January; other dates were her baptism, conversion, entry into Carmel etc. Moreover, within a week there was a dramatic divine acceptance of her offering: we shall later examine her profound mystical experience as she did the Way of the Cross.

Only a month before her death she stated: 'Very often, when

I am able to, I repeat my Act of Oblation.'[30] A week later she remarked to Sister Agnes: '...everything that I do, my actions, my looks, everything, since my Offering, is done through love.'[31] Hours before her death she said:

> All I wrote about my desires for suffering... Oh! it's true just the same! And I am not sorry for delivering myself up to Love... Oh! no, I'm not sorry; on the contrary!... Never would I have believed it was possible to suffer so much! Never! never! I cannot explain this except by the ardent desire I have had to save souls.[32]

She would utter only another few phrases before her death. The Offering summed up for her the whole meaning of her life.

Finally, her Act of Oblation is a later explication and development of the prayer she carried on her heart on the day of her profession: 'I ask You for nothing but peace and also love, infinite love without any limits other than yourself; love which is no longer I but You, my Jesus.'[33] The editors of the French omnibus volume of Thérèse's works noted that in her simple language she is asking for what is known in mystical theology as the transformation of love.[34]

My vocation is love

Clearly crucial for any understanding of the ecclesiology of Thérèse is a letter for her sister Marie, which forms part two of her autobiography (Manuscript B). The incident is one of the best-known in Thérèse and, though often studied, its full depths are not easily grasped.

The account was written in September 1896, just a year before Thérèse's death; the actual experience was a month or two earlier, in July or August. It was then just over a year after her Offering to Merciful Love. She recounts how she was reflecting on her vocation:

> To be your *Spouse,* to be a *Carmelite,* and by my union with You to be the *Mother* of souls, should this not suffice me? And yet it is not so. No doubt, these three privileges sum up my true *vocation: Carmelite, Spouse, Mother,* and yet I feel within me other *vocations.* I feel the *vocation* of the WARRIOR, THE PRIEST, THE APOSTLE, THE DOCTOR, THE MARTYR. Finally, I feel the need and the desire of carrying out the most heroic deeds for *You, O Jesus.* I feel within my soul the courage of the *Crusader,* the *Papal Guard,* and I would want to die on the field of battle in defence of the Church. I feel in me the *vocation of* the PRIEST. With what love, O Jesus, I would carry You in my hands when, at my voice, You would come down from heaven. And with what love I would give you to souls![35]

As we noted earlier, Thérèse had always been attentive to desires; she believed that 'God cannot inspire unrealisable desires'.[36] Hence she took seriously and followed the desires she felt within herself. They were a feeling about vocation, that is of the way God was drawing her; it was not, therefore, a self-induced desire. Moreover, it was not a simple wish, for she says 'my desires caused me a veritable martyrdom'.[37] The desires she felt at this time had a double focus: they were directed upward to God and outwards to others.

She considered four vocations. The first three are clearly ecclesial:

> I would like to enlighten souls as did the *Prophets* and the *Doctors.* I have the *vocation of the Apostle.* I would like to travel over the whole earth to preach Your Name and to plant Your glorious Cross on infidel soil. But *O my Beloved,* one mission alone would not be sufficient for me. I would want to preach the Gospel on all the five

continents simultaneously and even to the most remote isles. I would be a missionary, not for a few years only but from the beginning of creation until the consummation of the ages.[38]

Here there is a difference between the first two and the third. She would wish to be a prophet and doctor to enlighten others; in divine providence this was to be her gift after her death, in a way she could never have anticipated. The third, apostle or missionary, is absolute: 'I have the vocation of the Apostle.' But her missionary desires are unlimited and as such unrealisable in any obvious sense. She then goes on to the fourth vocation, that of a martyr. This too is unlimited; she would like all forms of martyrdom. Yet despite all the rational reasons against any realisation of these hopes, she is confident that God will answer them.

She then turned to chapter twelve of First Corinthians which speaks about charisms and love. The first thing to strike her was the diversity of vocations in the Church. Yet this did not satisfy her: 'The answer was clear, but it did not fulfil my desires and gave me no peace.'[39] Moving on to chapter thirteen, where Paul presents love as 'a more excellent way', she concludes:

> And the Apostle explains how all *the most PERFECT gifts* are nothing without *LOVE*. That *Charity is the EXCELLENT WAY* that leads most surely to God. I finally had rest. Considering the mystical body of the Church, I had not recognised myself in any of the members described by St Paul, or rather I had desired to see myself in them *all*. *Charity* gave me the key to my *vocation*. I understood that if the Church had a body composed of different members, the most necessary and most noble of all could not be lacking to it, and so I understood that the Church *had a Heart and that this*

Heart was *BURNING WITH LOVE. I understood it was Love alone* that made the Church's members act, that if Love ever became extinct, apostles would not preach the Gospel and martyrs would not shed their blood. I understood that LOVE COMPRISED ALL VOCATIONS, THAT LOVE WAS EVERYTHING, THAT IT EMBRACED ALL TIMES AND PLACES... IN A WORD THAT IT WAS ETERNAL! Then in the excess of my delirious joy, I cried out: O Jesus, my Love... my *vocation,* at last I have found it... MY VOCATION IS LOVE! Yes I have found my place in the Church and it is You, O my God, who have given me this place; in the heart of the Church, my Mother, I shall be *Love.* Thus I shall be everything, and thus my dream will be realised.[40]

The decisiveness of her repeated statement, 'I understood' (*je compris*) should be noted. It is a statement about an understanding reached in the past. The experience clearly reflects the kind of mystical understanding described by St John of the Cross, 'which is known through love and by which these truths are not only known but at the same time enjoyed.'[41] This understanding communicated to Thérèse is a grasp of the role of love in the Church and of her vocation to be that love, 'in the heart of the Church.' By love she will fulfil all the vocations to which she had aspired.

She goes on to develop the idea of love:

Why speak of a delirious joy? No, this expression is not exact, for it was rather the calm and serene peace of the navigator perceiving the beacon that must lead him to the port...I am only a child, powerless and weak, and yet it is my weakness that gives me the boldness of offering myself as *VICTIM of Your Love, O Jesus!* In times past, victims, pure and spotless, were the only ones accepted by the Strong and Powerful God. To satisfy Divine *Justice,* perfect victims were necessary, but the *law of Love* has succeeded the law of fear, and *Love* has chosen me as a holocaust, me, a weak and imperfect creature.[42]

Just afterwards she quotes from St John of the Cross a text that she had inscribed as the device or motto on her coat of arms, 'Love is repaid by love alone.'[43] Here she is clearly bringing together the Oblation to Merciful Love made just over a year earlier and a new comprehension of her vocation.

The meaning of love

But we must ask what the nature of that love is.[44] How are we to understand 'My vocation is love' and to see the meaning of the conclusion, 'in the heart of the Church, my Mother, I shall be Love'? We must proceed with care. We have to be alert to what Thérèse meant and probably understood, and what the theological realities might be, ones which she may not have articulated. We should look to her own explanations before attempting any further theological analysis.

Thérèse goes on in her text to develop the notion of love significantly. She is aware of the enormity of her longings, 'my desires of being everything, of embracing all vocations.'[45] She therefore invokes the angels and saints for a double spirit like Elijah (2 K 2:9) and to be adopted as their child. She is clearly startled by the audacity of her discovery: 'Jesus, I cannot fathom the depths of my request; I would be afraid to find myself overwhelmed [*accablée*] under the weight of my bold desires.'[46] She takes refuge in her weakness and places herself and her desires in the context of littleness and childhood and from that perspective she finds that she can love in small ways. We have to remember that she had discovered her Little Way two years earlier (autumn 1894); she thus had both an understanding and a language to express the meaning of her new identity and vocation.

> My excuse is that I am a *child,* and children do not reflect on the meaning of their words;...Well, I am the *Child of the Church* and the Church is a Queen since she is your Spouse, O divine King of kings... What this child asks for is Love. She knows only one thing: to love you O Jesus. Astounding works are forbidden to her; she cannot preach the Gospel, shed her blood; but what does it matter since her brothers work in her stead and she, *a little child,* stays very close to the throne of the King and Queen. She *loves* in her brothers' place while they do the fighting. But how will she prove her *love* since *love* is proved by works? Well, the little child will *strew flowers,* she will perfume the royal throne with their *sweet scents,* and she will sing in her silvery tones the canticle of *Love.*
>
> Yes, my Beloved, this is how my life will be consumed. I have no other means of proving my love for you other than that of strewing flowers, that is, not allowing one little sacrifice to escape, not one look, one word, profiting by all the smallest things and doing them through love. I desire to suffer for love and even to rejoice through love; and in this way I shall strew flowers before Your throne. I shall not come upon one without *unpetalling* it for You. While I am strewing my flowers, I shall sing, for could one cry while doing such a joyous action? I shall sing even when I must gather my flowers in the midst of thorns, and my song will be all the more melodious in proportion to the length and sharpness of the thorns.
>
> O Jesus, of what use will my flowers be to You? Ah! I know very well that this fragrant shower, these fragile, worthless petals, these songs of love from the littlest of

hearts will charm You. Yes, these nothings will please You. They will bring a smile to the Church Triumphant. She will gather up my flowers unpetalled *through love* and have them pass through Your own divine hands, O Jesus. And this Church in heaven, desirous of playing with her little child, will cast these flowers, which are now infinitely valuable because of Your divine touch, upon the Church Suffering in order to extinguish its flames and upon the Church Militant in order to gain victory for it.[47]

These sustained metaphors of childhood and flowers, for all their apparent artlessness or even naïvety, bring us into profound theological statements. Her vision is eccesial: her love is to serve the Church. But this love is directed primarily towards God, and from him flows back upon the Church. There seems a clear distinction between the love itself, and its proof; the latter is by small, almost insignificant acts. This love unites the theme of suffering that is central to Thérèse's spirituality. Offered to the Lord it becomes an abundant source for apostolic fruitfulness, showing its effectiveness in purgatory and on earth. Here we have in a mature form Thérèse's conception of herself as sustaining missionary effort; it is significant that she supports the work of missionaries by love.

She then develops more or less the same idea through a second metaphor of a little bird and a great eagle. Here the point is the security of divine love and the confidence she feels in its embrace. Therefore, she can move again into her victim language:

> [The little bird] wants to become the *prey* of Your Love. One day I hope that You, the Adorable Eagle, will come to fetch me, Your little bird; and ascending with it to the Furnace of Love, You will plunge it for all eternity into the burning Abyss of this Love to which it has offered itself as a victim.[48]

Thérèse herself is overwhelmed by the sublimity of her discovery. Characteristically she wants to share this with others. She ends the first part of her autobiography (Manuscript A) with a passage about these deep desires:

> O Jesus! why can't I tell all *little souls* how unspeakable is Your condescension? I feel that if You found a soul weaker and littler than mine, which is impossible, You would be pleased to grant it still greater favours, provided it abandoned itself with total confidence to Your Infinite Mercy. But why do I desire to communicate Your secrets of Love, O Jesus, for was it not You alone who taught them to me, and can You not reveal them to others? Yes, I know it, and I beg You to do it. I beg You to cast Your Divine Glance upon a great number of *little* souls. I beg You to choose a legion of *little* Victims worthy of your LOVE! (Signed) *The very little Sister Thérèse of the Child Jesus and the Holy Face, unworthy religious of Carmel.*[49]

Here we find united all the themes of the Little Way, divine love and mercy, victimhood, and her constant apostolic love for others.

We find various theological explanations of these passages in terms of the virtue of charity, exercised here to a high degree. Though that is undoubtedly true, it somewhat misses a more important point. We should rather seek an understanding in terms of the mystical transformation that Thérèse has received. God's love and her love are now so united that her desire for the Church is already God's; God's desire for the Church is hers. Such love can only be effective. In a profound sense Thérèse has become an incarnation of divine love in the Church. And just as the Incarnate Word lived out the mystery in the humdrum activities of Nazareth, and also in his public ministry through such human activities as walking, sleeping and eating as well as in miracles and teaching, so too Thérèse rightly senses that her proof of love will be by petals, not in themselves important, but receiving infinite value through God's acceptance.

In this way we can properly grasp the significance of her citation from St John of the Cross:

> O my Jesus! I love You! I love the Church, my Mother! I recall that *'the smallest act of PURE LOVE is of more value to her than all other works together.'* But is PURE LOVE in my heart? Are my measureless desires only but a dream, a folly?… these desires are the greatest martyrdom to me. However, I feel, O Jesus, that after having aspired to the most lofty heights of Love, if one day I do not attain them, I feel that I shall have tasted *more sweetness in my martyrdom and my folly* than I shall taste in the bosom of the *joy of the Fatherland.*[50]

The text of St John of the Cross is first found in the writings of Thérèse in a prayer of consecration to the Holy Face which she wrote on the feast of the Transfiguration (6 August 1896) for herself and her two companions in the novitiate who had the Holy Face as part of their religious names.[51] It is found in a letter which she wrote to her three sisters in Carmel about three months before she died,[52] and in one to her missionary brother, Fr Roulland, earlier in the year.[53] She had marked the text with a cross in the volume of St John of the Cross which she kept by her until her death.[54] Though she may have known the text from an earlier period, it would be safe to suggest that it had a special resonance for her after the discovery of her role in the Church. It is important to note the context in St John of the Cross: he is not talking about any love, but the 'pure love' characteristic of profound union with God.

We should not overlook the magnitude of this vocation: to be committed to 'not allowing one little sacrifice to escape, not one look, one word, profiting by all the smallest things and doing them through love' demands stark holiness in a truly heroic degree. The Little Way is a simple way to holiness and love; it is decidedly not an easy way. The third part of her autobiography (Manuscript C) shows how she proceeded to implement this decision; the *Last Conversations,* the account of her final months, shows too the intrepid steps she took to live and die according to this pattern of simple, but relentless loving. It is this, perhaps more than any other passage of Thérèse's writings, that gives the lie to any suggestion of a pallid, sweet figure; there is a flint-like quality in her unconditional loving, scarcely paralleled in the life of any saint. But because it is so simple, it can easily be missed.

In the third part of her autobiography we find further reflections on her vocation to love in all its concreteness. She develops her thoughts on love especially in the context of her work with the novices and of her dedication to the apostolate of her missionary brothers.[55] We should note too the significance of the long passage which she copied out from the Last Supper discourse in John 17:4-24. She was not content to refer to the passage, but despite her weakness she wished to share it and to savour Jesus' words as he prepares to depart and commits his followers to the care of the Father. She then writes, 'Yes Lord, this is what I would like to repeat after You before flying into Your arms.'[56]

But though what can at first be most easily recalled about these final pages of the autobiography may be the simple incidents, the profound theology of love has not changed. It is now nearly ten months since Thérèse has had her insight into her vocation, and she progressively deepened and simplified her understanding. A significant example of this is her comment on the text of the Canticle, 'Draw me, we shall run after you in the odour of your ointments' (Cant 1:3),[57] a commentary she never completed. One passage from it will suffice to show the direction of her thoughts.

O Jesus, it was not even necessary to say: *'When drawing me, draw the souls whom I love!'* This simple statement, 'Draw me' suffices; I understand, Lord, that when a soul allows herself to be captivated by *the odour of your ointments,* she cannot run alone, all the souls whom she loves follow in her train; this is done without constraint, without effort, it is a natural consequence of her attraction for You. Just as a torrent, throwing itself with impetuosity into the ocean, drags after it everything it encounters in its passage, in the same way, O Jesus, the soul who plunges into the shoreless ocean of Your love, draws with her all the treasures she possesses. Lord, You know it, I have no other treasures than the souls it has pleased You to unite to mine....[58]

We have to remember that all the time Thérèse was writing the second and third part of her autobiography, she was personally plunged into the deepest spiritual darkness. She can, however, for sake of others, speak in terms of suffused light.

As we draw this chapter to a conclusion we can suggest that though the critical experience from an ecclesiological point of view is her discovery of being love in the heart of the Church, the hermeneutical tool, the way to understand that insight, remains the Offering to Merciful Love, itself to be interpreted in the light of her Little Way of confidence and love. The remainder of this study will be devoted to drawing out the implications of Thérèse's vocation and of seeing the ways in which in the heart of the Church she received love from God and returned it to him as well as imparting this same love to others. We turn now to her teaching about, and her lived experience of the Communion of Saints.

Chapter Four

The Communion of Saints

The notion of the Communion of Saints is essential for any full or developed vision of the Church. It is of course quite traditional, being one of the articles of the Apostle's Creed. An exploration of its implications can open up for us more of the riches of Thérèse's intuitions concerning the Church. The Communion of Saints is a complex notion.[1] The words, 'Communion of Saints' (*communio sanctorum/koinonia tôn hagiôn*) are first attested in the late fourth century. The underlying reality is older. In the New Testament itself the members of the Church are called the 'saints' (e.g. Ac 9:13; Rm 16:2; 2 Co 1:1). The notion of communion is also well developed: it is vertical with God (1 Jn 1:3; 2 Cor 13:13), and horizontal among the disciples (Ac 2:42).

There is an ambiguity in the phrase for it can mean 'Communion of Holy Persons or of Holy Things'; the genitive plural can be either masculine or neuter in Greek or Latin. The earliest Greek usages seem to refer to sharing in the Eucharist, a meaning also found in the West. However, the West more frequently refers to holy persons, often denoting those in glory, those on earth, and later occasionally also those in purgatory. It is especially the anaphora (Eucharistic Prayer) in the East and in the Catholic West that gives a primary experience of the Communion of Saints: the Eucharist is celebrated with the explicit memory of Mary and the saints, with commemoration of the dead, as well as of the living. One of the significant deductions from the doctrine of the Communion of Saints is a rich theology of intercession and exchange of merits. It also opposes any tendency to see salvation purely in personal terms.

As an operative word in modern theology the notion of communion of saints needs some teasing out. It touches on several ecclesiological themes: the Church as the sacrament of salvation; Trinitarian life shared by its members; its communitarian dimension; the three states of the Church – heaven, earth, purgatory; the role of Mary and the saints; intercession. All of these insights of modern theology can be found in Thérèse, though some care is needed to uncover them in her language.

Her friends the saints
At every stage of her life, Thérèse had a profound sense of the intimacy between heaven and earth. An important summary of her sense of the Communion of Saints is found in the playlet she wrote on the Mission of St Joan of Arc (January 1894). She places these words on the lips of St Margaret of Scotland (d. 1093):

> Heaven is quite close to earth
> The Lord knows your desires
> The saints hear your prayer
> They gather up all your sighs;
> The Blessed and the Holy Angels
> Ceaselessly protect you;
> Of this all the heavenly host
> Have asked me to assure you.[2]

We could say that throughout her life Thérèse felt herself surrounded by her many friends in heaven. The list of saints that Thérèse mentions in her writings is extremely long; some indeed were canonised or beatified only after her own death, e.g. her beloved St Joan of Arc.

She cites and has a warmth towards various Old Testament figures:

Abraham, David, Ezekiel, Isaiah, Jeremiah, Judith, Moses. She invokes the angels Gabriel and Michael. She mentions or alludes to Saints Agnes, Margaret-Mary Alacoque, Alphonsus Liguori, Augustine, Bartholomew, Francis Borgia, Peter Canisius, Catherine, Catherine of Bologna, Cecilia, Céline, Charles Borromeo, Christopher, Crispin, Dominic, Elizabeth, Elizabeth of Hungary, Francis of Assisi, Francis de Sales, Francis Xavier, Genevieve, Gertrude, Hyacinth, Ignatius of Antioch, Ignatius of Loyola, Holy Innocents, James, Joan of Arc, John, John of the Cross, Jeanne de Chantal, Joachim, Joseph, Joseph of Cupertino, Claude de la Colombière, Louis, Louis de Gonzague, Luke, Mary Magdalene, Mark, Margaret, Mary Magdalene of Pazzi, Martha, Matthew, Maurice, Monica, Nicholas, Paul, Peter, Sebastian, Simon the Stylite, Stanislaus Kostka, Teresa of Avila, Thomas Aquinas and Veronica.

We could say that compared with the post-Vatican II Church, Thérèse had a rich culture of the saints. She did not appear to have extensive or lengthy devotions in their honour in any regular way, but from time to time she invokes some particular saint with special fervour. But from her writings and letters we see that she had a very extensive knowledge of hagiography so that she could unerringly point to some virtue or incident in the lives of the saints to help a correspondent or one of the community. Though in this area of the saints some may well not find Thérèse's reflections congenial, she has, none the less, something important to teach the Church of today.

In the liturgical reforms after Vatican II there was serious pruning of the calendar of the sanctoral cycle, the feasts of the saints. The reform of the calendar followed the norm of Vatican II, Constitution on the Liturgy:

> Lest the feasts of the saints overshadow the feasts which recall the mysteries of redemption, many of these should be celebrated by local churches, countries or religious communities. Only those which commemorate saints of universal significance should be kept by the universal church.[3]

The result was that being apostles, and hence presumably 'of universal significance', the feasts for example of Saints Matthias (24 May), Bartholomew (24 August) and Laurence (10 August) were retained, but many well-loved saints were dropped. More significant is the result of another norm to be found in the General Instruction for the *Roman Missal:*

> In accord with ancient tradition, images of Christ, Mary and the saints are venerated in churches. They should, however, be placed so as not to distract the faithful from the actual celebration. They should not be too numerous, there should not be more than one image of the same saint, and the correct order of the saints should be observed. In general the piety of the entire community should be considered in the decoration and arrangement of the church.[4]

This well-meaning regulation would be utterly incomprehensible to anyone from the Eastern Churches. Far from being a distraction, the sacred icons form part of the celebration; Eastern churches have many images, often of the same saint – a church may have a dozen or more icons of the Mother of God. These norms partly reflect Vatican II, but go far beyond what it demanded; the council had asked that the number of images be moderate (SC 125). The unfortunate result of the way in which these two reforms have been taken up by the Latin Church impoverishes piety to a very real extent. The rich yet restrained approach of Thérèse has still much to teach us today. Dull and drab churches are not conducive to piety or even liturgy; an overly intellectual approach to faith has not borne fruit since the council. Thérèse on the contrary is constantly aware of being surrounded by all her friends in heaven with whom she is on intimate terms. Thus some weeks before she died she remarks on the feast of St Joachim, 'It is grandpapa's feast today.'[5] Her guardian angel is 'my Brother, my Friend, my Consoler' and she invokes his intercession for others and asks him to mediate her love to them, as well as her sacrifices to God.[6]

Mary

Mary is central to Thérèse's life. Mary whom she constantly invokes as Mother has a special place for Thérèse. A full exposition of her rich mariology[7] would bring us very far afield indeed; a few brief indications can be given. She begins her autobiography by placing it under the guidance of the Virgin: she prays in front of the statue of the 'Virgin of the Smile'.[8] We find references to Mary throughout her works alluding to every phase of her life.

She tells us that she redoubled her devotion to Mary after her first confession;[9] she rejoiced to be enrolled as a Child of Mary when she was fourteen.[10] Her cure through the smile of the Virgin Mary from the strange psychosomatic illness which nearly killed her left an indelible mark on Thérèse's whole life and spirituality.[11] As we shall see later she had a major Marian experience at the shrine of Our Lady of Victories in Paris on her way to Rome.[12] There would seem to be four significant elements in Thérèse's approach to Mary. We should not, perhaps, overemphasise the title under which Mary brought healing to her, 'Our Lady of Victories', but neither should we ignore its significance. Mary is the one in whose protection Thérèse feels confident and safe. Secondly, what seems to have impressed Thérèse most about the statue vision was the beauty of Mary, and in the dark days ahead, she keeps repeating this: 'The Blessed

Virgin appeared very beautiful and I had seen her smile at me.'[13] Thirdly, Thérèse is firmly drawn to Mary as Mother, 'more Mother than Queen'.[14] Thérèse lost her own mother at the age of four and she found her foster mothers, Pauline and Marie, unreliable: both went off to Carmel when she felt she needed them. She transfers all her trust to Mary who was her constant companion and confidant. Fourthly, she has a deep passionate love for Mary. In the phrase that would later be used by Vatican II, Thérèse knew Mary as the one 'who occupies a place in the Church which is highest after Christ and also closest to us'.[15]

The May before she died she composed a long poem, 'Why I Love You, O Mary!'[16] Whilst it is not her finest poem from a literary point of view, it has a rich doctrinal and spiritual content. She signed the poem shortly before her death. A long conversation recorded by her sister Pauline, Mother Agnes, five weeks before she died records her saying 'In my poem, "Why I love you O Mary!", I have said everything I would preach about her.'[17] This narrative begins with an oft-quoted statement:

> How I would have loved to be a priest in order to preach about the Blessed Virgin! One sermon would be sufficient to say everything I think about this subject.[18]

She then goes on to outline her central intuitions about the Virgin Mother, what she would say in a sermon:

> I'd first make people understand how little is known by us about her life. We shouldn't say unlikely things or things we don't know anything about... For a sermon on the Blessed Virgin to please me and do any good, I must see her real life, not her imagined life. I'm sure that her real life was very simple. They show her to us as unapproachable, but they should present her as imitable, bringing out her virtues, saying that she lived by faith just

like ourselves, giving proof of this from the Gospel…We know very well that the Blessed Virgin is Queen of heaven and earth, but she is more Mother than Queen; and we should not say, on account of her prerogatives, that she surpasses all the saints in glory just as the sun at its rising makes the stars disappear from sight. My God! How strange that would be! A mother who makes her children's glory vanish! I myself think just the contrary. I believe she'll increase the splendour of the elect very much.[19]

Thérèse dwells on Mary failing to understand in the Gospel (Luke 2:50) before concluding with a flash of love and creative imagination:

What the Blessed Virgin has more than we have is the privilege of not being able to sin…, but on the other hand she wasn't as fortunate as we are, since she didn't have a Blessed Virgin to love. And this is one more sweetness for us and one less sweetness for her![20]

Yet we should note that on the previous day she had been sharing at length with Sister Agnes thoughts on the ordinariness of the Nazareth home when Jesus was a boy and on St Joseph. But nonetheless she could say:

I would like to be sure that she loves me; I mean the Blessed Virgin…. When I think of how much trouble I've had all my life trying to recite the rosary.[21]

The doubt or perhaps, better, her need for reassurance, reflects the trial of faith, the spiritual darkness that surrounded her in the last fifteen months of her life. However, her difficulties with the Rosary were, it seems, lifelong. Stating a preference for prayers in common she had remarked in her autobiography, about six weeks earlier:

I feel then that the fervour of my sisters makes up for my lack of fervour; but when alone (I am ashamed to admit it) the recitation of the rosary is more difficult for me than the wearing of an instrument of penance. I feel I have said it so poorly! I force myself in vain to meditate on the mysteries of the rosary; I don't succeed in fixing my mind on them. For a long time I was desolate about this lack of devotion which astonished me, for I love the Blessed Virgin so much that it should be easy for me to recite in her honour prayers which are so pleasing to her. Now I am less desolate; I think that the Queen of heaven, since she is my MOTHER must see my good will and she is satisfied with it…. The Blessed Virgin shows me she is not displeased with me, for she never fails to protect me as soon as I invoke her.[22]

Three weeks before her death, she wrote her last prayer in a weak hand. It is only twenty-five words in French and ends with triple exclamation marks and repeated stops:

O Mary, if I were the Queen of Heaven and you were Thérèse, I would want to be Thérèse so that you might be Queen of Heaven!!!….[23]

This somewhat whimsical thought shows something of the profound and intimate relationship between the two women. Clearly Thérèse's mariology is not theoretical. Thérèse does not so much tell us about Mary as communicate her lived experience of knowing Mary in the Communion of Saints.

The family of Thérèse

Thérèse's sense of the Communion of Saints, of our unity with those in heaven, was not restricted to canonised saints, but very much included her mother and father, two infant brothers and two sisters who had predeceased her. In a New Year letter to her sister Léonie she writes:

> With great joy I come to offer you my wishes at the beginning of this New year. The one which has just passed away has been very fruitful for heaven: our dear father has seen what 'the eye of man cannot contemplate.' …Dear little Sister, do you not find, as I do, that our father's departure has brought us close to heaven? More than half the family now enjoys the vision of God, and the five exiled ones on earth will not be long in flying away to their homeland.[24]

Since she was convinced of his sanctity, we are not be surprised that Thérèse sensed a particular affinity to her father after his death. Within a month of his release, she had written a family poem which celebrated the love of his children and his caring for them on earth and now beyond the grave with his wife:

> Remember that formerly on earth
> Your only happiness used to be to love us dearly.
> Grant your children's prayer.
> Protect us, deign to bless us still.
> Up there you have again found our dear Mother,
> Who had gone before you to our Holy Homeland.
> Now in Heaven
> You both reign.
> Watch over us.[25]

Somewhat the same sentiments are found in another letter to Léonie:

> I am thinking more than ever about you ever since our dear Father has gone up to heaven; I believe you are

experiencing the same feelings as ourselves. Papa's death does not give me the impression of a death but of a real *life*. I am finding him once more after an absence of six years, I feel him around *me,* looking at me, and protecting me... Dear little Sister, are we not more united now that we gaze on the heavens to find there a Father and a Mother who offered us to Jesus?[26]

Thérèse then not only looks at her family in glory, but she feels especially close to them. This vision was hers even from her youth. Thus she recalls that on her Communion day she was conscious of her mother being present.

The absence of Mamma didn't cause me any sorrow on the day of my First Communion. Isn't Heaven itself in my soul, and hadn't Mamma taken her place there a long time ago? Thus in receiving Jesus' visit, I received also Mamma's. She blessed me and rejoiced in my happiness.[27]

Elsewhere she shows herself conscious of her mother's intercession. She recalled her joy 'when I was able to pray at Mamma's grave and ask her to protect me always'.[28]

Thérèse's vision of the Communion of Saints is expressed very elaborately in a letter she wrote for her sister Céline's profession in 1896. Céline had a certain taste for embellishment, and Thérèse gave free rein to her imagination in describing how the whole court of Heaven would take part in the profession the following day: Mary, innumerable angels, many named saints are seen as celebrating with Céline. The text is flamboyant and was criticised by a theological censor at the beatification cause, who, as a modern editor noted, could have been 'better advised as to the literary genre of such a piece'.[29] But it contains deep insight and, behind its exuberance, we find again a profound theology and a lived experience of the Communion of Saints. Céline's profession will be an occasion for Mary to release many from purgatory. Thérèse sees their father and mother, their two sisters and two brothers who had died in infancy, as present in a special way and celebrating the profession with particular rejoicing.[30]

The Church is surely wise in being slow to declare people as holy too soon after their death. There is, however, a sense in which Thérèse's intuition is still valid today and could enrich us. We tend perhaps so to look to our duties of praying for our deceased relatives that we omit to consider sufficiently their care and intercession for us. A revitalised doctrine of the Communion of Saints has much to offer the Christian people. In a world where belief in life after death has weakened, Catholics can proclaim their experience of the love and care they expect from their departed loved ones.

Her role after her death

Thérèse saw not only her family as active members of the Communion of Saints, but she also gradually understood her own future role. As early as 1894 she wrote to Céline who was still outside the Carmel and concerned with their dying father: 'If I die before you, do not believe I shall be far from your soul, never shall we have been more united.'[31] Here we have a theme that would be greatly developed in Thérèse's final year. It emerged in the playlet which she wrote for the golden jubilee of Sister St Stanislaus of the Sacred Hearts (February 1897) on the topic of the latter's namesake, the young Jesuit saint, who had died as a Jesuit novice at the age of eighteen in 1568. At the close of the drama he is portrayed as having a vision of Mary and the Child Jesus. Stanislaus says to her:

> My beloved Mother, soon I shall see you on your immortal throne...I have regrets about nothing on earth, but I have one desire... a desire so great that I cannot imagine being happy in heaven if it is not realised... Ah! my dear Mother,

tell me if the blessed can still work for the salvation of souls… If I cannot work in heaven for the glory of Jesus, I prefer to remain in exile and still battle for Him! (Thérèse herself inserted the ellipsis points … as above).[32]

Mary replies, 'Yes, my child, the Blessed can still save souls; the gentle flames of their love draws hearts towards the heavens.'[33]

In a letter to her spiritual brother, Father Bellière, written a few weeks later, she used almost exactly the same words which she has placed on the lips of St Stanislaus:

> But rest assured, the only thing I desire is God's will, and I admit that if in heaven I were no longer able to work for his glory, I would prefer exile to the homeland…If Jesus realises my presentiments, I promise to remain your little sister up above…Then there will no longer be any cloister and grilles, and my soul will be able to fly with you into distant missions. Our roles will remain the same: yours, apostolic weapons, mine, prayer and love.[34]

One of the best-known sayings of Thérèse is surely her promise to spend her heaven doing good on earth. Like practically all of her insights, this one was slow in evolving. She made a private novena to St Francis Xavier ('Novena of Grace') from 4 to 12 March 1897 with the intention that she would be enabled to do good after her death.[35] We know from the testimony of her sister Marie, Sister Marie of the Sacred Heart, that she also prayed a week later to St Joseph on his feast for the same intention.[36]

Her famous phrase, 'I want to spend my heaven doing good on earth', is from her last conversations of 17 July and the following day.[37] But she had developed the idea with great clarity in her final letter to her other spiritual brother, Father Roulland, just three days earlier:

When you receive this letter, no doubt I shall have left this earth… Ah! Brother, I feel it, I shall be more useful to you in heaven than on earth, and it is with joy that I come to announce to you my coming entrance into that blessed city, sure that you will share my joy and will thank the Lord for giving me the means of helping you more effectively in your apostolic works. I really count on not remaining inactive in heaven. My desire is to work still for the Church and souls. I am asking God for this and I am certain He will answer me. Are not the angels continually occupied with us without their ever ceasing to see the divine Face and to lose themselves in the Ocean of Love without shores? Why would Jesus not allow me to imitate them?[38]

During her last months she thought several times about the state of the angels who could be 'continually interested in us without ever ceasing to see the divine Face.'[39] It is noteworthy that this insight is found in her last letter to her missionary brother, Father Roulland, when she was very conscious of her own approaching death. The idea is found elsewhere in these final months. Whilst it is not original – she may have found it in St Margaret Mary Alacoque – it is a very clear indicator of her thoughts as death approached.

In June before she died she foresaw what she termed a shower of roses coming after her death.[40] Five weeks later she said to Céline, 'I want to spend my heaven doing good on earth.'[41] Very soon after her death the shower of roses began, and the Carmel at Lisieux began to publish testimonies.

Intercession

Thus far we have seen two aspects of Thérèse's experience of the Communion of Saints, her relationship with those in heaven and her desire to serve those on earth especially after her death. There remains a third theme that will occupy most of the remainder of this volume, namely her role of intercession whilst she was still on earth.

She was always convinced of the power of intercession. She recalls that on one occasion, probably in 1895, Mother Gonzague, then Prioress, refused the request of one of the novices to enter into a spiritual correspondence with a view to converting her sister with the words, 'it was not through letters that Carmelites must save souls, but through prayer'.[42] This reply led to the novice having an experience of answered prayer similar to that of Thérèse herself at the age of fourteen when she prayed for the conversion of the murderer Pranzini and received a sign that her prayer had been efficacious.[43] Thérèse then goes on to develop at some length and with unusual passion an account of the wonder of prayer.[44]

Her ministry of intercession was above all concerned with priests. We see it in particular in regard to her two missionary brothers; she is also deeply committed to praying for sinners and for the souls in purgatory. Her means of intercession were prayer, suffering and love. The ministry of intercession of Thérèse extended to the whole Church, and is attested to by the wide range of people and circumstances mentioned in her letters. A remark during her final illness summarises her life and intercession: 'Everything I have, everything I merit, is for the good of the Church and for souls.'[45]

Part two of this study takes up these themes and examines how Thérèse in this way was totally inserted into the concerns of the Communion of Saints. After an examination of her teaching and experience of suffering, we look at the way in which through it and prayer she served the Communion of Saints. We conclude with an account of two other themes that illustrate her life in the Church, namely faith, and the gifts and charisms she received.

PART TWO

LIVING IN THE CHURCH

Chapter Five

Suffering

It is difficult to speak positively about suffering in our modern world. In face of the universal cry of humankind against suffering, it is surprising that some of the saints seem to welcome it. Many today would see as morbid, if not indeed psychologically aberrant, some writings of saints like Ignatius of Antioch or Catherine of Siena. There are several problems. One is the form and literary genre of much writing on suffering, which is strange to our mentality. Another difficulty is the current ideology of fulfilment and happiness that cannot comprehend a wish to suffer. A third issue is the fact that the only context in which desire for suffering makes sense is love. As a result care must be taken in presenting Thérèse's complex thought on the subject. We will see that she is in no way unhealthy in her approach, provided that we always keep in mind the perspective of love, which alone allows us to interpret her thought correctly.

A mystery

Suffering belongs to the realm of ultimate mysteries.[1] Philosophers and poets, theologians and saints, men and women from the dawn of history have faced the question of suffering. It raises not only the issue of how to cope with evil, but, more fundamentally, how a good and all-powerful God could permit evil. Suffering can come about from sickness or material circumstances; it may be physical, emotional, mental or spiritual; it can be individual or communitarian. Though it may also be caused by natural disaster or human malevolence, it is also inextricably linked with the nature of the universe, with its cycles of growth and decay. Every living thing eventually decays and dies.

In the Hebrew and Christian traditions there have been many attempts to find, if not solutions to the problem of suffering and evil, at least a way of seeing suffering as not devoid of some meaning. The Genesis story was an early attempt to make sense of suffering, seeing it as a punishment for sin (Gn 3:16-19); the history of the people is in part a history of sin and punishment (Jg 2:11-23). The psalms and the wisdom literature have another expression of this view, sometimes in the assertion that the good prosper and the wicked suffer (Pss 1:1-6; 37:25-29). But this simple position was contradicted by experience and by the dramatic story of the just Job who suffered terribly, and also by the teaching of Jesus (Jn 9:1-3; Lk 13:1-5). Job's response was to trust in God despite the apparent injustice of his suffering. The letter to the Hebrews saw suffering as God's discipline which yields 'the peaceful fruit of righteousness' and healing (Hb 12:5-13). Jesus himself suffered out of love, offering himself as a victim for the redemption of all, thus bringing to completion the spirituality of the Suffering Servant Songs (Is 42, 49, 50, 53). Thus the most profound human response to suffering in the New Testament is to see the possibility of being united to Christ in love through carrying the Cross (Lk 9:22-24) and to be risen with him in glory (see Rm 6:5-6). We can, with Paul, complete in our flesh 'what is lacking in Christ's afflictions for the sake of his body, that is the church' (Col 1:24). Vatican II suggests that suffering is meaningless except in and through Christ.[2]

All of these scriptural answers are valid in their own way, but different people will possibly find one or other more helpful in their particular situation. In the complex mystery of suffering more than one response is needed for different people and different situations, even suffering in union with Christ is recognised as having in itself some higher value and meaning.

Suffering in the life of Thérèse

Even the most superficial reading of Thérèse raises some serious questions. She wrote very frequently about suffering. The word 'trial' is found 173 times in her writings, the words 'suffer' or 'suffering' occur 228 times, almost half of the instances being in her letters. She spoke frequently about the joy of suffering, and in a letter written shortly before her death stated, 'I have a great desire to suffer.'[3] One might ask if there is not something disordered or psychologically unhealthy about such thoughts. Her teaching on suffering is extremely complex and has often been misunderstood.[4]

Thérèse's profound teaching on suffering arose from a life experience which was marked by an amount of suffering which was physical, spiritual and psychological. We can outline the various ways in which she encountered pain in her life. We need to read her texts carefully and note their development, if we are not to miss the hugely significant role it has in her life. As she began her autobiography in 1895 she looked back and noted:

> I find myself at a period of my life when I can cast a glance upon the past; my soul has matured in the crucible of exterior and interior trials. And now, like a flower strengthened by the storm, I can raise my head...[5]

At that time Thérèse saw her life as being divided into three separate periods:

> The first is not the least fruitful in memories in spite of its short duration. It extends from the dawn of my reason till our dear Mother's departure for heaven...[6]

After that she noted, 'I entered the second period of my existence, the most painful of the three.'[7] The torment of this period was undoubtedly increased by the fact that she had not yet discovered the depths of love that transform suffering.

Psychological suffering

Given her delicate sensibility Thérèse was particularly vulnerable to psychological pain at every stage of her life. Just after her birth there was the separation from her mother who was not able to look after her. She spent fifteen months with a wet-nurse, Rose Taillé, who had previously nursed two Martin babies who later died. After about a year Thérèse returned home, but when she was four-and-a-half her mother died, on 28 August 1877. Thérèse thus had three separations in her early years: from her mother in infancy; from Rose Taillé after a year; from her mother at her death. This pattern of painful separation would continue. On the death of her mother she adopted her eldest sister Pauline as her mother, but Pauline left to enter Carmel when Thérèse was nine. She recalls her feelings at the time:

> I understood that Pauline was going to leave me to enter a convent. I understood, too, she *would not wait for me* and I was about to lose my second *Mother!* Ah! how can I express the anguish of my heart! In one instant, I understood what life was; until then, I had never seen it so; but it appeared to me in all its reality, and I saw it was nothing but a continual suffering and separation. I shed bitter tears because I did not yet understand the *joy* of sacrifice.[8]

Everything was painful at the time, especially the parlour visits at Carmel.[9] She then adopted Marie as her 'third' mother.

The separation from Pauline undoubtedly was at least a partial cause of a serious illness which lasted for five months until her life was saved through the smile of the Virgin Mary when she was at the point of death (Pentecost 1883). During her illness

Thérèse was excessively sensitive, she suffered from insomnia, weakness, rashes, fevers, and some failure of her motor nerves so that she needed help even to move. We might judge it as psychosomatic with some element of infantile regression. Thérèse later judged it to have come from the devil, which was also the opinion of the Martin family.[10] Thérèse was long afterwards tortured by the thought that she became ill on purpose, which was, she said 'a real martyrdom for my soul.'[11] Even if one might point to Pauline's departure and suggest a psychosomatic illness, that would not mean either that Thérèse was responsible for the illness, nor that the demonic could be entirely ruled out.

Her school days were characterised by her hypersensitivity, and there is some hint of rejection or at least misunderstanding by her fellow pupils. She was not a normal child, happy at the rough and tumble of games and children's pastimes.[12] At the retreat before her First Communion the other pupils discovered that she was not fully adept at dressing herself; she could not comb her hair though she was then eleven.[13]

On Christmas Eve in 1886 when she was thirteen, she had her major conversion, when she was set free from a certain childish immaturity; she described it as a miracle, the grace of complete conversion.[14] The incident itself was small: she still expected Christmas gifts in the fireplace. But her need for the childhood way of marking Christmas was only a symptom of a more profound childishness. Instead of regressing and seeking relief in tears, she expanded into maturity. She was suddenly touched by God. She regarded this conversion as the beginning of the third period of her life, 'the most beautiful and the most filled with graces from heaven.'[15]

There was a period following at the family rented home, Les Buissonnets, when Céline and she were extremely happy. They bonded profoundly spiritually; then and later Thérèse shared her most profound thoughts with Céline. She would describe this youthful period as follows:

> It was the same soul giving us life. For some months, we'd enjoyed together the most beautiful life young girls could dream about…. I would say our life on earth was the *ideal of happiness.*[16]

Her desire to enter Carmel at the age of fifteen brought much more distress: the pain of telling her father; her initial reluctance to share her desire with Céline for fear of causing her pain;[17] the opposition of her uncle and of the religious authorities; the trip to Rome and the apparent failure of her appeal to the Pope to enter Carmel at the age of fifteen. The images she uses are significant: the three-day search by Mary and Joseph for Jesus, a desert, Jesus being asleep in her boat, Gethsemani.[18] God, it seemed to her, had abandoned her.[19] She had previously offered herself to Jesus to be like a ball or plaything; in Rome the ball was pierced, and she felt cast off.[20] Her soul, she says, 'was plunged into sadness.'[21]

She came into a new dimension of suffering with her father's illness. Already in childhood, at about the age of six, she had had a prophetic vision of her father, stooped and with his face covered.[22] When she was fourteen, he had a first attack of paralysis (May 1887). The following year he began to be seriously ill. It was surely a year of major psychological trauma for him. Thérèse left him to enter Carmel on 9 April; Marie took the veil on 23 May; about the same time Léonie indicated that she wished to try her vocation again; Céline told him on 15 June that she too wanted to enter Carmel. On the 23 June he went missing, to be discovered four days later in Le Havre by Céline and her uncle. During his absence a house that he had bought near Les Buissonnets was destroyed by fire. In September he had a serious relapse at Les Buissonnets, and again during a visit to Honfleur. He became subject to hallucinations and after an incident with a revolver at home, he was confined in the mental hospital at Caen (12 February).[23] He suffered the profound humiliation of being made equivalently a ward of court, when the administration of his estate was taken from him to protect him from reckless generosity. Shortly beforehand he had donated 10,000 francs for a new high altar at the cathredral (perhaps twelve years of earnings of a manual worker). Though he would leave the hospital in May 1892, he would never regain full health before his death on 27 July 1894. The last time Thérèse saw him was on 12 May 1892 when his only words were a farewell 'in heaven'. He kept his face covered, thus fulfilling the prophetic vision Thérèse had seen some twelve years earlier.

We can scarcely imagine the pain that this illness caused the closely united family. The disgrace of incarceration in a huge sixteen hundred bed mental hospital would have been extremely difficult at the time, especially for a family as prominent as the Martins. We need to keep in mind their bourgeois culture if we are fully to appreciate Thérèse's distress. Her account of this period is worth considering at some length:

> I recall that in the month of June, 1888, at the moment of our first trials, I said, 'I am suffering very much, but I feel I can bear still greater trials.' I was not thinking then of the ones reserved for me. I did not think that on February 12, a month after my reception of the Habit, our dear Father would drink the most *bitter* and *most humiliating* of all chalices. Ah! that day, I didn't say I was able to suffer more! Words cannot express our anguish… Papa's three years of martyrdom appear to me as the most lovable, the most fruitful of my life; I wouldn't exchange them for all the ecstasies and revelations of the saints. My heart overflows with gratitude when I think of this inestimable *treasure* which must cause a holy jealousy to the angels in the heavenly court. My desire for suffering was answered, and yet my attraction for it did not diminish. My soul soon shared in the sufferings of my

heart. Spiritual aridity was my daily bread, and deprived of all consolations, I was still the happiest of creatures since all my desires had been satisfied. O dear Mother! how sweet our great trial was since from our hearts came only sighs of love and gratitude.[24]

Here we have Thérèse seemingly in love with suffering. In a bold phrase, inspired perhaps by St Margaret Mary Alocoque, she speaks of the jealousy of the angels who cannot suffer.[25] She now feels that the desire for suffering was fully answered, and she notes the attraction to suffering still.

In letters to Céline at the time she develops a deep theology of suffering. To her intimate confidante Thérèse pours out her heart and her pain; at the same time Céline acknowledges the support and comfort these letters are to her.[26] In the most acute suffering Thérèse finds joy and wants Céline to share it. Some striking themes emerge in these letters: the privilege of suffering and sharing the Cross; suffering as a sign of the special favour of Jesus; the importance of weakness in carrying the Cross; the privilege of suffering; suffering as martyrdom. One remarkable passage which consists mostly of phrases and gaps gives us some insight into Thérèse's pain and her deepening insights:

Dear Céline, sweet echo of my soul!… If you only knew my misery!… Oh! if you only knew… Sanctity does not consist in saying beautiful things, it does not even consist in thinking them, in feeling them!… It consists in *suffering* and suffering *everything*. (Sanctity! We must conquer it at the point of the sword; we must *suffer*… we must *agonise!*) A day will come when the shadows will disappear.[27]

The words which Thérèse placed in brackets are taken from notes of a retreat given by Father Pichon in 1887. This letter, and many others, shows something of the distress of Thérèse. There is no romanticising or easy spiritualisation of her pain; she felt it profoundly.

It is perhaps strange that we do not find in the letters of this period any indication of the prayers and sacrifices for the recovery of their father; it is probably too obvious to need expression. The idea is rather that his illness and humiliation will be the source of great holiness for him. She also asserts that the sufferings of the family will reduce their father's sufferings or spare him greater ones.[28] There are some indications that people were saying that the daughters were responsible for the illness of their father, a charge which Thérèse found very distressing.[29] Thérèse progressively distanced herself from the opinions of others and by the time of her final illness she showed complete indifference: 'We receive compliments when we don't merit them and reproaches when we don't merit them either.'[30]

The community at Lisieux was in many ways far from ideal. With twenty-five sisters it was a good deal larger than the reformer, St Teresa of Avila, recommended. A number of the sisters had rather disturbed personalities or were otherwise unsuited for the Carmelite way of life. There were also some factions, and the Martins – four sisters and one cousin – were not appreciated by all. Pauline was elected as prioress, but served only one three-year term. It took, however, seven ballots before Mother Gongazue, with whom Thérèse had an ambiguous relationship, was re-elected. When Thérèse joined at fifteen, Mother Gonzague was determined that she would not become the spoiled pet of the community. The prioress constantly picked on her, humiliating her by public rebukes. She also had an intuition that Thérèse would suffer. In a letter to her Mother Gonzague warned:

> I'm not going to make you laugh, but we must tell the truth in all things! Jesus has formed my violet for suffering,

and I don't want to be a prophet today, but I can, nevertheless, say to my little daughter, that it is suffering and more sacrifice that will make you a great saint.[31]

These thoughts of the Prioress are confirmed by Thérèse's own statement. As Thérèse reflected on her entry into Carmel, she contemplated suffering in her life. She had no illusions about Carmel.

> I found religious life to be exactly as I had imagined it, no sacrifice astonished me and yet, as you know, dear Mother, my first steps met with more thorns than roses! Yes suffering opened wide its arms to me and I threw myself into them with love.... Jesus made me understand that it was through suffering that he wanted to give me souls, and my attraction to suffering grew in proportion to its increase. That was my way for five years; exteriorly nothing revealed my suffering which was all the more painful since I alone was aware of it.[32]

Though Thérèse does not specify, these sufferings were probably external from Mother Gonzague who treated her with severity,[33] from the other sisters, and from her refusal to become attached to her sister Pauline.

In a passage of remarkable insight written about four months before she died, we can see Thérèse's profound intuitions about suffering and about genuine values. As she helps the grumpy and very difficult Sister St Pierre to her place in the refectory, Thérèse hears the sound of distant music coming across the cold winter air. She imagines for a moment an elegant salon.

> Then my glance fell upon the poor invalid whom I was supporting. Instead of the beautiful strains of music I heard only her occasional complaints, and instead of the

rich gildings I saw only the bricks of our austere cloister, hardly visible in the faintly glimmering light. I cannot express in words what happened in my soul; what I know is that the Lord illumined it with rays of *truth* which so surpassed the dark brilliance of earthly feasts that I could not believe my happiness. Ah! I would not have exchanged the ten minutes employed in carrying out my humble office of charity to enjoy a thousand years of worldly feasts. If already in suffering and in combat one can enjoy a moment of happiness that surpasses all the joys of this earth, and this when simply considering that God has withdrawn us from this world, what will this happiness be in heaven...?[34]

This moment of lucidity merely makes explicit what Thérèse had been practising, and allows us to understand her sense of the joy that is to be found in suffering.

Spiritual suffering

Chapter ten looks at the great trial of faith that marked the final eighteen months of Thérèse's life, when all sense of heaven left her. But she suffered from spiritual trials throughout her life. The most serious one in her youth was surely the terrible distress of scrupulosity that afflicted her from May 1885 until the end of October 1886. It seems to have been triggered off by a retreat given by Father Domin in preparation for the renewal of her Second Solemn Communion. She described this as a veritable martyrdom. Scrupulosity is a form of anxiety and is marked by an inability to make balanced rational and objective judgements about moral issues; in Thérèse's case it centred on offending God, rather than the more common form which is about sin and the fear of divine punishments. Her sister Marie was her support at that time: Thérèse brought all her worries to her. But in August 1886, whilst the crisis of scrupulosity was still raging, she learned that Marie intended to enter Carmel. She was thus facing the loss of her third mother at a time when she was seriously in need. But the Lord looked after her, for within about a fortnight of Marie's departure for Carmel, Thérèse was set free from this trial through the intercession of her deceased brothers and sisters.[35] This grace probably influenced her profound sense of the Communion of Saints which we saw in an earlier chapter.

Belonging to the sphere of spiritual suffering were the trials of aridity in prayer, when Jesus seemed to be asleep in her regard, an image that she uses about various times of her life.[36] As we saw above, she regards herself as a ball that he does not wish to play with and leaves aside.[37]

Physical suffering and her final illness

Thérèse never enjoyed robust health. Apart from the serious illness of her childhood from which she was miraculously set free, she had a constant series of ailments. Almost casually she lets slip that she suffered almost daily from headaches.[38] In the convent she began to have poor health at least from spring 1894 when she was twenty-one; her throat ailments began then. They began to be concerned with a problem of huskiness in autumn of that year, and the doctor was consulted. She had her first haemoptysis on Good Friday 1896. Incredibly she felt the bubbling of blood coming to her lips, but did not bother to light a lamp to investigate it. In the morning she was overjoyed.[39] Her trial of faith began a few days later and her health deteriorated for the next eighteen months until her death.

The Carmelite life at the time was very severe. An outsider would immediately think of long hours of prayer, a monotonous regime of work, fasting and other ascetical exercises. But what seemed to have affected Thérèse most was the cold. It was only shortly before she died that she mentioned it. She also suffered intensely from chilblains on her hands and feet.

Thérèse's final illness is significant not only for what she suffered, but also for the understanding of suffering which emerges. The sources are the letters from May 1897 and the 'Yellow Notebook' of her sayings recorded by Mother Agnes from that time and published as *Last Conversations*. The text may not be always wholly reliable, but there is a profound consistency between the Thérèse of the *Last Conversations* and her other writings. The same Thérèse speaks in all. The period of her final illness has given rise to much misunderstanding and controversial interpretations. However, for our purpose of seeing Thérèse in the Church and her view on suffering, we can remain close to her texts and utterances.[40]

From May until her death on 30 September Thérèse suffered acutely at every level. On the spiritual level she remained in a thick darkness of faith. On the physical level she suffered enormously from tuberculosis which ate away at her lungs and her intestines. She became so emaciated that some bones protruded through her skin. Fever, dreadful pain and difficulty in breathing were constant. There were painful remedies, such as cauterizing with red hot needles[41] and a massage with horse-hair which was all the more painful due to the blistering of her skin.[42] On the psychological level she had all the humiliations associated with the collapse of bodily functions. The prioress, Mother Gongazue, refused to allow her morphine injections despite the doctor's strong recommendations; such an escape from suffering was, she considered, inappropriate for a religious. Though she has been judged harshly for this, she was consistent in that she refused morphine herself when dying from painful cancer.

Yet through all of this there was a serenity about Thérèse. She did not deny her suffering or seek to overspiritualise it. She displayed no self-pity and was constantly thinking of others. It is in the last sayings, many of which she could speak only with great difficulty and in extreme weakness, that we see the final lived theology of suffering. In the intimate sharing with Mother Agnes in these last conversations there are also some precious references to earlier experiences and intuitions.

We find the word 'suffering' occurring over fifty times in the *Last Conversations*. It is also frequent, twenty-six times, in her poetry. In both she is freely expressing her feelings without the constraint imposed by having to record her life story or reply to correspondents. In these we find some very important intuitions and notable statements.

One of Thérèse's most significant convictions, one that never wavered, was that God would support her in whatever trial might come her way. Thus in May 1897 as her health seemed to decline rapidly, though it was yet evident that she would not recover, she stated:

> I haven't any misgivings whatsoever about the final struggles or sufferings of this sickness, no matter how great they may be. God has always come to my aid; He has helped me and led me by the hand from my childhood. I count on him. I'm sure he will continue to help me until the end. I may really become exhausted or worn out, but I shall never have to suffer too much; I'm sure of this.[43]

Eleven weeks later when she was critically ill she repeated the same sentiments:

> God gives me courage in proportion to my sufferings. I feel at this moment I couldn't suffer any more, but I'm not afraid, since if they increase, He will increase my courage at the same time.[44]

She was very careful to suffer only in the present, to take each day as it came: 'I'm suffering only for an instant. It's because we think of the past and the future that we become discouraged and fall into despair.'[45]

She appreciated all that was done for her in her final illness, especially little luxuries like grapes, to which she frequently referred. Yet for one so sensitive it is perhaps surprising that she managed totally to avoid any sense of being a burden to the community. When asked about this she replied to Mother Agnes: 'So far as that is concerned, it is the least of my worries; it makes no difference to me at all'.[46] Here we have an example of a wider attitude of disregarding other people's judgement of her which she gradually learned and returned to frequently in the *Last Conversations*.

In her illness she appreciated the companionship of Mother Agnes, at one time saying: 'Remain with me, little Mother; it's like a support to have you'.[47] But she found incessant questions from the community very wearing; she felt like Joan of Arc before her judges.[48] One nun in particular, Sister St John of the Cross, used to come, stand at the end of her bed and laugh for a long time. Mother Agnes noted that this was intended in a kindly way, but one wonders, since Thérèse remarked, 'Yes, it's painful to be looked at and laughed at when one is suffering'. She then referred to the mockery of Jesus and added, 'This thought aids me in offering Him this sacrifice in the right spirit'.[49]

During the whole illness Thérèse showed no trace of self-pity. When she could she made light of her pains, saying at one time, 'I have only inconveniences to put up with, not sufferings'.[50] At other times she could not hide her distress. She frequently showed a whimsical humour as when she likened herself to a train: 'I cough and cough! I'm just like a locomotive when it arrives at the station.'[51] At another time she remarked how much nicer it would be to be buried in an elegant wooden box that had come from a famous firm in Paris than in a coffin.[52] She made light of her problems with various milk diets, not to mention a snail syrup prescribed for her.[53] She joked about the straw palliasse that she could smell; the sisters had got ready to lay her out and had indiscreetly left it in an adjoining room, a full two months before she died: 'Ah! there's our palliasse! It's going to be very close to place my corpse on…. My little nose was always good!'[54]

Her Attitude to Suffering

As the Abbé Combes and others have noted there is an evolution in Thérèse's view of suffering.[55] Quite early in life she had a desire for suffering; later she discovered a joy in suffering; she finally moved to emphasising God's will more and avoiding a preference either to suffer or not to suffer. But though these three stages are reasonably clear, there is an overlap: themes that are more common towards the beginning of her religious life do recur in her final illness. There are other views, such as conformity to Christ, that appear at all stages.

Her desire for suffering

There is in Thérèse's attitude to suffering and in her understanding of its place in her life a profound development. Though there is some overlapping, various stages can be seen. Here, as elsewhere in the study of Thérèse, we can grasp her thought accurately only if we pay close attention to its evolution.

The first time she mentions suffering in her autobiography is a reflection on the time when she grabbed all the dolls' dresses her sister Léonie offered to her and Céline with the words 'I choose all'.

> This little incident of my childhood is a summary of my whole life; later on when perfection was set before me, I understood that to become a saint one had to suffer much, seek out always the most perfect thing to do, and forget self.[56]

We have already noted the next references to suffering, which cluster around the departure for Carmel of Pauline, her second mother.

In her recollections after her First Communion we find a major reflection on suffering. She recalled Marie preparing her for Communions:

> I remember how once she was speaking to me about suffering and she told me that I would probably not walk that way, that God would carry me as a child. The day after my Communion, the words of Marie came to my mind. I felt within my heart a *great desire* to suffer, and at the same time the interior assurance that Jesus reserved a great number of crosses for me. I felt myself flooded with consolations so *great* that I look upon them as one of the *greatest* graces of my life. Suffering became my attraction; it had charms about it which ravished me without understanding them very well. Up until this time, I had suffered without *loving* suffering, but since this day I felt a real love for it. I also felt the desire for loving God, of finding my joy only in Him. Often during my Communions, I repeated these words of the Imitation: 'O Jesus, unspeakable *sweetness*, change all the consolations of this earth into *bitterness* for me'. This prayer fell from my lips without effort, without constraint; it seemed I repeated it not with my will but like a child who repeats the words a person he loves has inspired in him. Later I will tell you, dear Mother, how Jesus was pleased to realise my desire.[57]

We can easily understand how Marie would have considered her hypersensitive sister as not cut out for suffering. The charge of having a morbid interest in suffering could be made, were it not for the fact that we are dealing with a major mystical experience which has all the authenticity of the Ignatian 'consolation without previous cause', which comes unexpectedly.[58] Thérèse did not initially choose to suffer on her own initiative. She received a double communication: a future of suffering and overwhelming consolation. Further she was passively seized by an inner enlightening, through the impression within her of the words of the *Imitation of Christ* (3:26,3). The paradox of suffering and consolation sets off this experience as authentic. It will be continually verified until her death.

It is particularly important that we note the sacramental context of this experience: as she received Communion, she received a mystical insight into union with the Crucified. The next insight again comes in a sacramental context, this time confirmation. She looked forward to this sacrament:

> I awaited the Holy Spirit's visit with great happiness in my soul. I rejoiced at the thought of soon being a perfect Christian and especially at that of having eternally on my forehead the mysterious cross the Bishop marks when conferring the sacrament.... On that day, I received the strength *to suffer*, for soon afterwards the martyrdom of my soul was about to commence.[59]

The sufferings to follow soon would seem to be the scrupulosity which she describes here as martyrdom.[60]

A desire for suffering would stay with Thérèse for much of her life. But it never terminated merely in the suffering itself, which would be highly suspect from a psychological point of view. Through suffering she wished to express her love. It also had an ecclesial dimension as she saw its value for others.

There are some further insights from the time of her final illness. Thérèse does not ask for suffering. Just as she made an offering of herself to merciful love rather than to divine justice, so too she would not dare ask for suffering:

> I didn't expect to suffer like this; I'm suffering like a little child. I would never want to ask God for greater

sufferings. If He increases them, I will bear them with pleasure and with joy because they will be coming from Him. But I'm too little to have any strength through myself. If I were to ask for sufferings, these would be mine, and I would have to bear them alone, and I've never been able to do anything alone.[61]

It is one thing to have a desire for suffering when everything goes reasonably well; Thérèse, however, retained her desire for suffering when her physical pain and distress were most acute. When Mother Agnes wished her death to spare her further suffering, she said, 'Yes, but you mustn't say that, little Mother, because suffering is exactly what attracts me in life.'[62]

Suffering and the salvation of souls

Another discovery by Thérèse rather early in her spiritual growth is the power of sufferings and sacrifice in favour of another. She continually offers little sacrifices for others. A special case was the prayer for Pranzini. Here we have an example, common in the spiritual life, of the Lord teaching people how to intercede and to pray for someone and at the same time allowing them to see the results of their intercession. Later one is expected to pray in naked faith. In the case of Pranzini she had just previously had an experience which she described as 'I felt charity enter into my soul and the need to forget myself and to please others; since then I've been happy.' She describes this as Jesus making her a fisher of souls. She explains: 'I experienced a great desire to work for the conversion of sinners, a desire I hadn't felt so intensely before.'[63]

It is important that we note the context of these remarks and of the Pranzini incident: they were about the time of her Christmas Eve conversion. Thérèse was healed and at the same time given a mission for the salvation of others. At this time there was another profound grace which might or might not be described as mystical in the technical sense:

One Sunday, looking at the picture of Our Lord on the Cross, I was struck by the blood flowing from one of the divine hands. I felt a great pang of sorrow when thinking this blood was falling to the ground without anyone hastening to gather it up. I was resolved to remain in spirit at the foot of the Cross and to receive the divine dew. I understood I was then to pour it out upon souls.... As yet it was not the souls of priests that attracted me, but those of *great sinners.*[64]

In a letter to Céline at the beginning of their father's incarceration in the mental hospital, Thérèse wrote:

Let us really offer our sufferings to Jesus to save souls, poor souls... Jesus wills to make their salvation depend on one sigh from our heart.... What a mystery! If one sigh can save a soul, what can sufferings like ours not do?... Let us refuse Jesus nothing![65]

Again in a letter to Céline she touches profound depths and indicates her preferred apostolate, namely to priests:

Ah, here is great love, to love Jesus without feeling the sweetness of this love... this is martyrdom... Oh, Céline, let us live for souls... let us be apostles... let us save especially the souls of priests; these souls should be more transparent than crystal.... Alas, how many bad priests, priests who are not holy enough.... Let us pray, let us suffer for them, and on the last day, Jesus will be grateful. We will give him souls!... Céline do you understand the cry of my soul?... Together.... Together, always, Céline and Thérèse of the Child Jesus and of the Holy Face.[66]

Here we have a typical letter to Céline, rhapsodic, disjointed with gaps and repeated ellipsis dots. The letter is important not only as evidence of a growing awareness by Thérèse of the importance of suffering for souls, but especially as the first instance in which she writes about her commitment to priests.

Another example of the value of sufferings for others is the wise guidance by Thérèse of her cousin Marie Guérin, later Sister Marie of the Eucharist. Through her own experience of scruples Thérèse was able to write a model letter for dealing with such a problem.[67] The value of suffering for others is a constant theme of her final months as recorded in the *Last Conversations*.

This insight into the value of suffering deepens during Thérèse's last illness. Thus she says to Mother Gongazue: 'I hold nothing in my hands. Everything I have, everything I merit is for the Church and for souls.'[68] And, most significantly of all, a few hours before she died she said: 'Never would I have believed it was possible to suffer so much! never! never! I cannot explain this except by the ardent desires I have had to save souls.'[68]

Suffering as joy

Thérèse frequently speaks of suffering as joy. Thus in her last year she writes:

> God has deigned to make me pass through many kinds of trials. I have suffered very much since I was on earth, but, if in my childhood I suffered with sadness, it is no longer in this way that I suffer. It is with joy and peace. I am truly happy to suffer.[70]

Thérèse wrote this about June just four months before she died. She was already gravely ill, and had been enduring a trial of profound spiritual darkness from April of the previous year. We find the same ideas frequently in her poems, e.g. a poem she wrote for Sister Marie-Madeleine on her profession:

> If sometimes bitter suffering
> Should come to visit your heart,
> Make it your joy:
> To suffer for God... what sweetness!...
> Then Divine tenderness
> Will make you soon forget
> That you walk on thorns.[71]

But the idea of joy and suffering was one that grew only gradually with Thérèse. Writing to Céline in the early months of their father's illness she indicates something of her struggles. The repeated stops and gaps in the writing also gives an indication of an extended mediation:

> Your letter gave great sadness to my soul! Poor little Papa!... No the thoughts of Jesus are not our thoughts, and His ways are not our ways.... He is offering us a chalice as bitter as our feeble nature can bear.... Let us not withdraw our lips from this chalice prepared by the hand of Jesus... Let us see life as it really is.... It is a moment between two eternities.... Let us suffer in *peace!*.... I admit that this word peace seemed a little strong to me, but the other day, when reflecting on it, I found the secret of suffering in peace.... The one who says *peace* is not saying joy, or at least, *felt* joy.... To suffer in peace it is enough to will all that Jesus wills.... To be the spouse of Jesus we *must* resemble Jesus, and Jesus is all bloody, He is crowned with thorns.[72]

Though she has the paradoxical idea of joy and suffering, Thérèse never appears morbid about suffering, least of all in her last illness. On 19 May, some months before she died, she told her sister Agnes why she was so happy: 'Because this morning I had two 'little' pains. Oh! very sharp ones!... Nothing gives me 'little' joys like 'little' 'pains'.[73]

This theme of joy and suffering finds very dramatic expression in her last letter to her missionary brother, Father Roulland, when she is already very ill:

> The thought of heavenly beatitude hardly thrills my heart. For a long time, suffering has become my heaven here below, and I really have trouble in conceiving how I shall be able to acclimatise myself in a country where joy reigns without any admixture of sadness.[74]

This is not a passing thought; she says she has had it for 'a long time'. In a letter to her other missionary brother, the Abbé Bellière, a few days later she reiterates it:

> The thought of heavenly bliss not only causes me not a single bit of joy, but I even ask myself at times how it will be possible to be happy without any suffering. Jesus no doubt will change my nature, otherwise I would miss suffering and the valley of tears.[75]

We know that in this time Thérèse was in darkness and that the sense of heaven had left her. But there is more here: suffering has become for her the prime way of loving and she cannot see how she could she could be happy without this, for her, the ultimate expression of loving.

Suffering as union with Jesus

A theme that developed throughout her life was that of suffering seen as communion and union with Jesus. In one of her finest poems, and a favourite of her own, 'Why I love you O Mary', Thérèse sees suffering in a Marian perspective:

> Since the King of Heaven wanted his Mother
> To be plunged into the night, in anguish of heart,

Mary, is it thus a blessing to suffer on earth?
Yes, to suffer while loving is the purest happiness!...[76]

It is in another poem, 'My Joy', written when she had been in spiritual darkness for nine months, that we find some of the depths of her spirituality of suffering:

My joy is to love suffering
I smile while shedding tears.
I accept with gratitude
The thorns mingled with flowers....
If sometimes I shed tears,
My joy is to hide them well.
Oh! how many charms there are in suffering
When one knows how to hide it with flowers!
I only want to suffer without saying so
That Jesus may be consoled.
My joy is to see him smile...
My joy is to struggle unceasingly
To bring forth spiritual children.
It's with a heart burning with tenderness
That I keep saying to Jesus:
'For you, my Divine Little Brother,
I'm happy to suffer.
My only joy on earth
Is to be able to please you'.

One of the keys to Thérèse's views of suffering is her devotion to the Holy Face of Jesus. She had added 'and of the Holy Face' to her name at her clothing in 1889. This devotion had come to the Lisieux Carmel through revelations given to a young Carmelite nun in the Carmel of Tours, Sister Mary of St Peter (1816-1848). Whereas her emphasis was on making reparation to Jesus, Thérèse saw in devotion to the Holy Face a way of resembling him. Several other poems draw out this theme.[77] It also embraces her whole concern for sinners:

> Living on Love is wiping your Face,
> It's obtaining the pardon of sinners...[78]

Finally, it is again within the perspective of love that Thérèse sees devotion to the Holy Face. With the other two bearing this name she made an act of consecration on the feast of the Transfiguration in 1896, at a time when she was in profound darkness.[79]

Beyond the desire – love alone

Thérèse says several times that the Lord always fulfilled her desires. 'He has not willed that I have one single desire which is not fulfilled.'[80] Thérèse was constantly developing her insights. Her teaching on suffering makes no sense except in the perspective of love. From every other point of view it would indicate some psychological pathology. But seen as love it has an overwhelming rightness. When, however, she comes into a deeper understanding of love towards the end of her life, she will no longer desire suffering, but remain indifferent to it. This is the final transformation of her being. The key passage is found towards the end of Manuscript A when again she is speaking about her desires, and about the fact that her beloved Céline could enter the Lisieux Carmel:

> And now I have no other desire except *to love* Jesus unto folly. My childish desires have all flown away.... Neither do I desire any longer suffering or death, and still I love them both; it is love alone that attracts me, however. I desired them for a long time; I possessed suffering and believed I had touched the shores of heaven, that the little flower would be gathered in the springtime of her life.

Now abandonment alone guides me. I have no other compass! I can no longer ask for anything with fervour except the accomplishment of God's will in my soul.[81]

The profound teaching here is given more poetic expression in the ecstatic colloquy with Jesus which concludes her letter to Marie (Manuscript B):

> Yes, my Beloved, this is how my life will be consumed. I have no other means of proving my love for you other than that of strewing flowers, that is, not allowing one little sacrifice to escape, not one look, one word, profiting by all the smallest things and doing them through love. I desire to suffer for love and even to rejoice through love; and in this way I shall strew flowers before Your throne. I shall not come upon one without unpetalling it for You. While I am strewing my flowers, I shall sing, for could one cry while doing such a joyous action? I shall sing even when I must gather my flowers in the midst of thorns, and my song will be all the more melodious in proportion to the length and sharpness of the thorns.[82]

This passage, written about ten months after the previous one, shows no rejection of suffering. Despite what she said at the end of Manuscript A the desire for suffering is still there, but now it is within the context of love.

Conclusion

We have insisted throughout this chapter that Thérèse is in no way deviant or unhealthy in her approach to suffering, provided her insistence on love is kept uppermost. But there is one question that can still be asked about her attitude to her own body, about which there would appear to be some ambiguity. At one level she can joke during her last illness on seeing the picture of her two missionary brothers, 'I am much prettier than they are'.[83] But on the very same day she had said earlier: 'My body has always embarrassed me; I've never been at ease in it... even when very small, I was ashamed of it.'[84] There are some other indications of a less than healthy approach to her body but they are rather too few to allow any definite conclusions. Thus she would seem to have regarded as a failing of some kind to have enjoyed using eau-de-Cologne before she entered the convent.[85] The context of this remark is, however, an examination in preparation for Extreme Unction of any possible sins connected with any of the senses. More significant perhaps is the remark on looking at her emaciated hands, 'I'm becoming a skeleton already, and that pleases me'.[86] This comment was on the same day. The available evidence would seem to point to some lack of appreciation of her body, but it does not indicate any serious psychological distortion, nothing that would invalidate her profound theology of suffering.

Though there is development in Thérèse's understanding of suffering, there is also a consistency and a coherence. What she grasped as a child eventually comes into mature expression in detachment and confidence. A few days before she died she said to Mother Agnes:

> O Mother, it's very easy to write beautiful things about suffering, but writing is nothing, nothing! One must suffer in order to know![87]

The teaching on suffering may well disturb those who see Thérèse as presenting a nice way to holiness, one that anyone can follow. In reply one must insist that her texts speak for themselves. There is no way that her stern vision can be watered down. Nor can one escape by imputing psychological illness to her. The problem here arises partly from a tendency to make Thérèse ordinary. She was not. She was called to very great holiness, to the most profound love. Most of the rest of us who are not called to such heights may in all likelihood escape such suffering. But we can learn from her some meaning for human pain, and a way of transmuting the dross of suffering into the gold of love.

> Let us profit from our one moment of suffering!… Let us see only each moment!…A Moment is a treasure…. One act of love will make us know Jesus better… it will bring us closer to Him during the whole of eternity.[88]

Chapter Six

Thérèse and the World

St Thérèse of Lisieux had a very sheltered life both in her family home and in the Carmel. The question arises about her knowledge of, and involvement in, the world of her time. In chapter two we saw that her view of the Church tended towards triumphalism, and that her family had something of the citadel mentality characteristic of the times. It can be shown that Thérèse was not unaware of the world and that through her mission of intercession she entered deeply into many of its concerns.

The biblical world

The world is an extremely complex notion in the Bible; there must be no reductionism of its essentially ambiguous state.[1] The world as created by God is good (Gn 1-2; Pr 8:22-31). The world moves to a final destiny planned by God, the Lord of history, which will be a new heaven and a new earth (Is 65:17; 66:22; Rv 21). But the world is infected with sin, almost from the beginning (Rm 5:12). The world can be said to be in darkness (see Ep 6:12). Indeed, for John the world stands for all that is opposed to Jesus and its leader is Satan, ruler of this world (Jn 12:31; 14:30). In a profound sense neither Jesus nor his followers belong to the world (Jn 17:14-16). Jesus, however, takes away the sin of the world (Jn 1:29) and gives his flesh for the life of the world (Jn 6:51). Whilst on earth the Christian must be on guard from the contamination of the world (Jm 1:27); one must not love the world or the things of the world (1 Jn 2:15), for friendship with the world involves enmity with God (Jm 4:4).

The three enemies of holiness, indeed of salvation, are the world, the flesh and the devil.

Ambiguity of the world

In the opening chapter we considered the hostile civil authority of the Third Republic.[2] Thérèse saw the attacks on religious life as a serious danger. It even fanned her desire for martyrdom again, and she wondered if perhaps this dream might come about even in France. Thus one reaction to the contemporary world was to see it as hostile, offering perhaps the possibility of martyrdom. Another response was that of her redoubtable uncle, the pious and wealthy Isidore Guérin, who entered Catholic politics and wrote editorially on current events at home and abroad for the monarchist paper *Le Normand* from 1891. He was always ready to defend the Church whenever it was attacked. Thérèse spoke of him with real warmth in her letters and she was impressed with his holiness.[3] Her close relationship with him and his wife ensured that Thérèse was not ignorant of the affairs of the world.

Thérèse's writings well reflect the ambiguity of the world. She uses the word 'world' 221 times, and, apart from idiomatic phrases such as *tout le monde* (everybody), generally in a negative sense. Two incidents from her childhood might be seen as pointers to her attitude. She recalled that when she was about eight she found an ideal game for herself and her cousin Marie, which was to play at being hermits withdrawn from the world having only simple work with a vegetable garden and a life of constant prayer.[4] Whilst such an incident should not be overemphasised, it should be remembered that Thérèse recalled it later in detail and with pleasure and that it would be consistent with the some of the deepest desires of her life.

The other incident is more significant, this time with Céline. On the pilgrimage to Rome Thérèse and her sister visited the Colosseum, commonly believed to have been a place of Christian martyrdom. They searched for the place marked with a cross where the martyrs were said to have fought:

> We soon found it and threw ourselves on our knees on this sacred soil, and our souls were united in the same prayer. My heart was beating hard when my lips touched the dust stained with the blood of the first Christians. I asked for the grace of being a martyr for Jesus and felt that my prayer was answered![5]

Thoughts of martyrdom, the most radical form of rejection of the world, were to be with Thérèse all her life.

Very early in her autobiography she speaks of God's protection: 'In his love He wished to preserve His little flower from the world's empoisoned breath.'[6] Sometime later she referred in the following terms to the new stage of her schooldays which for her were not happy times:

> I was undoubtedly big enough now to commence the struggle, to commence knowing the world and the miseries with which it is filled.[7]

Whilst we must be aware that Thérèse's memories of youth are seen from the later perspective of an enclosed Carmelite who had abandoned the world, we would probably be right in seeing the bitter-sweet account of her childhood as reflecting fairly accurately the vision both of Thérèse and of her family. Her account of her first return to Alençon gives the impression of recalling an insight given at the time rather than being merely a later interpretation retrojected and imposed on the past. There is, however, some element of later reflection.

> My joy was very great when seeing the places where I had spent my childhood days and especially when I was able

to pray at Mamma's grave and ask her to protect me always. God gave me the grace of knowing the *world* just enough to despise it and separate myself from it. I can say that it was during my first stay at Alençon that I made my *first entrance* into the *world*. Everything was joy and happiness around me; I was entertained, coddled, and admired; in a word, my life during these two weeks was strewn only with flowers. I must admit that this type of life had its charms for me. [...] At the age of ten the heart allows itself to be easily dazzled, and I consider it a great grace not to have remained at Alençon. The friends we had there were too worldly; they knew too well how to ally the joys of this earth to the service of God.[8]

She goes on to cite the 'all is vanity' text from Ecclesiastes (2:11) before adding: 'perhaps Jesus wanted to show me the world before His *first visit* to me in order that I might choose freely the way I was to follow.'[9] The rather negative view of this stay in her original home town contrasts with the extraordinary delight with which she immediately speaks about he First Communion ('His first visit'). Such sentiments can be found at every stage of her life.

It is surely significant that just before her strength failed totally she transcribed into her life story a long passage from John 17:4-26 which revolves around belonging to the world or to Jesus and the Father.[10] Thérèse is quite convinced that God withdrew her from the contamination of the world. As she recalled the lessons with her tutor Mme Papineau, she was exposed to flattery, which she found quite attractive:

Oh! how I pity souls that are lost! It is so easy to go astray on the flowery paths of the world. Undoubtedly, for a soul a little advanced spiritually, the sweetness which the world offers is mixed with bitterness, and the *immense* void of the *desires* cannot be filled by the praises of an instant. However, if my heart *had not been raised to God from the dawn of reason,* if the world had smiled on me from my entrance into life, what would have become of me?... Did [the Lord] *not draw me from the world before my spirit was corrupted by its malice and before its deceitful appearances had seduced my soul* (Wis 4:11)? The Blessed Virgin, too, watched over her little flower and, not wanting her to be tarnished by contact with worldly things, drew her to *her mountain* before she blossomed.[11]

The text from the Book of Wisdom was one of the passages copied out by Céline into the notebook of Old Testament texts that she brought with her to Carmel. If Céline had copied out this text, it must have struck her too. The reference to the mountain is obviously to Mount Carmel, a synonym for her vocation.

Another aspect of the world on which Thérèse reflects frequently is its transitoriness. She alludes several times to the text of Paul: 'For the present form of this world is passing away' (1 Co 7:21).[12] Within this vision her Carmelite life represents security and an embracing of what is truly worthwhile and eternal. She would seem to suggest that it was some kind of worldly wisdom that led her uncle to oppose her early entry to Carmel.[13] Entry into Carmel is seen by her as leaving the world.[14]

Thérèse is aware that her knowledge of the world is very incomplete. Apologising for having missed Céline's feast-day she says, 'the life in Carmel is so eremitical that the poor little hermit never knows what the date is'.[15] Again, she begins retailing an amusing incident about the convent's ignorance about how to cook a lobster to her missionary brother, Father Roulland, by stating: 'Carmel... is a country foreign to the world where one loses the world's most elementary usages.'[16]

Insights with Céline

Elsewhere we have noted that throughout her life Thérèse shared her deepest thoughts with Céline. We know that she was very anxious that her favourite sister Céline would enter the Lisieux Carmel. There were formidable difficulties. It would have meant another member of the Martin clan, a fifth, joining the convent where there was already some resentment of them. Moreover, Father Pichon, her spiritual director, wanted Céline to join him as a missionary in Canada. Whilst retaining her desire that Céline join her,[17] Thérèse eventually accepted God's will in the matter.[18] But she was determined that Céline in exile, Thérèse's word,[19] would be protected from the world. Céline had being receiving attentions from a lawyer and she was torn between her desire to belong totally to God and the thought of marriage. Thérèse went so far as to storm heaven to prevent Céline dancing at a family wedding. She recalls her satisfaction at hearing that Céline became foot-tied on the dance-floor to the embarrassment of both herself and her partner.[20]

Elsewhere she admits that she knew little about the situation of Céline: 'I had already suffered very much when knowing she was exposed to dangers in the world which were unknown to me.'[21]

Martyrdom

Her central intuition into martyrdom can perhaps be found in the expression: 'love comprised [*renfermait*] all vocations' in the Church; martyrdom is surely included.[22] In Thérèse's writings martyrdom is much more an expression of total love for God than a gesture of defence of the faith. In a letter to Céline in 1889 she wrote: 'Let us make our life a continual sacrifice, a martyrdom of love, in order to console Jesus.'[23] On her profession day, 8 September 1890, she carried a letter on her heart:

Jesus, I ask You for nothing but peace, and also love,

infinite love without any limits other than Yourself; love which is no longer I but You, my Jesus. Jesus may I die a martyr for you. Give me martyrdom of heart or of body, or rather give me both.[24]

A year later, perhaps inspired by the wave of anti-clericalism then sweeping France and Italy, she returns to the theme of martyrdom in another letter to Céline, under the image of a flower being taken up:

> Céline, when will Jesus pluck His little flower? Perhaps the pink colour of its corolla indicates that this will be by means of martyrdom! Yes, I feel my desires are reborn. Perhaps after having asked us love for love, so to speak, Jesus will want to ask blood for blood, life for life.[25]

The contemporary situation seems to have inspired another reference to martyrdom during the financial and other harassment of religious congregations by a Masonic government administration from 1895. She writes to her aunt, Mme Céline Guérin, quoting a sentence from a sermon she heard:

> 'Times similar to those of Achab's persecution are about to begin again.' We seemed to be flying already to martyrdom. What joy, dear little Aunt, if our whole family were to enter heaven on the same day.[26] [The biblical reference is 1 K 18:20-40.]

Such expressions proliferate in Thérèse's writings. They are implicitly both a choice made in love and a rejection of the values of the world.

Carmel and the World

There is no doubt but that Thérèse regarded Carmelite life as
quite preferable to life in the world. She rejoices 'to be always a
prisoner in Carmel'.[27] She describes the temptation against her
vocation in ways that allow us to see the interaction of Carmel
and the world:

> I found life in Carmel to be very beautiful, but the devil
> inspired me with the assurance that it wasn't for me....
> The darkness was so great that I could see and understand
> one thing only: I didn't have a vocation.... I wanted to do
> God's will and return to the world rather than remain in
> Carmel and do my own will.[28]

Recalling God's care for her vocation she remarked, 'Before my
entrance into Carmel I had many experiences of life and the
miseries of the world.... Today, when I am enjoying Carmel's
solitude..., I find I paid very little for my happiness.'[29] She saw
herself as 'expanding on the fertile mountain of Carmel'.[30] She
sometimes used phrases like 'the solitude of Carmel'.[31] She
returned several times to the grille, which at different times has
received various interpretations in Carmel: is it to keep the nuns
in or the world out? Speaking of Céline still in the world looking
after her father, she said: 'Ah! far from separating us, Carmel's
grilles united our souls more strongly.'[32] There is also a positive
view of the Carmelite vocation, as when Thérèse remembered a
quotation from a retreat, 'the zeal of a Carmelite embraces the
whole world'.[33] More specifically Thérèse saw the Carmelite
vocation as praying for sinners and for priests.

Sin and Thérèse

The question must be asked how close Thérèse is to the world
and its concerns. Hans Urs von Balthasar developed a thesis
that Thérèse was stunted by the declaration after a general

confession of Father Pichon that she had never committed a mortal sin..[34] He stated:

> From now on, obedient soul that she is, she never speaks of her sins but only of 'imperfections'. Her sense of sin had been destroyed. The most fateful effect on her mission was that, at a vital moment, she had been withdrawn from the community of sinners, divided off from them and banished into a lifelong exile of sanctity.[35]

Though Balthasar was sharply criticised for this view, he never revoked it, and repeated it at the prestigious Paris celebration of the centenary (1973).[36] The problem here would seem to be his use of inadequate texts and of some prejudice arising from the influence of Adrienne von Speyr, herself a translator from the earlier unsatisfactory French text of the *Story of a Soul*. Against the distinguished Swiss theologian one would have to draw attention to significant texts in which Thérèse truly feels herself a sinner. In her meditation on herself as a little bird, she speaks of her misdeeds and her infidelities and takes consolation from the love of him who came to call not the just but sinners (Mt 9:11).[37] But most explicitly in recounting her trial of faith she sees herself at the table at which sinners eat and adds, 'Can she not say in her name and in the name of her brothers, 'Have pity on us, O Lord, for we are poor sinners!' (Lk 18:13).[38] Though they are not frequent, there are sufficient texts in which Thérèse aligns herself with sinners to demand a reconsideration of Balthasar's views. Thus, in 'Why I Love You, O Mary', a late poem of quite some depth, she says 'Refuge of sinners, He leaves us to you' – a statement which can hardly be seen as distancing herself from sinners.[39] Indeed she speaks of the greatness of preventative mercy:

> I know that without him, I could have fallen as low as St

Mary Magdalene, and the profound words of Our Lord to Simon resound with great sweetness in my soul. I know that *'he to whom less is forgiven, LOVES less'* (Lk 7:47), but I also know that Jesus has *forgiven me more than St Mary Magdalene* since He forgave me *in advance* by preventing me falling.[40]

She then goes on to give an analogy. A doctor could set his child's broken limb; this would be great love. But if the doctor saw the stone on which the child might trip and removed it, he would be showing even greater love, even though the child might not know it. She then concludes:

> Well, I am this child, the object of the *foreseeing love of a Father* who has not sent his Word to save the *just* but *sinners*. He wants me *to love* Him because he *has forgiven* me not much but *ALL*.[41]

In another of her great poems we find:

> Living on love is wiping your Face,
> It's obtaining the pardon of sinners.
> O God of Love! may they return to your grace,
> And may they forever bless your name…
> Even in my heart the blasphemy resounds.
> To efface it, I always want to sing:
> I adore and love your Sacred Name.
> I live on in love.[42]

At first sight she seems here to distance herself from sinners, the 'they' of the poem. The fifth line is difficult: 'Even in my heart the blasphemy resounds' *(Jusqu'à mon coeur retentit le blasphème)*. The poem is from February 1895 and thus before her trial of faith during which she was assailed by blasphemous thoughts.[43] So the sense would seem to be that the blasphemies of sinners touched her profoundly and with them or on their behalf she wishes to make reparation through an act of adoration and love. It does not support any idea that Thérèse was not at one with sinners.

Prayer for sinners

Thérèse continually returned to the theme of praying for sinners; it occurs over fifty times in her writings. This mission can in a sense be said to have been established with her prayer for the triple murderer Pranzini. The story is familiar. Thérèse learned that he was unrepentant as he faced the death sentence. She was profoundly drawn to intercede for him and just before his death he gives a sign of repentance by kissing the crucifix at the actual guillotine.[44] This answer to her prayer coming so soon after her profound intuition into the blood of Jesus and his thirst for souls,[45] gave her a deep, lifelong commitment to pray for sinners: 'to pray for sinners attracted me' *(me ravissait).*[46] The thought of praying for sinners is a frequent theme in her letters and poems, e.g.

> I want to pray unceasingly for sinners.
> That I came to Carmel
> To fill your beautiful Heaven, Remember....[47]

We would need to look somewhat more closely at her prayer for the world. She was certainly aware of sin and scandal in the Church as some illustrations will make clear. A few weeks before she died she offered up her trial of faith for an in-law, René Tostain, who had no faith.[48]

Two incidents of public sin touched her deeply. The first was the Diana Vaughan affair. In 1895 a woman calling herself Diana Vaughan published a document retelling the story of her conversion from Freemasonry and satanism, due to the influence of Joan of Arc. Catholics, who saw their Church locked in mortal combat with Masonry, were enthralled. Thérèse's uncle was very much involved writing about the convert; it was even rumoured that she was thinking of entering a monastery – could it be Lisieux? The convent there was kept informed about the whole matter, largely through Isidore Guérin.

At the same time the Lisieux Carmelite community was still bruised after the difficult elections that reappointed Mother Gonzague on the seventh ballot. Thérèse wrote a playlet to entertain the community, her seventh, 'The Triumph of Humility' which was a reflection on the conversion of Diana Vaughan.[49] Thérèse saw Diana's conversion as reflecting the cosmic struggle between good and evil, and she peopled her play with three novices and a variety of demons. The central message of the play was that the great weapon of Carmelites was humility; if accompanied by self-love, religious vows and virginity do not disturb Satan.[50]

The interest in Diana continued in the Carmel. Mother Agnes asked Thérèse to send her a poem, but for once her inspiration dried up. She sent her a photograph of herself dressed up as Joan of Arc, through whose intercession Diana had been converted. But an awful surprise awaited them all. An infamous Mason, Léo Taxil, had made a public conversion, and had been absolved from excommunication by the Nuncio. He called a meeting of journalists and others for 19 April 1897. He had a blown-up copy of the photo of Thérèse dressed as Joan of Arc projected on the wall. He proceeded to tell the packed audience that he had made up the story of Diana; she never existed. Moreover, his conversion was feigned. It was all a practical joke stretching over twelve years that had fooled clergy, religious, politicians, bishops and even the Vatican. Protected by the police, Taxil disappeared amid boos. Thérèse was devastated. Her values and her beloved Joan of Arc had been publicly mocked. She tore up the letter she had received from 'Diana,' who was Taxil. She did not burn the scraps, but instead buried them in the convent dung-heap. She does not seem to have referred directly to this incident afterwards, though it is surely echoed behind the passage towards the end of her autobiography:

> Jesus made me feel that there were really souls who have no faith, and who, through the abuse of grace, lost this precious treasure, the source of the only real and pure joys.[51]

Taxil would provide an even greater challenge to her prayers than Pranzini.

We have more evidence of Thérèse's feeling in the case of another sinner, the complex character of Father Hyacinthe Loyson.[52] He had tried his vocation with the Sulpicians and Dominicans before becoming a Discalced Carmelite. A fine preacher, he eventually became provincial of the order. In 1869, just before Vatican I, he left his order and the Church, married a Protestant widow, and preached Gallican views, especially throughout the north of France. From about 1891 the Carmel received several newspaper cuttings concerning his activities.

Thérèse took up his cause: here surely was a soul to be won. She writes to Céline and the difficult syntax gives some idea of her distress:

> Yes, dear Céline, suffering alone can give birth to souls for Jesus… Is it surprising that we are so favoured, we whose only desire is to save a soul that seems lost forever?…. The details interest me very much, while making my heart beat very fast…. Dear Céline, he is really culpable, more culpable than any other sinner ever was who was converted. But cannot Jesus do once what he has not yet ever done? And if He were not to desire it, would He have placed it in the hearts of His poor little spouses a desire that He could not realise?[53]

Her restrained language is noteworthy: she calls Loyson 'this poor stray sheep' and elsewhere 'the unfortunate prodigal'. At the same time there were those in the Catholic papers and in the Carmel using expressions like 'renegade'. It is not quite clear why she regarded his sin as the greatest; it may be because by seeking to establish an alternative Church, he was leading others astray. She prayed constantly for him and offered her last Communion on 19 August 1897 for him. Mother Agnes noted: 'This conversion had preoccupied her all through her life.'[54] The Carmel sent him a copy of Thérèse's autobiography and other documents in 1911. He replied in a courteous way, stating that he had been very impressed by Thérèse, though not fully convinced. He died in 1912 whispering the name of Jesus and kissing the crucifix. His death thus mirrored that of Pranzini whom Thérèse regarded as her first child.

Reparation

In the nineteenth century the spirituality of reparation had been developing strongly; it had origins in the Catholic reaction to the intellectual excesses of the Enlightenment and to the anti-religious excesses of the Revolution. It had, of course, roots further back in the apparitions of the Sacred Heart to St Margaret Mary Alacoque (1673-75) and even earlier. Though Thérèse only uses words like 'reparation' very infrequently (ten times), she is very much in the current of its spirituality. It could perhaps be argued that this is a French emphasis rather than a Carmelite one. The most characteristic expression of Thérèse is that of 'consoling Jesus'.[55] This complex theme of consolation is perhaps best seen in terms of love. One would not be happy with the idea that the glorified Jesus is pained by sin. Pain belongs only to this earth. But just as Thérèse at an early age was distressed to see the blood of Jesus being poured out with nobody to gather it,[56] so too she sees the love of Jesus rejected. Consoling Jesus, or making reparation to him, seems to be her affective response to this rejected love of Jesus. Reparation or consolation is most profoundly Thérèse being conscious of the world and bringing its pain and its sin to the healing mercy of God.

By way of conclusion we can look to some of the prayers which Thérèse wrote. She had been enrolled in two confraternities: The Reparation Archconfraternity of Saint-Dizier (1885) and the Confraternity of the Holy Face at Tours (1876). The apparitions at La Salette also increased the theme of reparation. In her prayers some of these current ideas are to be found. In her 'Homage to the Most Holy Trinity' she prays:

> O my God, we prostrate ourselves before you. We have implored the grace of working for your glory. The blasphemies of sinners remain in our ears.[57]

One of the aspirations that Thérèse taught the novices was to say at the elevation of the Host at Mass: 'Holy Father, look on the face of your Jesus and of all the sinners that you make the elect.'[58] In the Consecration to the Holy Face which she and the others with the name of Holy Face pronounced on the feast of the Transfiguration 1896, we find:

> Souls, Lord, we must have souls...above all the souls of apostles and martyrs so that through them we may embrace with your love the multitude of poor sinners.[59]

In summer 1896 she collected four prayers around images of Jesus. On a picture of the Holy Face she recalled one of the promises given to the visionary of the Holy Face, Sister Mary of St Peter in 1845.[60] In response to the sixth promise that those who invoke the Holy Face will receive what they pray for, it is interesting what Thérèse chose to ask for:

> Eternal Father, since you have given me as a heritage the

Adorable Face of Your Divine Son, I offer it to you and ask you in exchange for this infinitely precious part that you forget the ingratitude of souls who are consecrated to you and that you pardon all sinners.[61]

Thérèse is constant in her prayer for sinners. She sees it in a double perspective: she wishes to make reparation to God for the sins committed against him and to give him glory through the conversion of sinners. But in her commitment to sinners and the world, she is not only loving God, but she is passionately in love with those who need her prayer and the divine mercy. She finds this double focus of love of God and love of others especially in her deepening attraction to the mystery of the Holy Face. Withdrawn from the world she carried the world in her heart, especially sinners and priests. Her extraordinary mission to priests is the theme to which we will now turn.

Chapter Seven

Priests

Thérèse's sister and former prioress, Mother Agnes, testified to her commitment to priests at the diocesan process for her beatification:

> Later (after the Pranzini affair) the souls of priests drew her more and more, because she knew that they were dear to Our Saviour and more capable of drawing hearts to him. She several times said to me after the journey to Rome, during which she had seen with astonishment that if their sublime dignity raised them above the angels, they are nonetheless weak and frail men. She afterwards constantly prayed for priests and spoke of the necessity of obtaining graces for them. She was very happy to offer especially prayers and mortifications for two missionaries, to whose works the mother prioress had assigned her.[1]

Leaving to the next chapter the question of Thérèse's two missionary brothers, we shall examine here Thérèse's remarkable apostolic dedication to priests.[2] It will be helpful firstly to indicate briefly the tradition of priestly spirituality that Thérèse inherited, before outlining her main encounters with priests. These two points will provide the context in which we can best understand what she says about priests and her absolute commitment to prayer and suffering for them.

Tradition and priesthood
The tradition about priests inherited by Thérèse is very ancient

in the Church. It may be said to go back to the fourth century and St Gregory of Nazianzus' defence of his temporary flight from sacerdotal responsibilities – he had earlier been ordained priest against his will by his father.[3] It is a veritable treatise on the nature and responsibilities of the priesthood. St John Chrysostom (d. 407) took it as a model for his Six Books on the *Priesthood*;[4] it also inspired the *Pastoral Rule* of Pope St Gregory the Great (d. 604).[5] In these classics we see several themes recurring: awe at the holiness of the priestly ministry and the holiness to be cultivated by the priest; teaching and preaching as primary priestly tasks; wonder at the Eucharistic mystery; humility, prayer, ascesis and charity as marks of the priest's life; the need to avoid all immorality. These classical works presented the ideal of the priesthood that would be dominant for centuries. After the patristic period the most significant teaching on priestly spirituality was the French School of spirituality, notably P. de Bérulle (1575-1629) and J. J. Olier (1608-1657) who proposed that the priesthood should be seen in relation to the Incarnation and the Eucharist. The other significant themes of this tradition are those of the priest being *alter Christus* (another Christ) and of his acting *in persona Christi* (in the person of Christ), the latter only being used by Vatican II.[6] Thérèse was influenced by this tradition throughout her life, even though her experience of priests was not always positive.

Priests in the life of Thérèse

Thérèse's own direct contacts with priests were somewhat limited, yet of sufficient diversity to enable her to have quite an ample appreciation of their vocation and ministry. It is unlikely that she ever met a Discalced Carmelite priest; during her Roman pilgrimage she encountered a friar of the Ancient Observance who beckoned her to leave when out of curiosity she had penetrated the reserved cloister.[7] Despite their standing in the town the Martin family do not seem to have entertained priests at their home, except perhaps Father Pichon. She recalls the curate Father Ducellier visiting,[8] but until the Roman pilgrimage priests must have been rather distant figures for Thérèse.

There is little doubt but that Thérèse was seriously disedified by priests when at the age of fourteen she went on pilgrimage to Rome with her father and Céline. About one quarter of the 197 pilgrims were members of the lesser nobility and included seventy-five priests. Later commenting on the Carmelite vocation to pray for priests she recalled her experience:

> Having never lived close to them, I was not able to understand the principal aim of the reform of Carmel. To pray for sinners attracted me, but to pray for the souls of priests whom I believed to be as pure as crystal seemed puzzling to me!... How beautiful is the vocation, O Mother, which has as its aim the *preservation* of the *salt* destined for souls! This is Carmel's vocation since the sole purpose of our prayers and sacrifices is to be the *apostle* of the *apostles*. We are to pray for them while they are preaching to souls through their words and especially their example.[9]

She was apparently quite shocked by seeing another side of priests previously viewed only in sacred functions.[10] A young priest's excessive attentions to herself and Céline would have been an unwelcome surprise.

As we read biographies of Thérèse,[11] her writings and the literature surrounding her, we notice the names of quite a number of priests who touched her life only fleetingly. Thus Father Roger de Teil, postulator for the cause of the Compiègne Carmelites martyred in 1794, gave a talk on them to the community in 1896. This fired Thérèse's enthusiasm and interest in them.[12] Later in fact he would be the vice-postulator for her own cause of beatification.

Father Alcide Ducellier was curate at St Peter's in Lisieux where he heard Thérèse's first confession. She was too tiny to be seen when kneeling and she recalls that he told her to stand. She was firmly convinced that through him she was confessing to God and that the 'tears of Jesus were going to purify' her soul.[13] Well instructed by her sister, Marie, she already had the idea of the priest's acting in *persona Christi*. Thérèse also recalled that a sermon by this priest on the Passion was the first one she ever understood.[14] He testified at the diocesan process that he had the impression that she was a very pure soul, very devout and greatly afraid of offending God in the least things.'[15]

A missionary priest, Armand Lemonnier, gave three retreats in the convent. Mother Agnes asked his opinion on Thérèse's *Offering to Merciful Love*. Having consulted with his superior he approved it, but with a change that Thérèse regretted: he wanted her to use 'immense desires' instead of 'infinite desires'.[16] She described his retreat in 1893 as beautiful and she noted in particular his words on union with Jesus and on the value of the contemplative life.[17] He testified at the beatification process, paying special tribute to her wise direction of the novices, her confidence and faith, and the high esteem in which she was held, especially by the chaplain Father Youf.[18]

When Thérèse left the Benedictine Abbey school, her confessor was Father Louis Lepelletier. At the time we must remember one could receive Communion only with the permission of one's confessor. He rather unusually allowed Thérèse to communicate four or even five times a week. But so well did Marie counsel Thérèse that neither he nor Father Domin, her confessor at the Abbey, suspected the terrible onslaught of scruples that would last for about a year and a half from May 1885.

Father Faucon, who heard her last confession in the absence of Father Youf, does not seem to have influenced her; he remarked on the beauty of her soul before she died. Another priest, Father Gombault, was to be very important for Thérèse's admirers. Entering the cloister to oversee some construction project, he brought a camera and gave the world the striking picture of Thérèse as a white-veiled novice embracing a large cross in the garden of the convent.

Given Thérèse's great dedication to priests throughout her life it is important to note that her encounters with priests were by no means all positive. Some were quite negative, others mixed or ambiguous. Father Leconte, curate at St Peter's, was the source of some scandal on the pilgrimage to Rome. He, however, was probably the one who arranged for Thérèse and Céline to have Communion at the Holy House at Loreto.[19]

Father Louis-Victor Domin was chaplain at the Benedictine Abbey. He was a distant cousin of Thérèse. He gave her much affirmation at catechism lessons, calling her 'his little doctor'.[20] She was not afraid to ask for permission, exceptional for the time, to receive her second Communion within a month of her First; he permitted it.[21] But he was to have a very negative influence on her. He preached a retreat for those preparing for First Communion. He gave terrifying talks on topics like Hell, The Last Judgment, Sacrilegious Communion, Death. Thérèse does not seem to have been affected at that time, but a year later (1885) a retreat (again by Father Domin) in preparation for the Solemn Communion saw the beginning of the attack of scruples which Thérèse called a martyrdom.[22] To the end of her life the thought of retreats left her apprehensive. He was a good but rather severe man. Because he heard Thérèse praised in her presence by Mother Agnes, he ceased visiting the Carmel; by the time of the beatification process he had been won over by her autobiography and readily admitted his mistake. He recalled too Thérèse asking him one time after receiving absolution 'Do you believe that Jesus is content with me?' He was of the opinion that she never committed a fully deliberate fault.[23]

About May 1890 Thérèse told a Jesuit retreat director, Father

Laurence Blino, that she wished to be a great a saint and to love God as much as St Teresa of Avila. He was nonplussed at her audacity and advised moderation. From Mother Agnes we have Thérèse report of the interview. He told her:

> Confine yourself to correcting your faults, to offending God no longer, to making a little progress in virtue each day, and temper your rash desires.[24]

The two priests who probably caused her most pain were the ecclesiastical or religious superior of the Carmel, Canon Jean-Baptiste Delatroête (d. 1895), and the Vicar General, Father Maurice Révérony (d. 1891). The religious superior, who was largely the bishop's representative, had made some mistakes in the past by allowing quite unsuitable persons to join religious communities. Having had his fingers burned, he was quite adamant about rejecting the idea of Thérèse's entry at the age of fifteen. Indeed, he demanded more than did Church law, by suggesting that she stay at home until she was twenty-one. His opposition was unrelenting and even when his hand was forced and Thérèse was admitted, he remained hostile and quite ungenerous in his comments afterwards. It was only when he saw Thérèse in action in December 1891 when all but three of the community were bedridden with influenza and there were several deaths, that he began to realise her worth.[25] He should not be judged too harshly, as if Thérèse's desire to enter the Carmel at fifteen were so patently obvious as being from God that only the stupid or the prejudiced could fail to appreciate it. Canon Delatroête knew the Carmel, the many unbalanced personalities it contained, the equivocal temperament of its superior, Mother Gonzague. Even Thérèse's own sister Marie, already in Carmel, took some time to be convinced of the prudence of such an early entry.

Father Révérony, though initially opposed to her entry, does not appear to have been quite so negative. He was quite annoyed at Thérèse's audacity in appealing to the pope about her entry to Carmel. Thérèse sensed that he watched her closely during the pilgrimage. She felt intimidated by him; having to ask for a ride in his coach at Assisi made her feel, she said, 'like a squirrel caught in a trap'.[26] But he was obviously impressed by her during the pilgrimage and on the way home at Nice, he promised his support for her entry. She reminded him later of this promise.[27] On his return, he attempted to mediate between the Carmel who wanted Thérèse admitted and the redoubtable and still intractable Canon Delatroëtte.

The bishop throughout all Thérèse's life was Mgr Flavien Hugonin, a gentle scholarly man, who was highly esteemed in the French Church. He had opposed the definition of infallibility at Vatican I, but accepted it when it was passed. He confirmed Thérèse, he received her and her father at his residence at Bayeux when she requested to enter at fifteen. On her return from Rome she wrote several times to him.[28] Eventually he gave permission. A month before she died he was in Lisieux and there was talk of his visiting Thérèse. Her response was typical: 'How I wish the Bishop wouldn't come to see me…. However, a bishop's blessing is a grace.'[29] Shortly before he died in 1898 he gave the necessary imprimatur for the publication of the *Story of a Soul*.

Several priests had a very positive influence on Thérèse, one of whom, Father Alexis Prou, she met only during the retreat of October 1891; the other was Father Almire Pichon, spiritual director of Marie, Céline and Thérèse herself. During her last illness she said:

> I'm very grateful to Father Alexis; he did me much good. Father Pichon treated me too much like a child; however he did me much good by telling me I'd not committed a mortal sin.[30]

The convent were expecting a Franciscan provincial to give the retreat. He had to send a replacement, Father Alexis Prou, who had a great reputation as a preacher for crowds and sinners. Thérèse did not expect much and tells us that she was the only one in the community who appreciated him. Approaching him was one of the great graces of her life:

> At the time I was having great interior trials of all kinds, even to the point of asking myself whether heaven really existed. I felt disposed to say nothing of my interior dispositions since I didn't know how to express them, but I had hardly entered the confessional when I felt my soul expand. After speaking only a few words, I *was understood* in a marvellous way and my soul was like a book in which this priest read better than I did myself. He launched me full sail upon the waves of *confidence and love* which so attracted me, but upon which I dared not advance. He told me that *my faults caused God no pain and that holding as he did God's place,* he was telling me *in his name* that God was very much pleased with me.[31]

She would have loved to speak to him again, but Mother Gonzague, in a not untypical abuse of authority, forbade a second encounter; Thérèse obeyed. In a few moments God had used this unlikely visitor to the convent to touch her life profoundly. In time she would articulate this grace in her spiritual doctrine of the Little Way. We can note here again the sense of the priest representing Jesus. Indeed this event is recounted to explain how Thérèse sensed that Jesus was to be her director.

Father Pichon, a Jesuit, was ordained the year of Thérèse's birth.[32] He was the director of two of her sisters, Marie and Céline, but except for a few crucial times, Thérèse did not find him very helpful. She first met him in August 1883, when she was ten. To be like her sisters she asked him to be her spiritual director in 1887,[33] but it did not work out, largely because he departed for Canada. It was agreed that she would write monthly, but he only replied once a year to her letters. Unfortunately, he did not keep any of perhaps fifty letters she wrote to him; he wrote fifteen times to her.

He was one of the priests who had a profound influence on her in one significant meeting. He had personally been well prepared to help her; as he had suffered intensely from scruples as a youth, he was always eager to calm those disturbed. His published retreat notes show him as steeped in the best traditions of spirituality, with a sharp eye for human foibles and the ability to use a vivid and telling phrase.[34] Thérèse was not long in Carmel when he came to give a retreat on the occasion of Marie's profession. Thérèse made a general confession. Father Pichon was the instrument of two major graces. Firstly, at that confession she was set free from the gnawing anxiety that she had brought upon herself the serious illness which had been cured by the smile of the Virgin.[35] More important still, despite the difficulty she had in expressing herself, he spoke solemnly to her in words that Thérèse highlights with capitals and underlining:

> *'In the presence of God, the Blessed Virgin, and all the saints,*
> *I DECLARE THAT YOU HAVE NEVER COMMITTED*
> *A MORTAL SIN.'* Then he added: 'Thank God for what
> He has done for you; had he abandoned you, instead of
> being a little angel, you would have become a little
> demon'.[36]

His own experience of scruples would have shown him the value of such a solemn formula. Thérèse again recognised God speaking through a priest for she added:

> ...such an assurance, coming from the mouth of a
> director such as St Teresa desired, i.e. one combining

knowledge and virtue, it seemed to me to be coming from the mouth of Jesus himself.[37]

Twice more in letters Fr Pichon had to speak authoritatively to her about relapsing into scruples.[38] Thérèse and he were on opposite sides about Céline: he wanted her in Canada; she wanted her in the Lisieux Carmel. Thérèse won, for when her father died, and after much opposition from within the Carmel and from Canon Delatroëtte, Céline entered in September 1894, becoming one of Thérèse's novices. Father Pichon gave important testimony at the process of her beatification;[39] we shall examine what he said about her writings in the Epilogue.

It is difficult to assess the influence of Father Louis Youf on Thérèse. He was chaplain at the Lisieux Carmel from 1873 until his death just a week after that of Thérèse. He was the ordinary confessor of the convent. A dedicated priest who enjoyed poor health, he would have been the priest Thérèse saw most often as a Carmelite. She would always be grateful for his advice to go to speak to the bishop in Bayeux about entering Carmel. He supported her case, as well as Céline's. Though he was her regular confessor, she did not record any great lights she received through him. He was perhaps a bit too anxious personally to be able to reassure her. Earlier he had scolded her for her dryness, distraction or sleep during prayer. The nuns knew about his own fear of death, and Thérèse did not always find his words to her very helpful.[40] Indeed when she told him about her temptations against faith, he seems to have taken fright. Mother Agnes recalled Thérèse's words:

> Father Youf told me with reference to my temptations against the faith: 'Don't dwell on these, it's very dangerous'. This is hardly consoling to hear, but happily I'm not affected by it. Don't worry, I'm not going to break my 'little head' by torturing myself. Father Youf also said:

'Are you resigned to die?' I answered: 'Ah! Father, I find I need resignation only to live. For dying, it's only joy I experience.'[41]

She took great pleasure in a comment he made after hearing her confession two months before she died: 'If the angels were to sweep heaven, the dust would be made of diamonds.'[42] We do not know the context sufficiently to be clear about what he meant.

Canon Alexander Maupas succeeded Canon Delatroëtte as ecclesiastical superior of the Carmel. In the narrow, almost grudging administration of Extreme Unction of the time, he took a strict view of the danger of death necessary for its reception. When Thérèse had already been gravely ill and had asked for the sacrament after confessing to Father Youf on 5 July,[43] Canon Maupas did not judge her to be sufficiently near death. He did anoint her on 30 July. He testified at the beatification process that on account of the illness of Father Youf he had visited her five or six times during her last two months and found her radiant and smiling.[44]

The Premonstratensian, Father Godefroid Madelaine, preached three retreats in Carmel. In October 1896 Thérèse confided in him her temptations against faith. He advised her to write out the *Creed* and carry it on her heart, so that she could touch it when tempted; she wrote it out in her own blood, and placed it in her copy of the gospels.[45] He read her *Story of a Soul* and approved it for publication. He also recommended chapter divisions, suppression of some rather intimate family matters, and the title of the autobiography. During the process for beatification he testified warmly to her holiness. He noted the veneration in which she held the pope and her own bishop.[46] His comments on her writings can be noted in the Epilogue of this work.

Some priests whom Thérèse did not know touched her by

their deaths. Father Frédéric Mazel, a companion of her missionary brother, Father Roulland, was killed in China by looters at the age of twenty-six. Thérèse regarded him as a martyr.[47] In particular she was drawn to the Venerable Théophane Vénard, martyred in 1861 and subsequently beatified in 1909. Thérèse read his life and kept his picture before her pinned to the curtain of her bed during her last illness. She wept with joy when she was given his relic.[48] She referred to him frequently during her last illness: she admired his ordinariness.[49] In February 1897 she wrote a poem in his honour in which she identified with his suffering, his missionary zeal, his desire for the salvation of sinners.[50] In a special farewell letter to her three sisters in the convent, written perhaps in June before she died, she used phrases from Théophane to express her thoughts.[51]

Finally, we do not know if she had much devotion to the Lazarist, Jean-Gabriel Perboyre, who was martyred in China and beatified in 1889; she kept a holy picture of him.

Love of priesthood

We know that Thérèse had a deep appreciation of the priestly vocation and everything associated with it. She delighted in sacristy work and took great pleasure in looking after the sacred vessels. In a poem written for Sister Marie Philomena who made altar hosts, 'The Sacristans of Carmel', she outlines her joy in this ministry and sees her association with Christ:

> We must help the apostles
> By our prayers, our love.
> Their battlefields are ours.
> For them we fight every day.[52]

It is not easy to interpret some sayings in which she expressed a desire to be a priest, one she seems to have shared with her Mother, Teresa.[53] Some have invoked her as patroness of the cause of the ordination of women. The best known passage is where she searches for her own vocation and considers the various vocations in the Church, especially warrior, priest, apostle, doctor and martyr and says:

> I feel in me the *vocation of* the PRIEST. With what love, O Jesus, I would carry You in my hands when, at my voice, You would come down from heaven. And with what love would I give you to souls! But alas! while desiring to be a *Priest,* I admire and envy the humility of St Francis of Assisi and I feel the *vocation* of imitating him in refusing the sublime dignity of the *Priesthood.*[54]

Seeing that she sees as a vocation both being a priest and refusing the priesthood, we cannot take this text as indicating a serious envy of priests. One should note that her vision of the priest here is above all as minister of the Eucharist, which accords with the tradition she inherited.

This desire does not seem to be isolated. There are several significant texts during her last illness. She regretted the multiplicity of translations of the Bible, and she states:

> Had I been a priest, I would have learned Hebrew and Greek, and wouldn't have been satisfied with Latin. In this way, I would have known the real text dictated by the Holy Spirit.[55]

Again, she reflected on presiding at the Liturgy of the Hours:

> How proud I was when I was hebdomadarian during the recitation of the Divine Office, reciting the prayers aloud in the centre of the Choir! I was proud because I remembered that the priest said the same prayers during Mass, and I had the right, like him, to pray aloud before the Blessed

Sacrament, giving the blessings and the absolutions, reading the Gospel when I was first chantress.[56]

On another occasion during her last illness she said:

How I would have loved to have been a priest in order to preach about the Blessed Virgin. One sermon would be sufficient to say everything I think about this subject.[57]

None of these texts suggests any deep frustration at not being a priest. We can get more insight by considering how she viewed aspects of the priestly ministry.

Quite fundamental to her spirituality is her concern for sinners, which we studied in chapter six. After the profound experience at her Christmas night conversion she was given deep insight into the cry from the Cross, 'I thirst' (Jn 19:28), a text to which she would return several times.[58] She would certainly have loved to preach the gospel: only a mission without limitations of time or space would satisfy her.[59] She was deeply appreciative of the permission she got from priest confessors and ecclesiastical superior to receive Communion frequently, even daily, during the influenza epidemic in the winter 1891/92.[60] She expressed delight when Rome removed from local superiors the authority to allow their subjects to receive Communion or to prohibit them from doing so. Rome, seeking to correct abuses, gave this authority only to the ordinary or extraordinary confessor and forbade superiors to interfere in this matter.[61]

In the end Thérèse transcended any immediate desires about priesthood in her all-encompassing vision of being 'love in the heart of the Church'. Indeed she said about that discovery: 'Thus I shall be everything.'[62] But even earlier in a letter to Céline she deliberately eschewed envy of priests:

Is not the apostolate of prayer, so to speak, more elevated

than that of the word? Our mission as Carmelites is to form evangelical workers who will save thousands of souls, whose mothers we shall be.... I find that our share *(notre part)* is really beautiful, what have we to envy in priests?[63]

Intercession for priests

Given Thérèse's deep appreciation of the priestly vocation it clearly pained her to see priests who did not seek God with undivided love. In her last illness she laments: 'Oh, how little God is loved on this earth, even by priests and religious! No, God isn't loved very much'.[64] She was particularly pained as we have seen by the apostasy of Father Hyacinthe Loyson. Her ministry of intercession was above all concerned with priests.[65] Thérèse is very taken up with a specific Carmelite charism of prayer for priests (and theologians), which is derived from Teresa of Avila.[66] At the formal examination of her motivation before her profession, she stated: 'I came to save souls and especially to pray for priests.'[67] She recognised that this desire had been sharpened by some of the disedifying incidents she had witnessed on her Rome pilgrimage. She reflects afterwards about the vocation of being an apostle to the apostles: 'We are to pray for them while they are preaching to souls through their words and especially through their example'.[68] The same ideas occur in several of her letters, especially to Céline, e.g.

> Oh! Céline, let us live for souls... let us be apostles... let us save especially the souls of priests; these souls should be more transparent than crystal.... Alas, how many bad priests, priests who are not holy enough.... Let us pray, let us suffer for them, and, on the last day, Jesus will be grateful.[69]

Again,

> 'Dear Céline, I *always* have the same thing to say to you. Ah! Let us pray for priests; each day shows how few the friends of Jesus are…. It seems to me that this is what he must feel the most, ingratitude, especially when seeing souls who are consecrated to him giving to others a heart which belongs to Him in so absolute a way.'[70]

These two letters are typical of her correspondence with Céline: passionate, occasionally disjointed, with great use of ellipsis. The vision of Thérèse is what is sometimes today called 'a multiplier'; by helping priests she was helping a vast number touched by their ministry.

In another rather discontinuous letter to Céline in 1889, she wrote about the intercessory power of love. She feels that she is at one with her sister and that the latter will understand her perfectly:

> Let us love him, then unto folly; let us save souls for Him. Ah! Céline, I feel that Jesus is asking *both of us* to quench *His thirst* by giving him souls, the souls of *priests* especially. I feel that Jesus wills that I say this to you, for our mission is *to forget* ourselves and to reduce ourselves to nothing…. We are so insignificant… and yet Jesus wills that the salvation of *souls* depends on the sacrifices of our love. He is begging souls from us.[71]

Her commitment to priests was lifelong. Thus in her last illness she offered her suffering for The Abbé Joseph de Cornière, then a seminarian. He wrote a letter to her which deeply touched her:

> Oh, what consolation this letter brought to me! I saw that my sufferings were bearing fruit. Did you notice the sentiments of humility the letter expresses? It's exactly what I wanted.[72]

There is, of course, a wider dimension of her apostolate on behalf of priests, namely missionaries; we will turn to that in the next chapter.

Conclusion

There can be no doubting Thérèse's appreciation of priests and of their vocation. Even though, as we shall see, she was richly gifted with charisms and in a sense had only Jesus as her director,[73] she nevertheless received significant help from priests at critical stages of her spiritual journey. In most of these there was that typical element of surprise, which often authenticates spiritual experience, as she was not expecting the grace she received. She was very much aware of the possibility of doing good which priests have, and she knew that one priest helped can indirectly help many more. She was also in the great tradition of seeing that holiness should arise out of the sacred ministry of priests. She had clearly been disappointed by the behaviour of priests, not least that of Hyacinthe Loyson. She experienced in her own life and surroundings the need for the ecclesial vocation of Carmelites, already established by Teresa of Avila, to pray for priests. Her intercession was an act of love for God whose ministers they were, for the priests themselves, and for the Church which depended on their ministry.

Chapter Eight

Missions and Missionaries

When, on 12 December 1927, Pope Pius XI declared St Thérèse of Lisieux principal patroness of the missions and of all missionary men and women on a par with St Francis Xavier, he was saying something important about contemplatives in the Church and about the life and mission of Thérèse. The fecundity of mission work depends not only on the active work of missionaries like Francis Xavier, but also on the support of prayer and sacrifice that has a primary expression in contemplative institutes, although open to all Christians at all times. There are three important issues concerning Thérèse and the missions: her own sense of missionary vocation; her commitment to the missions by prayer, sacrifice and suffering; her two missionary brothers.

Missionary vocation

The nineteenth century was a time of great missionary expansion. Confining ourselves to Thérèse's own country we see that three major missionary congregations had their origins then: The Congregation of the Holy Spirit (Spiritans), the Oblates of Mary Immaculate, the White Fathers (Missionaries of Africa). And there were many more. French missionaries went to all four continents outside Europe. The Lisieux Carmel itself was responsible for the planting of Carmel in Indo-China (Saigon 1861). The view of missions then was the traditional one of saving souls rather more than of planting the Church. Thus, as she begins her autobiography, Thérèse is musing on the inequalities in God's creation:

> I was puzzled at seeing how Our Lord was pleased to caress certain ones from the cradle to the grave, allowing no obstacles in their way... I wondered why poor savages died in great numbers without even having heard the name of God pronounced.[1]

Her answer was, as always, theologically very accurate: God loves all; 'He created the poor savage who has nothing but the natural law to guide him'; 'Perfection consists in doing His will, in being what he wills us to be.'[2] Thérèse's view of the missions will be within the perspective of love. A question constantly comes up in relation to her desire for the salvation of others: is it only out of love of God that she is concerned, or does she genuinely love those in need of redemption? It is clear that both are operating, even though the former may seem to predominate. Here her anxiety about what was called at the time 'the poor savages' (*sauvage* is less harsh in French) indicates her genuine love for them.

Thérèse's missionary vocation was clearly nurtured in her family home.[3] We know that her father and mother made regular contributions to the missions. Almost casually Thérèse herself tells us that on big feasts she withdrew coins from her money box when there were collections for the Propagation of the Faith.[4] When she was on retreat for her First Communion she said that she made a show of herself by quite ostentatiously wearing a large cross that she wore in her cincture like a missionary.[5] The clearest indication is recalled by her sister Céline:

> During our pilgrimage to Rome when Thérèse was only fourteen years old, I saw her put aside a missionary almanac after she had read only a few pages. 'I had better not go on with this,' she told me, 'for it might only intensify my yearning for the life of the missions. I have deliberately sacrificed it for the hiddenness of Carmel,

where I can suffer more through the monotony of an
austere life and thereby win more souls for God.[6]

The origin of Thérèse's missionary vocation was her profound
concern for the salvation of souls, which was strongly awakened
by a moment of deep intuition when seeing a picture of the
Crucified, an event which we considered in the earlier chapter on
suffering. That fifth chapter is the indispensable context for an
understanding of her missionary dedication. We will see that her
attraction for, and commitment to, the missions is lifelong.[7]

The key text is one that we have already considered in a
number of contexts, her discovery of her special vocation to be
'love in the heart of the Church'. One of the vocations that had
most attracted her apart from martyrdom was the impossible one
of being a missionary, one, indeed, with no limits as to mission:

> I have the *vocation of an Apostle*. I would like to travel
> over the whole earth to preach Your Name and to plant
> Your glorious Cross on infidel soil. But *O my Beloved,* one
> mission alone would not be sufficient for me. I would
> want to preach the Gospel on all the five continents
> simultaneously and even to the most remote isles. I would
> be a missionary, not for a few years only but from the
> beginning of creation until the consummation of the
> world. But above all, O my Beloved Saviour, I would shed
> my blood for You even to the very last drop.[8]

But as she finds her vocation to be 'love in the heart of the
Church' she realises that the missionary task of the Church
depends utterly on love for 'if love ever became extinct, apostles
would not preach the Gospel'.[9]

All her life Thérèse longed to be an actual missionary,
especially in the Carmel in Saigon or the more recently established
convent at Hanoi (1895); she expressed a hope of being able to go

there even during the last year of her life.[10] There was also talk of her sister Pauline and others going there, and Thérèse sensed the pain this break would cause.[11] She quotes Mother Gonzague to the effect that 'a very special vocation is necessary to live in foreign Carmels. Many believe they are called to this, but it isn't so.'[12] She professed herself ready to leave Lisieux, with no illusions either about what this would cost her.[13] As late as November 1896 there was talk of her going. A novena to the martyr the Venerable Théophane Vénard was begun to obtain a sign of God's will: before it was over there was a clear relapse of her health. When Sister Geneviève remarked to her within a month of her death,'When I think they are still waiting for you at the Carmel of Saigon,' Thérèse replied, 'I shall go; I shall go very soon; if only you knew how quickly I will make my journey!'[14] This rather cryptic response seems to refer to her death and the consequent possibility of a new presence to the nuns in China.

Thérèse's sense of missionary vocation found expression in her prayer and suffering for missions and missionaries, and in her remarkable relationship with her two missionary brothers.

A life for missionaries

One of the best-known stories about Thérèse is found in Marie's memoirs, appended to the main text of the *Last Conversations* which was composed mostly of the notes taken by Mother Agnes ('the Yellow Notebook'). A few months before Thérèse died she was asked by the infirmarian to walk daily in the garden; she remarked to her sister Marie who told her she would be better to rest:

> It's true, but do you know what gives me strength? Well, I am walking for a missionary. I think that over there, far away, one of them is perhaps exhausted in his apostolic endeavours, and, to lessen his fatigue, I offer mine to God.[15]

It was later confirmed that Bishop Breynat (1867-1954), then a missionary priest of the Oblates of Mary Immaculate in the North American Arctic, got the strength to continue an almost impossible journey at the same time that Thérèse was 'walking for a missionary.' This missioner who believed that he was the recipient of this grace, would later with his Oblate confrères be a chief instigator in having Thérèse declared Patroness of the Missions.

During her last illness Thérèse's thoughts were never far from missionaries. She spoke frequently about her missionary brothers and about the martyred missionary the Venerable Théophane Vénard. About ten week before she died, when she was already terribly ill, she spoke of what she was feeling:

> I can't think very much about the happiness of heaven; only one expectation makes my heart beat, and it is the love I shall receive and I shall be able to give. And I think of all the good I would like to do after my death: have little children baptised, help priests, missionaries, the whole Church. But first console my little sisters.[16]

The first sentence reflected the deep interior darkness which she had experienced for about fifteen months. Three days later she expressed her famous desire: 'I want to spend my heaven in doing good on earth.'[17] Her concerns here are quite remarkable: babies, which is probably a missionary desire, priests, missionaries, the whole Church, and a special affection for her sisters, by which she most probably meant her community.

On the same day her sister Marie recorded the same sentiments in somewhat different words. The idea is so striking that Thérèse may well have spoken twice about it to two different sisters:

> If you only knew the projects I'll carry out, the things I shall do when I'm in heaven....I will begin my mission.[18]

When Marie asked 'What are your projects?', Thérèse replied,

> Projects such as coming back with my sisters, and going over there to help missionaries, and then preventing little pagans from dying before being baptised.[19]

Elsewhere she showed her concern for unbaptised babies when thinking of her funeral and recalling that of Mother Geneviève, the foundress of the Lisieux Carmel:

> After my death, I don't want to be surrounded with wreaths of flowers as Mother Geneviève was. To those who want to give these, you will say that I would rather they spend this money in the ransom of black babies. This will please me.[20]

We have elsewhere noted some of the cures prescribed by her physicians that caused her great distress and did her little good. Quite early in her last illness she reflected on these treatments:

> I'm convinced of the uselessness of the remedies to cure me; but I have made an agreement with God so that He will bring profit from them for poor, sick missionaries who have neither the time nor the means to take care of themselves. I've asked Him to cure them instead of me through the medicines and the rest that I'm obliged to take.[21]

Her deep love for missionaries nowhere comes across more clearly than in the remarkable correspondence with her two missionary brothers.

Her missionary brothers

Thérèse's relationship with her two missionary brothers led to her developing some of her most mature thoughts on suffering, on intercession, on the Communion of Saints, on the missionary task. But if we are fully to appreciate this exceptional exchange of letters we have to be aware of what this relationship meant to Thérèse. Writing for Mother Gonzague in the last months of her life she said:

> For a very long time, I had a desire which appeared totally unrealisable to me, that of having *a brother as a priest*. I often thought that had my little brothers not flown away to heaven, I would have had the happiness of seeing them mount the altar; but since God chose to make little angels of them, I could not hope to see my dream realised. And yet, not only did Jesus grant me the favour I desired, but He united me in the bonds of the spirit to two of his apostles, who became my brothers. [...] Mother, it would be impossible for me to express my happiness. My desire, answered in this unexpected way, gave birth in my heart to a joy I can describe only as that of a child. I would really have to go back to my childhood days to recapture once more the memory of joys so great that the soul is too little to contain them, and not for years had I experienced this kind of happiness. I felt my soul was renewed; it was as if someone had struck for the first time musical strings left forgotten until then.[22]

When she penned these rapturous lines her health had seriously deteriorated; she would write only for another few days before leaving her manuscript unfinished on 8 July 1897. This passage gives us a key to interpret the letters and invites us to take their warmth seriously and to give full attention to the spiritual visions which unfold in them

Indeed, some of Thérèse's most profound thoughts on mission come in the context of her two missionary brothers, Maurice Bellière and Adolphe Roulland.[23] There are many ways in which Thérèse's correspondence with them can be studied. It can be helpful to consider the themes that run through the eighteen letters. But as we have available their letters to Thérèse and her letters, the correspondence, when taken as a whole, reveals much not only about Thérèse's spirituality of mission, but also about her own affectionate personality. However, reading her letters would never cause one to suspect that she was already far into the darkness of the trial of faith which began at Easter 1896. Thérèse is very aware that this kind of correspondence can easily be useless and she warned about it for the future. In her final illness she said to Mother Agnes:

> Any Sister could write what I have written and would receive the same compliments, the same confidence. But it's only through prayer and sacrifice that we can be useful to the Church. Correspondence should be very rare, and it musn't be permitted at all for certain religious who would be preoccupied with it, believing they're doing marvels, and would be doing nothing really but harming themselves and perhaps falling into the devil's subtle traps.[24]

But despite this guarded view of correspondence, Thérèse appears very human in her letters. She wanted each of them to tell her the significant dates of their lives and she gave them hers.[25] She wanted their photographs, and when she got them she looked at their rough, bearded countenances and said: 'I'm much prettier [*gentille*] than they are.'[26]

We will consider Thérèse's correspondence with each of the brothers, noting especially indications of her theology of mission and other suggestions of her vision of the Church. We will find, often presented with new depth, many of the intuitions and reflections that we have seen in previous chapters.

Father Maurice Bellière

Thérèse's first missionary brother was Father Maurice-Marie-Louise Bellière (1874-1907). As a seminarian he was given as a 'spiritual brother' in 1895. She wrote eleven letters to him. The prioress read to Thérèse from a letter he had written to the Carmel. He felt in some sense inspired by St Teresa of Avila:

> He was asking for a Sister who would devote herself especially to the salvation of his soul and aid him through her prayers and sacrifices when he was a missionary so that he could save many souls. He promised to remember the one who would become his sister at the Holy Sacrifice each day after he was ordained. Mother Agnes of Jesus told me she wanted me to become the sister of this future missionary.[27]

He left for Algiers and entered the novitiate of the White Fathers (Missionaries of Africa) the day before Thérèse died. His mother had died when he was a week old, and his father did not appear until he was eleven, at which age he discovered that his 'father and mother' were really his aunt and uncle. His upbringing resulted in his being extremely sensitive and somewhat lacking in decisiveness. Thérèse found that he needed much support and encouragement; her letters to him combine both firmness and warmth. These letters to him show her to be a spiritual director of great understanding and delicacy. Even when, after 8 July 1897, Thérèse became too weak to continue the writing of her autobiography, she made a supreme effort to send him four more letters.

Despite her assurance of caring for him after her death, he was to know many tribulations. He went to Africa and was almost immediately appointed an area superior, a task for which he proved quite inept. He lost his way between the colonial culture and his task as missionary in Nyassa. He returned to France in

1904, in poor health after only two years as a missionary, and eventually had to leave the White Fathers. He seems to have suffered a mental illness not unlike that of Thérèse's own father. More remarkably still, he died in the same mental hospital at Caen as M. Martin. Father Bellière's death in 1907 at the age of thirty-three may have been as a result of a cerebral tumour, rather than the sleeping sickness hitherto generally proposed.[28]

We begin with a letter from July 1896 that he wrote to Mother Agnes, unaware that she was no longer prioress. He asked for renewed prayer from Thérèse whom he had been given as a sister nine months previously. He planned to abandon the seminary for a military career.[29] Mother Gonzague soon entrusted him directly to Thérèse. She wrote a first letter in October 1896. It has a formal greeting, *'Monsieur l'abbé'*. She rejoices that her prayers for him have been answered and consoles him with the thought that temptation comes to all, especially to those specially chosen. She tells him:

> I am asking Him that you may be not only a *good* missionary but a *saint* all on fire with the love of God and souls; I beg you to obtain also for me this love so that I may help you in your apostolic work. You know that a Carmelite who would not be an apostle would separate herself from the goal of her vocation and would cease to be a daughter of the Seraphic Saint Teresa who desired to give a thousand lives to save a single soul.[30]

Father Bellière replied to this letter at the end of November, addressing Thérèse as 'Good Little Sister.' He was encouraged by her letter.[31] She replied after Christmas, assuring him of her prayers and of her confidence that he will receive the graces he needs, 'since Our Lord never asks sacrifices from us above our strength'. She referred to his desire for martyrdom, but said, 'martyrdom of the heart is no less fruitful than the pouring out of one's blood, and now this martyrdom is yours.' She then shared some of her most profound insights. She understood his needs but drew him into a higher vision:

> *Monsieur l'Abbé,* you come seeking consolations from her whom Jesus has given you as a sister, and you have the right. Since Reverend Mother allows me to write to you, I would like to respond to the sweet mission entrusted to me, but I feel the surest means of reaching my goal is to pray and to suffer...Let us work together for the salvation of souls; we have only the one day of this life to save them and thus to give the Lord proofs of our love.[32]

She concluded the letter 'Let us remain close to the crib of Jesus through prayer and suffering.'[33] Already she can be seen operating according to the spiritual principles she enunciated later in conversation with Mother Agnes as noted above. Thérèse never doubts the efficacy of prayer and suffering. Here too we find the notion of saving souls as an expression of her love for the Lord. Elsewhere there is the complementary notion of love for those redeemed.

The next letter, in February 1897, still has a formal greeting, but Thérèse reveals something more of her regard towards her brother: 'Truly you will know only in heaven how dear you are to me; I feel our souls are made to understand one another.' Almost incidentally she reveals her deepest inspiration: 'the only thing I desire is God's will.' She looks to a future, perhaps soon when she will die and for the first time shares with him her sense of deep union in the Communion of Saints:

> I do not know the future; however, if Jesus realises my presentiments, I promise to remain your little sister up above. Our union, far from being broken, will become more intimate. Then there will be no longer any cloister

and grilles, and my soul will be able to fly with you into distant missions. Our roles will remain the same; yours apostolic weapons, mine, prayer and love.[34]

Here we have already the germ of the vision about spending her heaven doing good on earth that will only be articulated fully six months later. Elsewhere, for 'prayer and love' she writes 'prayer and suffering'.

Two months later she addresses Father Bellière for the first time as 'Dear little Brother.' She speaks again about the bond between them: 'It seems to me that the divine Saviour has seen fit to unite our souls in working for the salvation of sinners,' and she compares the two of them with Father Claude de la Colombière and Blessed Margaret Mary. She discusses his desire for martyrdom, and says, 'the Lord seems to will to grant me only the martyrdom of love'. She later reflects on Joan of Arc and adds,

> ...instead of voices from heaven inviting me to combat, I heard in the depths of my soul a gentler and stronger voice, that of the Spouse of Virgins, who was calling me to other exploits, to more glorious conquests, and into Carmel's solitude. I understood my mission was not to have a mortal king crowned but to make the King of heaven loved, to submit to Him the kingdom of hearts.[35]

Clearly her sense of mission is continually deepening.

On 9 June she wrote a farewell letter which, since her condition later improved, was not sent. In it she further developed her sense of the Communion of Saints in which she and her brother will be still more closely united:

> Your little sister will be united forever to her Jesus; then she will be able to obtain graces for you and to fly with you into distant missions. Oh, dear little brother, how

happy I am to die! [...] Brother, I shall go soon to offer your love to all your friends in heaven, begging them to protect you. Dear little Brother, I would like to tell you many things that I understand now that I am at the door of eternity; but I am not dying, I am entering into life, and all that I cannot say to you here below, I will make you understand from the heights of heaven.[36]

The next letter later in June is very important for the insight it gives into Thérèse as a sensitive but firm spiritual director.[37] It has little of interest for our concerns about her mission spirituality and her teaching on the Church.

By the time she writes again on 13 July she has already ceased writing her autobiography; she has been moved to the infirmary and had asked to be anointed. Her articulation of her role is even clearer as she takes up some of the thoughts of the unposted letter of 9 June:

I am happy to die because I feel that such is God's will, and that much more than here below I shall be useful to souls who are dear to me, to your own in particular [...]. I shall do more than write to my dear little Brother, more even than speak to him in the fatiguing language of this earth I shall be very close to him, I shall see all that is necessary for him... When my dear little Brother leaves for Africa, I shall follow him no longer by thought, by prayer; my soul will be always with him, and his faith will be able to discover the presence of a little sister whom Jesus gave him, not to support him for barely two years but *right up to the last moment of his life.*[38]

She is referring to the two years during which she had been Father Bellière's Little Sister, but it is surprising in view of his actual destiny. She goes on to give one of her clearest statements on suffering:

All these promises, Brother, may perhaps appear to you a little chimerical; however, you must begin to realise that God has always treated me like a spoiled child. It is true that His Cross has followed me from the cradle, but this Cross Jesus has made me love with a passion. He has always made me desire what he wanted to give me.[39]

Five days later she wrote again: 'The thought of heavenly bliss not only causes me not a single bit of joy, but I even ask myself at times how it will be possible to be happy without any suffering.' She is alluding to her trial of faith, which, however, she had never shared with either of her missionary brothers. The paradoxical statement that she did not quite know how she could be happy without suffering, that is, the opportunity it allowed of showing the deepest love, must surely have surprised him. But she went on to reiterate her view on their vocation: 'I feel it, we must go to heaven by the same way, that of suffering united to love.' She proceeded to take up again a theme of deeper communication after her death: 'I explain myself so poorly that I must wait for heaven in order to converse with you about this happy life...' And further, 'I beg you, dear little Brother, try like her (Sister Agnes) to convince yourself that instead of losing me you *will find* me, and that I will no longer leave you.'[40]

A letter from the Abbé Bellière crossed Thérèse's in the post.[41] Shocked at the imminence of Thérèse's death, he writes in a sad, rather self-pitying vein, much more centred on his loss than on Thérèse or how she may have been suffering or feeling. She writes on 26 July when she was already desperately ill. Since he had become resigned to her death, she can give him astonishing assurances:

Ah! Brother, allow me to say it: God is reserving for your soul very sweet surprises; you have written, it is 'little accustomed to supernatural things,' and I, who am not your little sister for nothing, I promise to have you taste after my departure for eternal life the happiness one can find in feeling a friendly soul next to oneself. It will not be this correspondence, more or less distant, but it will be a fraternal conversation that will charm the angels, a conversation that creatures will be unable to reproach since it will be hidden from them.[42]

Despite her weakness she shared with him details about her family and gave him careful spiritual direction about his view of himself and his sinfulness.

On 10 August she managed to send him a last letter. She had already been anointed, and she alluded to some grace of learning from her father that she was soon to die. She wrote a farewell and instructed him still again about weakness and the divine mercy.[43] Her final communication was only a picture, the last one she had painted, and a single-line greeting.[44]

Father Adolphe Roulland

A seminarian at the Foreign Mission Society, Father Adolphe Roulland (1870-1934) was ordained on 28 June 1896 and left for China on 2 August. He had been given to Thérèse as her second 'spiritual brother' on 30 May of that year.[45] The arrangement was somewhat strange. Mother Gonzague wanted the community to think that Father Roulland was her own spiritual brother, and commanded Thérèse to keep confidential the fact that it was she and not the prioress who did the writing. Only in May 1897 did Mother Gonzague allow Thérèse to tell her sister Pauline about Father Roulland and herself.

Father Roulland visited the Carmel on 3 July 1896 and met Thérèse. Despite the grille he saw her once – during the parlour visit Mother Gonzague told him that Thérèse would be last up for Communion; Thérèse at the same time told him that Mother Gonzague would be the first communicant in line. Thérèse wrote seven letters to him while he was in China. She wished to obtain the key dates of his life, so that she would be united with him in celebrating God's graces in him. Their lives were certainly bound together by one common date, the Birthday of Mary, 8 September 1890, Thérèse's profession; on that very day, troubled by vocational doubts, he received a profound interior confirmation of his missionary calling at the Marian shrine of Notre Dame de la Déliverande.[46] Father Roulland was a much stronger character than Father Bellière. His greatest fear was that he would be assigned missionary promotion work in Paris and not be an active missionary, but Thérèse gently taught him the way of abandonment to God's will. After his return to France in 1909, he was to be an active proponent of Thérèse's Offering to Merciful Love

As we survey Thérèse's seven letters to Father Roulland we shall not note all the passages which repeat insights found already in the correspondence with the Abbé Bellière.

The first letter is rather formal, addressing him as 'Reverend Father', but then he was Mother Gonzague's missionary, and she would presumably be reading the letter before posting it. Thérèse writes:

> I feel very unworthy to be associated in a special way with one of the missionaries of our adorable Jesus [...]. I shall be happy to work with you for the salvation of souls. It was for this purpose I became a Carmelite nun; being unable to be an active missionary, I wanted to be one through love and penance just like Saint Teresa, my seraphic Mother.[47]

By the very next letter the address is less formal, 'Brother (*Mon frère*)'. She reflects on their joint apostolate:

> ... distance will never be able to separate our souls, death

itself will make our union more intimate. If I go to heaven soon, I will ask Jesus' permission to go to visit you at Su-Tchuen, and we shall continue our apostolate together. In the meanwhile, I shall always be united to you by prayer.... I would even wish that my brother always have consolation, and I trials; perhaps this is selfish? But, no, since my only *weapon* is love and suffering and since your sword is that of the word and apostolic works.[48]

In the next letter, written nearly five months later, Thérèse develops the bond of 8 September 1890. She says of herself:

Bidding an everlasting *adieu* to the world, she had one goal, to save souls, especially the souls of apostles. From Jesus, her divine Spouse, she asked particularly for an apostolic soul; unable to be a priest, she wanted that in her place a priest might receive the graces of the Lord, that he have the same aspirations, the same desires as herself [...] I believed I would meet only in heaven the apostle, the brother whom I had asked from Jesus. [...] I did not know that for six years I had a *brother* who was preparing himself to become a missionary; now that this brother is really His apostle, Jesus reveals it to me in order no doubt to increase in my soul the desire of loving him and making him loved.[49]

We notice here that the missionary aim is expressed as 'loving Jesus and making Him loved'. The theme of priesthood is notable here, especially Thérèse's sense of identification with it. Like the texts we saw in the previous chapter it does not give any real sense of envy or even profound regret at not being a priest. She then thinks of praying for the gift of martyrdom for Father Roulland, the gift that we know she would most of all like to have herself.

Indeed she continues to pray for this gift for him, even to saying in her last letter that when she gets to heaven she 'will ask for the palm of martyrdom' for him.[50] After sharing details of her own vocational story, she brings in a new expression of their relationship:

> Like Joshua, you are fighting on the plain, and I am your little Moses, and incessantly my heart is lifted up to heaven to obtain the victory.[51]

The letter of 19 March is one of the most important of the series; we have already drawn from it in previous chapters. It has an important statement on suffering derived from *The Imitation of Christ* 2,12,11:

> When you find suffering sweet and when you love it for the love of Jesus Christ, you will have found paradise on earth. This paradise is really that of the missionary and the Carmelite; the joy that worldlings seek in the midst of pleasures is only a fleeting shadow, but our joy sought and tested in works and sufferings is a very sweet reality, a foretaste of the happiness of heaven.

Thérèse told him of her desire to have been a missionary in China and about her not being concerned with future purgatory for herself. It is also a most human letter, with a long, humorous account of the attempt of the Lisieux cook to deal with a live lobster which had been given to the community.[52]

The next letter is largely taken up with the question of purgatory: Father Roulland was afraid of a stern sentence in purgatory if he were to die violently on the mission. We shall examine Thérèse's reassurance in the next chapter. But she not only dealt with the issue of purgatory, she developed her own spirituality: 'my way is all confidence and love'. She then outlined her Little Way of childhood. The letter has also another major insight on the interrelation of heaven and earth:

> I am also deeply touched and grateful for your remembrance of my dear parents at Mass. I hope they are in possession of heaven to which all their actions and desires were directed; this does not prevent me praying for them, for it seems to me these blessed souls receive a great glory from the prayers offered for them and which they can use for other suffering souls.[53]

She goes on to refer to their desire for a missionary son, which has now been fulfilled, and she looks forward to the union of herself and him and both sets of parents. She concluded with a fresh exposition of their joint mission with a conceit based on the number nought:

> ...let us work together for the salvation of souls. I can do very little, or rather nothing, if I am alone; what consoles me is to think that at your side I can be useful for something. In fact, zero by itself has no value, but when placed next to a unit it becomes powerful, provided, however, that it is placed at the *right side,* after and not before.[54]

Her last letter to Father Roulland is a prolonged reflection on her death and her continuing apostolate afterwards.

> When you receive this letter, no doubt I shall have left this earth. The Lord in his infinite mercy will have opened His kingdom to me, and I shall be able to draw from His treasures in order to grant them liberally to the souls who are dear to me. Believe, Brother, that your little sister will hold to her promises, and, her soul, freed from

the weight of the mortal envelope will joyfully fly toward the distant regions you are evangelising. Ah! Brother, I feel it, I shall be more useful to you in heaven than on earth, and it is with joy that I come to announce to you my coming entrance into that blessed city, sure that you will share my joy and will thank the Lord for giving me the means of helping you more effectively in your apostolic work.[55]

She continued immediately:

I really count on not remaining inactive in heaven. My desire is to work still for the Church and for souls. I am asking God for this and I am certain he will answer me. Are not the angels continually occupied with us without their ever ceasing to see the divine face and to lose themselves in the Ocean of love without shores? Why would Jesus not allow me to imitate them? [.....] What attracts me to the homeland of heaven is the Lord's call, the hope of loving Him finally as much as I have desired to love Him, and the thought that I shall be able to make Him loved by a multitude of souls who will bless him eternally.[56]

Conclusion

It seems clear that in this chapter we see all the major themes of Thérèse's spirituality and her vision of the Church. When we look at her ecstatic discovery of her vocation of being love in the heart of the Church in Manuscript B, it is clear that she is describing a moment of transforming insight. But though this intuition came suddenly into clear perception, it had already been partially emerging, especially in her reflections on missions and in her correspondence with her missionary brothers. The translator of her poems, Donald Kinney, is surely right in supporting the suggestion of the editors of the poems that one written for Father Roulland on 16 July 1896 is a step towards the vision of Manuscript B. He notes that it is addressed to 'Our Lady of Victories, Queen of Virgins, Apostles and Martyrs', as the shrine of Our Lady of Victories, visited by Thérèse on her way to Rome, was a favourite place for missionaries to pray for their apostolates. We can end with this entire poem which can be seen as summarising not only this chapter, but most of the chapters preceding it.

> You who fulfil my hope,
> O Mother, hear the humble song
> Of love and gratitude
> That comes from the heart of your child...
>
> You have united me forever
> With the works of a Missionary,
> By the bonds of prayer,
> Suffering and love.
>
> He will cross the earth
> To preach the name of Jesus.
> I will practise humble virtues
> In the background and in mystery.
>
> I crave suffering.
> I love and desire the Cross...
> To save one soul,
> I would die a thousand times...
>
> Ah! for the Conqueror of souls
> I want to sacrifice myself in Carmel.
> And through Him to spread the fire
> That Jesus brought down from Heaven.

Through Him, what a ravishing mystery,
Even as far as East Szechuan
I shall be able to make loved
The virginal name of my tender Mother!...

In my deep solitude,
Mary... I want to win hearts.
Through your Apostle, I shall convert sinners
As far as the ends of the earth.

Through Him, the holy waters of Baptism
Will make of the tiny newborn babe
The temple where God Himself
Deigns to dwell in his love.

I want to fill with little angels
The brilliant eternal abode...
Through Him hosts of children
Will take flight to heaven!...

Through Him, I'll be able to gather
The palm for which my soul yearns.
Oh what hope! Dear Mother,
I shall be the sister of a Martyr!!!

After this life's exile,
On the evening of the glorious fight,
We shall enjoy the fruits of our apostolate
In our Homeland.

For Him, Victory's honour
Before the army of the Blessed.
For me... the reflection of His Glory
For all eternity in the Heavens!...

The little sister of a Missionary.[57]

Chapter Nine

Purgatory

The possibility of some purification after death is an ancient Christian belief, though the word 'purgatory' may be medieval.[1] The amount of Church teaching is extremely limited: two truths viz. the existence of a state of purification and the efficacy of prayer or pious works for the deceased.[2] From the Middle Ages there has been quite an amount of unhealthy fascination with purgatory and a disordered fear of its purification. From about the thirteenth century theologians began to use the word 'punishment' about purgatory: its pains were described as resembling those of hell, except that they would end, whereas hell was eternal.[3] Official Church teaching, however, has always avoided the word 'punishment' with regard to purgatory. In his great poem, *The Divine Comedy,* Dante Alighieri (d. 1321)gave equal space to heaven, purgatory and hell. His masterpiece fired the medieval imagination.

Prayer for the dead became a major feature of medieval and modern spirituality. The feast of All Souls, of Cistercian origin, was established in the mid-eleventh century. An Augustinian, St Nicolas of Tolentino (d. 1305) was recognised as the patron of those in purgatory. There was a fascination with indulgences which could help oneself or others to avoid or lessen purgatory. There were many devotional works and pious associations concerned with helping the dead. There was also an extensive literature on how to live and die in such a way as to avoid or reduce one's term in purgatory. Such works continued up to the time of Vatican II and beyond.[4]

What became known as the 'Heroic Offering' or the 'Heroic

Act' is of uncertain origins: it is clearly attested from the sixteenth century, but it may well date from earlier.[5] It was a spontaneous offering in favour of the souls in purgatory of all the works of satisfaction during one's life, and even of the prayers of others made for oneself after death. Sometimes these spiritual goods were given to the Virgin Mary, so that she might dispose of them in favour of whatever souls she might choose. In the nineteenth century this heroic act was propagated in England by the Oratorian and devotional writer, Father Frederick Faber (d. 1863).

Thérèse

Two saints in particular have made a critical contribution to the understanding of, and correct approach to purgatory. Catherine of Genoa (d. 1510) and Thérèse[6] both grasped the crucial fact that purgatory can only be properly understood in terms of love. The spirituality at the time of Thérèse was individualistic, even rather selfish. There was enormous interest in storing up merits for one's future blessedness. Thérèse's concerns on the contrary were wholly centred on the entire Communion of Saints. As we have seen she was very conscious of the profound relationship with her friends the angels and saints. She was also totally committed to prayer, suffering and intercession for those in need on earth. But her vision was not only about the Church in glory and the Church militant; she was also devoted to the Church suffering. Many people of her time, even within her own community, were concerned to accumulate indulgences and good works to shorten their stay in purgatory. Thérèse had a supreme disdain for such considerations and, as we shall see later, she declared herself uninterested in whatever purgatory might await her, even though she has an intuition that she may well escape it. Thus, recalling her Act of Oblation to Merciful Love on Trinity Sunday 1895, she wrote:

> Ah! since that happy day, it seems to me that Love

penetrates and surrounds me, that at each moment this Merciful Love renews me, purifying my soul and leaving no trace of sin within it, and I need have no fear of purgatory. I know that of myself I would not merit even to enter that place of expiation since only holy souls can have entrance there, but I know that the Fire of Love is more sanctifying than is the fire of purgatory.[7]

She was, however, very concerned to help those who might be in purgatory. In the beginning of the Act of Oblation we saw that she expressed a desire 'to work for the glory of Holy Church... by liberating those suffering in purgatory'.[8] About her profession day she said, 'I wanted to deliver all the souls from purgatory and convert all sinners.'[9]

Thérèse spoke frequently about purgatory, and it would seem clear that both the sisters in the convent and her correspondants had some trepidation in its regard. Thérèse, however, came to lose all fear of purgatory. It was with her new insights into merciful love that she found a different perspective. She clearly saw divine love as purifying before death, so that purgatory would be superfluous. But we would need to note the very high holiness that she had reached at this point, and could not necessarily conclude that all others could likewise escape purification after death. We would also have to remember the intense physical suffering of her final illness as well as the profound spiritual night in which she was enveloped, all of which were surely a penetrating purification of her whole being. In June or October of the same year as the Act of Oblation she wrote a poem to the Sacred Heart of Jesus in which the same sentiments can be found:

> To be able to gaze on your glory,
> I know we have to pass through fire.
> So I for my purgatory,

Choose your burning love, O heart of my God!
On leaving this life, my exiled soul
Would like to make an act of pure love,
And then, flying away to Heaven, Its Homeland,
Enter straightaway into your Heart.[10]

In one of her finest poems, 'Living on Love!', she developed further the idea of the purification by divine Love:

Living on Love is banishing every fear,
Every memory of past faults.
I see no imprint of my sins.
In a moment love has burned everything...
Divine Flame, O very sweet Blaze!
I make my home in your hearth.
In your fire I gladly sing:
'I live on Love!...'[11]

Her missionary brothers

We find some important teaching on purgatory in her letters to her missionary brothers. The reason would seem to be that as her health declined she focused more on purgatory, rejoicing to be able, through her sufferings, to help people detained there. Furthermore, Father Roulland would appear to have had something of the absorbtion with purgatory characteristic of his time. In a letter of March 1897 she refers to his promise to pray for her after her death. Her attitude is complex: she is more concerned with being able to love God and to help others than about herself:

I am not at all worried about the future; I am sure that God will do his will, it is the only grace I desire.... I hope, Brother, that if I were to leave this exile, you would not forget your promise of praying for me... I do not want you to ask God to deliver me from purgatory; Saint Teresa said to her daughters when they wanted to pray for her: 'What does it matter to me to remain to the end of the world in purgatory, if through my prayers I save a single soul?' These words find an echo in my heart. So I would be happy if you were to say then instead of the little prayer you were saying and which will always be realised: 'My God, allow my sister to make you still loved.'[12]

In another letter to the same missionary brother a few months before her death, Thérèse reflected at some length on divine justice and mercy. It would seem that Father Roulland was worried about his future state if he were to be murdered by the native peoples. Some missionaries to China had indeed been martyred around that time. Thérèse proceeded from the very fact of divine justice, which frightens so many people, to find it a profound source of consolation:

> I know one must be very pure to appear before the God of all holiness, but I know, too, that the Lord is infinitely just; and it is this justice which frightens so many souls that is the object for my joy and confidence.[13]

She developed her reversal of common norms:

> To be just is not only to exercise severity in order to punish the guilty; it is also to recognise right intentions and to reward virtue. I expect as much from God's justice as from his mercy.[14]

Thérèse then outlined her conviction that as missionaries are totally self-sacrificing, they of all people should expect to avoid any purgatory:

How can we doubt that God will open the doors of His kingdom to His children who loved Him even to sacrificing all for him, who have not only left their family and their country to make Him known and loved, but even desire to give their life for Him whom they love... How would He purify in the flames of purgatory souls consumed in the flames of divine love?[15]

She went on to express her confidence in Mary's intervention for such missionaries:

If there remains in their soul at the moment of appearing before God some trace of human weakness, the Blessed Virgin obtains for them the grace of making an act of perfect love, and then she gives them the palm and the crown that they so greatly merited.[16]

This letter places in perspective the attitude of Thérèse to purgatory, one which she had consistently adopted, though with ever-increasing clarity as she approached her own death. The viewpoint she adopted here about missionaries, that through the very generosity of the missionary vocation they would be spared purgatory, is not one that is found in theological or spiritual writing. Thérèse might have been on surer ground if she grounded the hope on the fact of martyrdom. There is some theological reflection that suggests that martyrs should escape purgatory; hence Father Roulland need not have worried about purgatory in the event of his being martyred.

Purgatory for herself
Though she referred to purgatory frequently, she was not herself very much concerned about it. Her approach might be summarised by saying that she sought God's will, all the time relying on his merciful love, and consequently she, as it were, let

purgatory look after itself. Thus, a few months before her death she said:

> I don't know whether I'll go to purgatory or not, but I'm not in the last bit disturbed about it; however, if I do go there, I'll not regret having done nothing to avoid it. I shall not feel sorry for having worked solely for the salvation of souls. How happy I was to learn that our holy Mother, St Teresa, thought the same way![17]

Clearly she had escaped the morbid fascination with the avoidance of purgatory which had been a characteristic of western spirituality since the Middle Ages.

Another vision emerged shortly before she died. She shows confidence that she will not have to suffer, but is open to whatever God chooses. But a new element is an intuition that perhaps she might undergo purgatory for others:

> If only you knew how gentle God will be with me! But if he is the least bit not gentle, I'll still find him gentle…. If I go to purgatory, I'll be very content, I'll do like the three Hebrews in the furnace, I'll walk around in the flames singing the canticle of love. Oh, how happy I will be, if when going to purgatory I can deliver other souls, suffering in their place, for then I would be doing good, I would be delivering captives.[18]

Three weeks later she remarked: 'I would not want to have picked up a pin to avoid purgatory. Everything I did was done to please God, to save souls for Him.'[19]

In her last illness purgatory was frequently on her mind. In the Last Conversations it is found seven times. On 8 July 1897 her cousin, Sister Marie of the Eucharist, writes in a letter on to M. Guérin, 'She had a very bad night, and this morning she was telling us that the souls in purgatory couldn't burn any more than she did, her fever was so strong.'[20] Her intense suffering continued and she thought three weeks later that death was imminent:'Well, "baby" is about to die! For the last three days, it's true that I've suffered very much; tonight, it's as though I were in purgatory.'[21]

Love for those in purgatory

Love for those detained in purgatory was characteristic of Thérèse throughout her life. Her sister, Céline (Geneviève of St Teresa) stated at the process for Thérèse's beatification:

> The Servant of God aided the souls in purgatory by every means in her power, principally by gaining indulgences. She had made the 'Heroic Act' and placed in the hands of the Holy Virgin all her merits of each day, so that Mary could apply them as she willed, as well as all the prayers that would be offered for her after her death. The only prayers which she allowed herself to apply for a particular intention were for Pranzini, the sinner who had been converted by her prayers and sacrifices. Each time our family offered to give her something on the occasion of a feast or an anniversary, she asked for money, and with the permission of our mother, had Masses said for the repose of the soul of Pranzini: 'He is my child,' she used to say, 'I must not neglect him now.' On the day of her profession she asked the good God that he empty the prisons of purgatory. She said daily the prayer, *O Good and Most Kind Jesus,* the six *Our Fathers* and *Hail Marys* of the Scapular of the Immaculate Conception, and until her death she fulfilled a certain practice of devotion which she had been told was richly indulgenced. When, being too ill, and she did not any longer say vocal prayers, people wanted her to be dispensed from this latter, she on

the contrary entreated: 'I can do nothing more for the souls in purgatory, and it is so little.' She was left free. So long as she was able, she was faithful to the Stations of the Cross several times per week.[22]

In this passage we note that Thérèse embraced the most radical form of the heroic offering, viz. including also the prayers that would be said for herself after her death, and that she placed all her merits in the hands of Mary; but, none the less, she made a special exception in praying specifically for her 'first-born' Pranzini, the murderer for whose conversion she prayed in her youth.[23] Sister Thérèse de Saint-Augustin, the sister who did not realise how much she irritated Thérèse,[24] stated at the same process:

> If souls exposed to losing eternal happiness were the object of the care of Sister Thérèse of the Infant Jesus, those who found themselves detained in the expiatory flames did not arouse less compassion. She hastened to hand them over to the Sovereign Good; for this she drew from the treasury of the Church and asked that after her death the stations of the Cross be made frequently for her intentions, so that she would have a way of helping them.[25]

Her love for the souls in purgatory continued in her last illness. Three weeks before she died she asked her sister, 'Will you hand me my Crucifix so that I can kiss it after the Act of Contrition, in order to gain the plenary indulgence for the souls in purgatory; I can give them no more than that.'[26] A month previously she was conscious of not being able to say the offices for the dead which were a feature of Carmelite liturgy and said:

> Then I made this prayer to God: O my God, I beg You,

pay the debt I have acquired with regard to the souls in purgatory, but do it as God, so that it will be infinitely better than if I said my Offices for the Dead.[27]

Thérèse had a profound sense of the value of her life and prayer for those in purgatory. On the day of her profession she stated, 'What graces I begged for on that day!... I wanted to deliver all the souls from purgatory.'[28] She carried a letter on her heart that day in which she prayed, 'Jesus, allow me to save very many souls; let no soul be lost today; let all the souls in purgatory be saved.'[29] In the letter for Céline's profession noted above, Thérèse envisioned an emptying of purgatory on the occasion: 'With an all-motherly care she (the Virgin Mary) will open the abyss of purgatory.'[30]

She was also very keen to encourage others not to fear purgatory, and even to hope to escape it. This view was very much opposed to ones current in the Church and even in the Lisieux Carmel at the time. Thus she recalls a conversation with the saintly Mother Geneviève, the foundress of the Lisieux Carmel, shortly before she died in 1891:

> While she was still living, I said to her one day, 'Mother, you will not go to purgatory!' She answered gently: 'I hope not.' Ah! surely God does not disappoint a trust so filled with humility.[31]

Conclusion

When we compare Thérèse's teaching with that of the other major theologian of purgatory, St Catherine of Genoa[32] there are some obvious similarities and differences. Both saints see purgatory as a manifestation of divine love rather than as a place primarily of punishment. But Thérèse practises and counsels a sublime indifference to being placed there, and she prefers to commit herself to God's will in this life and leave the future to his love, to his mercy and, paradoxically for her time, to his justice which will take account of our weakness. When compared with St Catherine, she is not so interested in reflecting on the actual purgation. Neither saint contradicts the other; both are necessary for an integral view of purgatory.

In recent years there has been a general decline in interest in purgatory. There has also been much questioning by theologians.[33] Inquiry centres around several issues: the mythological ideas of the 'place' of an intermediate state of purgatory; the problems of 'time' in the other world; the status and meaning of individual judgment; the problem of punishment; the need for a satisfactory presentation of the doctrine in the light of sound Christology, soteriology and anthropology. It may not be unfair to suggest that current theological reflection is stronger when indicating problems than when presenting purgatory in a way that is both accurate and up-to-date as well as being pastorally helpful.

Thérèse can in this context be seen to make a double contribution to a contemporary theology and spirituality of purgatory. She gives us the only parameter in which purgatory may be considered, viz. love. Her own life, and especially her eighteen months of darkness, allow us to grasp in a concrete way the suggestion made about an understanding of purgatory by the Vatican International Theological Commission in 1992. This important document on eschatology set out clearly the need for complete purity in the one who would be united fully with God; it reiterated the traditional teaching and warns against any parallel between purgatory and hell. It pointed to the teaching of St John of the Cross as a more helpful parallel:

> The Holy Spirit as 'the flame of living love' purifies the soul to enable it to reach the perfect love of God, both on earth and, where necessary, after death. In this way, he established a certain parallelism between the purification

associated with the so-called 'dark nights' and the passive purification of purgatory.[34]

Thérèse's trial of faith is surely a clear example of this purification already accomplished on earth. In the next chapter we shall see something of the extent of this trial of faith.

Chapter Ten

Living by Faith

Faith is a complex notion with various aspects, so that its meaning has to be carefully ascertained in any particular book of scripture or other source.[1] One major distinction is between the objective truths believed *(fides quae)* and the act by which we believe, that is the subjective commitment to God *(fides qua)*. Nowadays there is more emphasis on the divine Person who is encountered in faith than on a series of propositions that are to be held. Faith 'is the letting-go by which I surrender my own securities and take Christ alone as my rock'.[2] Faith involves, therefore, three acts: we believe truths; we hand ourselves over to God; we live in a practical obedience of faith. Increasingly in the literature on faith we find Thérèse of Lisieux cited as one who has something to teach about living by faith.[3]

Her time knew a crisis of faith. From the time of the Enlightenment there was a rationalistic rejection of faith in the name of science and reason; there was also a defensive retreat into pietism. Just before Thérèse was born, the First Vatican Council (1869-70) reaffirmed the authentic nature of faith, indeed its possibility. The society of her time was marked by a militant anti-clericalism and atheism. But, as Michael Paul Gallagher has pointed out in many contexts,[4] the ground has shifted once more. Marx, Nietzsche and Freud in their own ways dismissed belief in the name of human dignity. Our contemporary society has moved still further: people do not actively oppose faith, they ignore it. Militancy has given way to apathy.

We approach Thérèse's contribution to faith by outlining her faith story before concentrating on her trial of faith. There are many features in the life of Thérèse that belie the pietistic image of her as a simple nun to whom nothing exceptional ever happened. One of these is surely this mysterious trial of faith. It needs quite an amount of teasing out if we are to discover what it was, how Thérèse dealt with it and how it fits in with her mission in the Church.

Background

Thérèse's home had certainly an atmosphere of faith. Father Godefroid Madelaine, who knew the Martin family quite well, spoke of Les Buissonnets as being like a convent in which Thérèse kept all the commandments of God and of the Church.[5] In terms of faith we can distinguish several periods in Thérèse's life. In her early youth there was an ambience of serene, certain faith. We have already seen how she felt surrounded by the saints and angels; she had a vivid sense of the Communion of Saints especially as peopled by her own family – her departed mother, two little brothers and sisters, and later her father. Thus she felt her mother very close to her at the time of her First Communion. The symbol of heaven was important then: her friends were in heaven; her name was written in heaven; she liked as a small girl to dwell on thoughts of eternity. Indeed heaven is a very common word in the writings of Thérèse: it is found over sixty times in her *Last Conversations* and 709 times in her other writings, sometimes as a symbol, e.g. for Carmel.

A second phase in her faith journey was the eighteen months of scruples which disturbed her equilibrium. She does not seem to have taken up the image of the harsh God, the God who is on the look-out for sin, which we often find associated with scrupulosity. It was rather that her intense love of God led to a tortured fear of offending him. But then, the sermons of the retreat master, Fr Domin, did emphasise fear and judgment.

After her recovery from scrupulosity there is a new phase of certain faith. This lasted until Easter 1896 with, however, at least two recurrences of some scruples. There were some key moments of grace in her early years in the Carmel. In autumn 1894 she discovered the texts in Céline's notebook that were to be the basis of the Little Way. On 9 June of the following year, she made her Oblation to Merciful Love. Within a week she received a divine confirmation of her offering in the mystical experience of wounding by divine love (perhaps on 14 June). The year 1895 was a year of great graces for her. In addition to these two major experiences, she wrote almost the whole of Manuscript A. On Good Friday in the following year, 3 April 1896, she suffered her first haemoptysis, and at Easter she entered her trial of faith which would last eighteen months until her death on 30 September 1897.

It was a time of extraordinary creativity. The Abbé Bellière was given to her as a spiritual brother on 17 October 1895; the eleven letters to him begin eleven months later, on 21 October 1896 when Thérèse had been in darkness for over six months. The seven letters to Fr Roulland began on 23 June 1896, seven weeks after the trial had begun. Two major parts of her autobiography, Manuscripts B and C are from this period of trial also, as well as eighty letters (LT 186-266) and about twenty-four poems (PN 29-52). Thus apart from the first part of her autobiography, Manuscript A, all her major writings are from this period.

The trial

At Easter 1986 Thérèse entered the trial of faith which would last until her death.[6] She describes the beginning of this trial in her autobiography:

> At that time I was enjoying such a living faith, such a clear faith, that the thought of heaven made up all my happiness, and I was unable to believe there were really impious people who had no faith. I believed they were actually speaking against their inner convictions when

they denied the existence of heaven [...] During those very joyful days of the Easter season, Jesus made me feel that there were really souls who have no faith, and who, through the abuse of grace, lost this precious treasure, the source of the only real and pure joys.[7]

Though she was concerned to pray for those with no faith, such as her cousin's husband, René Tostain, her uncle Isidore's former assistant and later politician, Henri Cheron, and especially Hyacinthe Loyson, she was up to then unable to empathise with them. Significantly, in the passage above, when she said 'Jesus made me feel,' she used the word *'sentir'*, which for her means 'he made me experience'. The depth of this perception is made clear in various descriptions.

He permitted my soul to be invaded by the thickest darkness, and that the thought of heaven, up until then so sweet to me, be no longer anything but the cause of struggle and torment. The trial was to last not a few days or a few weeks, it was not to be extinguished until the hour set by God himself, and this hour has not yet come. I would like to be able to express what I feel, but alas! I believe this is impossible. One would have to travel through this dark tunnel to understand its darkness.[8]

Through this experience she finds a new mission in an identification with unbelievers:

Your child, O Lord, has understood Your divine light, and she begs pardon for her brothers. She is resigned to eat the bread of sorrow as long as you desire it; she does not wish to rise up from this table filled with bitterness at which poor sinners are eating until the day set by You.

> Can she not say in her name and in the name of her brothers, *'Have pity on us, O Lord, for we are poor sinners!'* Oh! Lord, send us away justified. May all those who are not enlightened by the bright flame of faith one day see it shine. O Jesus! if it is needful that the table soiled by them be purified by a soul who loves You, then I desire to eat this bread of trial at this table until it pleases You to bring me into Your bright Kingdom. The only grace I ask of You is that I never offend You![9]

This deeply moving passage surely puts paid to any suggestion that Thérèse regarded herself as aloof from sin and sinners; she is with those she calls 'my brothers.' It is as we see other descriptions of the trial that we can appreciate the bread of sorrow she ate at the table of sinners. Thérèse does not use the word 'doubt' about her experience, but rather 'trial' *(épreuve)* and 'torment' *(tourment)*. Various images cast light on its agony. It is like being in a country covered by a thick fog;[10] it is darkness,[11] a wall,[12] a tunnel.[13]

There are other indications from the *Last Conversations,* mainly recorded by Mother Agnes. Thérèse told her about the trial of faith only during her last illness; Mother Agnes says she was only vaguely aware of Thérèse's ordeal until August 1897 – within weeks, therefore, of her death.[14] Mother Agnes testified about the nature of the trial at the beatification process: 'Her soul remained until the end plunged in a veritable night, because of her temptation against the existence of heaven.'[15] Though the trial of faith, which mainly concerned the existence of heaven, seems to have burst suddenly on Thérèse, there had been earlier indications. Referring to October 1891 she said 'I was having great interior trials of all kinds, even to the point of asking myself whether heaven really existed.'[16]

Mother Agnes recorded several important sayings of Thérèse during her illness:

My soul is exiled, heaven is closed to me, and on earth's side it is all trial too.[17]

I admire the material heaven; the other is closed against me more and more.[18]

All the saints whom I love so much, where are they 'hanging out'? Ah! I am not pretending, it's very true that I don't see a thing. But I must sing very strongly in my heart.[19]

Look! Do you see the black hole [in the chestnut trees] where we can see nothing; it's a similar hole that I am in as far as body and soul are concerned. Ah! what darkness! But I am at peace.[20]

There were other ways in which her faith was tested even before the great trial of faith, for example her concern about her sister Léonie, who had very special needs. Thus in July 1895 when Léonie left the Visitation convent after her third unsuccessful attempt at religious life she wrote: 'We were plunged into a very great sorrow because of our dear Léonie, it was like a real agony. God who willed to try our faith, was sending us no consolation whatever.'[21]

Thérèse shared her trial with very few. Indeed her behaviour and outer demeanour would seem to belie any such trial. She was conscious of this and wrote to Mother Gonzague after describing her ordeal:

My dear Mother, I may perhaps appear to you to be exaggerating my trial. In fact, if you are judging according to the sentiments I express in my little poems composed this year, I must appear to you as a soul filled with consolations and one for whom the veil of faith is almost torn aside; and yet it is no longer a veil for me, it is a wall which reaches right up to the heavens and covers the starry firmament. When I sing of the happiness of heaven and of the eternal possession of God, I feel no joy in this, for I sing simply of what I WANT TO BELIEVE.[22]

The trial had some intermittent moments of light, an aspect of the spiritual journey which we shall see is well documented by St John of the Cross. Thus she says:

It is true that at times a very small ray of the sun comes to illumine my darkness, and then the trial ceases for an instant, but afterwards the memory of that ray, instead of causing me joy, makes my darkness even more dense.[23]

One such respite came from the dream of the Venerable Anne of Jesus in May 1896. She described the effect when she awoke:

O Jesus, the storm was no longer raging, heaven was calm and serene. I *believed*, I *felt* there was a heaven and that this heaven is peopled with souls who actually love me, who consider me their child.[24]

Again, when asked during her last illness if the trial of faith had passed she replied, 'No, but it seems to be suspended; the ugly serpents are no longer hissing in my ears.'[25] Shortly afterwards, recalling the love of God and of those who surrounded her, she remarked, 'I'm very much touched by this, for it's like a ray, or rather a flash of lightning in the midst of darkness; but only like a flash of lightning.'[26] Another indication of the intermittent nature of the trial, or perhaps of the shafts of light that pierced the darkness, are the two experiences of her discovery of her place in the Church and the dream of the Venerable Anne, which along with love, are the main topics of Manuscript B.

The severity of these temptations becomes clear in the light of her sayings about suicide, which would seem to be particularly significant:

> Watch carefully, Mother, when you will have patients a prey to violent pains; don't leave them any medicines that are poisonous. I assure you, it needs only a second when one suffers intensely to lose one's reason. Then one would easily poison oneself.[27]

Again, perhaps a month later when she was within a week of dying: 'Yes! What a grace it is to have faith! If I had not had any faith, I would have committed suicide without an instant's hesitation.'[28] Suicide becomes easier when one has no faith in an after-life; Thérèse was being tempted precisely on this score; hence the intensity of the suicide temptation.

In the texts we have already seen it seems that Thérèse's trial of faith was to be primarily about the existence of heaven, so that she could say: 'Now it is taking away everything that could be a natural satisfaction in my desire for heaven.'[28] But though her trial seemed to centre on heaven, there are some mysterious texts that speak of blasphemous thoughts. Mother Agnes told Sister Léonie who was a nun in the Lisieux Carmel (1919-82) that Thérèse felt herself attacked with such violence by a spirit of blasphemy that she bit her lips forcefully in order not to speak the impious words that came to her despite herself.[30] There are other confirmatory indications. She shared in some detail her trial of faith with her sister, Mother Agnes, only a few times. One of the most significant was in the August before her death:

> If only you knew what frightful thoughts obsess me! Pray very much for me in order that I do not listen to the devil who wants to persuade me about so many lies... O little

Mother, must one have thoughts like this when one loves God so much.[31]

These sayings are hard to evaluate. Quite naturally, perhaps, Thérèse does not elaborate them, but they were clearly very intense. We know that such thoughts come to many people. Thérèse's sensitivity and deep love for God would make these more distasteful to her than to most. But there is something deeper in these blasphemous thoughts, and we would be wrong to play them down, as when she said about the trial:

Dear Mother, the image I wanted to give you of the darkness that obscures my soul is as imperfect as a sketch is to the model; however, I don't want to write any longer about it; I fear I might blaspheme; I fear even that I have already said too much.[32]

Just before that she had referred to a mocking voice speaking to her of eternal nothingness.[33]

Her response to the trial of faith

Thérèse has much to teach people today about how to respond to difficulties of faith. Some of her strategies were traditional, some of them quite her own. In Thomistic language we might say that Thérèse was tempted against an article of faith, that is, eternal life. St Thomas Aquinas insisted that confession of faith is necessary when faith is in danger.[34] Thérèse certainly felt her faith in danger, and she responded in the traditional manner and very robustly. Thus, during her retreat from 8 to 15 October 1896 she shared her trial of faith with Fr Godefroid Madelaine, a Premonstratentian, who advised her to write the Creed and carry it on her heart. She wrote the Apostles' Creed in blood and attached it to her copy of the gospels.[35] In June/July 1897 she wrote one of her last prayers in pencil, less than twenty words:

'My God, with the help of your grace, I am ready to shed all my blood to affirm my faith.'[36]

We can see why she was reserved about telling people about her temptations against faith. She did not want to shock or scandalise others. Occasionally she let those especially intimate have some idea, but even then she is restrained. In the letter to Marie which forms the first part of Manuscript B she said: 'Do not believe I am swimming in consolations; Oh no! My consolation is to have none on earth.'[37] When Marie felt disturbed and inadequate on the receipt of this letter, Thérèse hastened to reassure her. She spoke of her only treasure being 'the blind hope I have in his mercy.' She went on to give the core of her spiritual doctrine:

> I beg you, understand your little girl, understand that to love Jesus, to be His *victim of love,* the weaker one is, without desires or virtues, the more suited one is for the workings of this consuming and transforming Love. [...] Let us remain then *very far* from all that sparkles, let us love our littleness, let us love to feel nothing, then we shall be poor in spirit, and Jesus will come to look for us, and *however far* we may be, He will transform us with flames of love... Oh! how I would like to be able to make you understand what I feel!... It is confidence and nothing but confidence that must lead us to Love...[...Jesus] will to give us His heaven *gratuitously.*[38]

Marie would, of course, have had no idea of the depth of emptiness and darkness out of which these words were written, yet they do not belie Thérèse's state; she was experiencing supreme weakness and littleness, out of which she held on only to confidence and love.

Again, when she did share her distress, she did not always receive much help. Thus, in the month of June before she died she recalled that Father Youf, the chaplain, told her with reference to her temptations against faith: 'Don't dwell on these. It's very dangerous.' She added, 'This is hardly consoling to hear, but happily I am not affected by it.'[39]

She made constant acts of faith. About seven weeks before her death she told Mother Agnes about a bad night during which she hoped she would die: 'I never ceased looking at the Holy Face. I repelled many temptations. Ah! how many acts of faith I made!'[40] She stated that she did not always directly attack the enemy, but preferred to sidestep:

> [Jesus] knows very well that while I do not have *the joy of faith*, I am trying to carry out its works at least. I believe I have made more acts of faith in this past year than all through my whole life. At each new occasion of combat, when my enemy provokes me, I conduct myself bravely. Knowing it is cowardly to enter into a duel, I turn my back on my adversary without deigning to look him in the face; but I run towards my Jesus. I tell him I am ready to shed my blood to the last drop to profess my faith in the existence of *heaven*. I tell Him, too, I am happy not to enjoy this beautiful heaven on this earth so that He will open it for all eternity to poor unbelievers.[41]

This last quotation shows another of the ways in which Thérèse responded: she offered this distress for others, for her favourites – missionaries, priests, sinners. At least from 1891 she gave evidence of a concern of the danger to the faith of her cousin, Marguerite-Marie Maudelonde, niece of Madame Guérin. She was then married eighteen months to René Tostain.[42] The latter, while giving proof of a great moral rectitude, said he was an atheist. Thérèse prayed for him up to her last months, offering 'especially' for him her trial against faith.[43]

She was not unaware of the problems of unbelief. She described as coming from the devil disturbing thoughts:

It's the reasoning of the worst materialists, which is imposed on my mind: Later, unceasingly making new advances, science will explain everything naturally; we shall have the absolute reason for everything that exists and that still remains a problem, because there remain very many things to be discovered, etc.[44]

This reflects the classical atheism of the Enlightenment. But she knew another problem of unbelief, as when she said: 'Finally, I offer up these very great pains to obtain the light of faith for poor unbelievers, for all who separate themselves from the Church's beliefs.'[45] She is surely thinking of the unfortunate Carmelite Hyacinthe Loyson, discussed in a previous chapter. His problem was precisely Church authority and Church teaching. As early as 1870 John Henry Newman was in correspondence with him on the question of Ultramontanism, the extreme papalism that some people wanted defined by the First Vatican Council. Newman was appalled that Loyson had attacked the Church even in its Ultramontanist members, through an extreme liberal Protestant paper. He, however, wrote him a kindly letter advising patience and quoting the tessera from Augustine that had been the lodestone in his own search: 'The multitude judges securely.'[46] Likewise, Thérèse's sense of the Communion of Saints was at the opposite remove from any individual's assertion of private, personal truth.

Another way in which Thérèse responded in her distress was through her poetry and letters. These can be seen in two ways. She always rose above her own pain to answer the needs of others, whether through letters or through the poems that sisters kept requesting from her. Here we have a model for ministry in the Church: those who care for or serve others need to have a detachment and objectivity that enables them not to impose on people what they may be going through at a particular time. But the poetry in particular is quite defiant when read against the background of her faith trial. She cloaks her feelings, so that the poetry is an affirmation of what she believes. Even when she reflects her deepest feelings, the poem is so constructed that, had we not known about her problems with faith we would never suspect them from her verse; knowing however, her inner state at the time enables us to see the deeper poignancy of her expression. Thus, in the poem written for Mother Agnes in January 1897, 'My Joy,' she said, 'I love the night as much as the day.' But she went on:

> If sometimes I shed tears.
> My joy is to hide them well.
> Oh! how many charms there are in suffering
> When one knows how to hide it with flowers!
> I truly want to suffer without saying so
> That Jesus may be consoled.
> My joy is to see him smile
> When my heart is exiled...[47]

Knowing what we know about her state of soul we can perhaps get some idea of what the eighteen letters to his missionary brothers cost her; all of them were written during her trial of faith. To this we should add the smiling disposition of so much of her last illness, her wry humour, her complete lack of self-pity. Taken all together, her response to the inner trials of the final eighteen months is clearly heroic.

The meaning of the trial

It remains to consider what the nature of this trial was. We have already seen that it was about the existence of heaven. But it might be possible to understand it more deeply through the mystical tradition, especially St John of the Cross to whom we know that Thérèse was very devoted. At the age of seventeen and eighteen, she tells us, 'I had no other spiritual nourishment.'[48]

But she does not draw parallels between her states and his writings. She would probably have thought such considerations inappropriate for her littleness. Given that St John of the Cross is a doctor of the spiritual life, we could seek light from his teaching.

Her trial of faith was quite different from aridity, which is normal in the spiritual journey. Thérèse knew dryness in prayer. Referring to her first years in Carmel around the time of her reception of the habit and of her father's first illness she recalled: 'My soul soon shared in the sufferings of my heart. Spiritual aridity was my daily bread and, deprived of all consolations, I was the happiest of creatures since all my desires had been satisfied.'[49] Her descriptions of aridity would seem to reflect what St John of the Cross writes about the passive night of the senses, the first great development in prayer, when God begins to work deeply in darkness.[50]

Her trial of faith, however, would seem to belong to the passive night of faith. Thérèse herself indicates that God did not allow it to happen until she was quite mature:

> Never have I felt before this, dear Mother, how sweet and merciful the Lord really is, for He did not send me this trial until the moment I was capable of bearing it. A little earlier I believe it would have plunged me into a state of discouragement. Now it is taking away everything that could be a natural satisfaction in my desire for heaven.[51]

St John of the Cross frequently indicates the anguish of the passive night of the spirit which he describes in book two of *The Dark Night of the Soul*. Elsewhere he describes it as 'dark, obscure, dreadful'.[52] He contrasts the night of the senses with 'the more oppressive night of the spirit',[53] 'the frightful night of contemplation'.[54] He gives a summary of the effects of the night:

> God divests the faculties, affections and senses, both spiritual and sensory, interior and exterior. He leaves the intellect in darkness, the will in aridity, the memory in emptiness, and the affections in supreme affliction, bitterness and anguish by depriving the soul of the feeling and satisfaction it previously obtained from spiritual blessings.[55]

Though Thérèse does not use this kind of technical language, it would seem that the state of her soul, as described in Manuscripts B and C, accurately reflects the teaching of St John.

There are many parallels between the two saints. One immediate correlation is the passage in which St John of the Cross speaks about blasphemy:

> At other times a blasphemous spirit is added; it commingles intolerable blasphemies with all one's thoughts and ideas. Sometimes these blasphemies are so strongly suggested to the imagination that the soul is almost made to pronounce them.[56]

This would immediately recall the statements of Mother Agnes to Sister Léonie above.

Another significant teaching of St John of the Cross concerns the fact that the person being tried in the passive night of the spirit can feel abandoned by God. We do not have sufficient texts of Thérèse to draw parallels point by point; as we have already noted, Thérèse is quite reticent about her trial of faith. But there is one indication which allows us perhaps to generalise about her state. We look first at the text of John where he speaks about a burning with love. This, he remarks, is not given at the beginning of the night, 'because the fire of love has not begun to catch.' He goes on to say:

Nevertheless, God gives from the outset an esteeming love by which he is held in such high favour that, as we have said, the soul's greatest suffering in the trials of this night is the anguish of thinking that it has lost God and been abandoned by him.... The soul is aware that the greatest suffering it experiences in these trials is this fear. If such persons could be assured that all is not over and lost but that what they suffer is for the better – and indeed it is – and that God is not angry with them, they would be unconcerned about all these sufferings; rather, they would rejoice in the knowledge that God is pleased with them. Their love of esteem for God is so intense, even though obscure and imperceptible, that they would be happy not only to suffer these things but even to die many times in order to please him.[57]

This teaching of St John of the Cross would surely recall the dream of Thérèse in which the Venerable Anne of Jesus appeared to her. Thérèse notes that 'the storm was raging very strongly in my soul'; she gives an indication that this storm was concerned with 'the clouds which were covering my heaven'. The dream can be dated at 10 May 1896, that is about five weeks after the trial of faith began. She was immeasurably consoled in the dream by the smile and the caresses of the Venerable Anne; but they were so realistic that she says, 'I believe I can still feel the caresses she gave me at that time.' But perhaps more significant are the two questions that Thérèse asks. The first is about death: 'O Mother! I beg you, tell me whether God will leave me for a long time on earth. Will He come soon to get me?' So, though the trial of faith was about an absence of any sense of heaven, she could still place a question precisely reflecting her faith. In fact she stated about the Venerable Anne and her two unnamed companions, 'I did understand clearly that they came from heaven.' But the second question is even more significant: 'Mother, tell me further if God is not asking something more of me than my poor little actions and desires. Is he content with me?'[58] This question seems to reflect exactly the anxiety that St John of the Cross described above.

Thérèse suffered these trials alone. St John of the Cross notes that neither spiritual directors nor doctrine are of any use at this stage.[59] Thérèse had found this out for herself; only the Gospels and the *Imitation* gave her any support.[60] But neither of these treated explicitly of her condition.

The accounts of the graces associated with the night of the senses accords well with what Thérèse says about the intermittent moments of light that broke into her trial. What Thérèse knew is found also in St John of the Cross when he speaks of the alternation of darkness, some comfort and renewed darkness and purgation.[61] The parallel is quite striking. Thérèse says in describing the darkness:

> It is true that at times a very small ray of the sun comes to illumine my darkness, and then the trial ceases for *an instant,* but afterwards the memory of that ray, instead of causing me joy, makes my darkness even more dense.[62]

By then she knew that the ordeal would be long-lasting:

> This trial was to last not a few days or a few weeks, it was not to be extinguished until the hour set by God Himself and this hour has not yet come.[63]

St John of the Cross gives a more ample description of the state:

> But if it [dark purgation] is to be truly efficacious, it will last for some years, no matter how intense it may be; although there are intervals in which, through God's dispensation, this dark contemplation ceases to assail the soul in a purgative mode and shines upon it

illuminatively and lovingly... Sometimes the experience is so intense that it seems to the soul that its trials are over. [...But] when a person feels safest and least expects it, the purgation returns to engulf the soul in another degree more severe, dark and piteous than the former, lasting for another period of time, perhaps even longer than the first. Such persons believe thereby that their blessings are gone forever.[64]

Again St John notes that in spite of the trials there is peace. He notes that peace is at various levels: a former peace which appeared to be both sensory and spiritual which must eventually give way to what he calls in the *Spiritual Canticle* 'perfect spiritual peace'[65] In Thérèse's case she seemed surprised by the quality of the peace she enjoyed: despite what she elsewhere calls torment, she said, 'I'm always in my trial [of faith]...but also in peace.'[66] Even more strongly, within a week of her death she repeated: 'My soul, in spite of this darkness, is in an astonishing peace.'[67]

At a most profound level we can see the parallels between the teaching of Thérèse and that of John of the Cross, not so much in the texts about darkness but in the texts about love. In the concluding pages of *The Dark Night of the Soul* John of the Cross explains in some detail the line 'Fired with love's urgent longings'.[68] The corresponding passage of Thérèse is surely 'desire', seen in her insatiable desire to love God and to find her place in the Church, both amply documented in Manuscripts B and C. We find in Thérèse's later experiences what John calls an illumination of the intellect and an enkindling of love.[69]

Conclusion

Along with her teaching on the Little Way, Thérèse's living in faith is perhaps the aspect of her spirituality that resonates most with modern readers, for many reasons. Many people find difficulty with faith at some stage of their life. Thérèse shows us how to live in the chiaroscuro of faith and emptiness. Her cousin, Marguerite-Marie Tostain, married to an atheist, began to doubt her faith around the time of Thérèse's death. On reading the *Story of a Soul,* she learned how to cope: not by reasoning with the doubt, but by submitting to God and continuing to act as though she had a dazzling light before her eyes.[70] The approach of Thérèse is not to panic, but to hold on and act as if the difficulty did not exist.

This teaching is of particular importance in the case of terminal illness. It is the experience of many good people that there seems to occur a time lasting several days or more, when they are assailed by the most disturbing doubts about faith. Very frequently these are not voiced, as the person feels a moral guilt or shame about the experience. The trial passes and, usually quite quickly, the person dies. Though for most people this trial or final purification before death may not last as long as it did for Thérèse, her experience can be an assurance that such darkness does not mean that one is abandoned by God.

Her sense that God is faithful and merciful so that one can safely turn to him with confidence, is a major contribution to the modern malaise about faith. So often people reject not the living God, but an idol of their own making or a distorted image unfortunately, perhaps, communicated through the Church. Thérèse's Little Way can lead to a new appreciation of the saying of Julian of Norwich, 'All will be well and all manner of things will be well.' Her example also teaches that from our own difficulties in faith we are not to turn in on ourselves, but rather to realize the enormous possibilities for intercession and compassion that can arise from the very difficulties experienced.

There are two further ways in which the writings and example of Thérèse enrich the Church. In her simple, unadorned way, she provides a living commentary on the teaching of St John of the Cross on the dark night of the spirit, so that his mystical thought becomes more widely available in the Church.

An age that has often failed to find God present in concentration camps, in gulags, in continuing genocide, can look to Thérèse who has walked in the absence of God. In a remarkable lecture for a centenary congress on Thérèse, Cardinal Cahal Daly drew attention to one text, which he said would be difficult to parallel in any existentialist literature:

> ... It seems to me that the darkness, borrowing the voice of sinners, says mockingly to me: 'You are dreaming about the eternal possession of the Creator of all these marvels; you believe that one day you will walk out of this fog which surrounds you! Advance, advance; rejoice in death which will give you not what you hope for but a night still more profound, the night of nothingness.[71]

When ultimate questions are asked, Thérèse's is often the only way, 'hoping against hope' (Rm 4:18).

Chapter Eleven

Charisms and Other Gifts

As we look at the life of St Thérèse of Lisieux we can be so struck by the ordinariness of it, the perennial 'littleness', that it is easy to miss the profound graces that she received. But we have two major advantages over those who studied her earlier: we have the important teaching of Vatican II on charism; and we have a heightened awareness of charism as a result of the insights of the Charismatic Renewal for the past three decades. Thérèse herself would not have known the word 'charism,' but we can see that she was endowed spectacularly with charisms, although they were so quietly and discreetly exercised that many people wrongly concluded that there was nothing extraordinary in Thérèse's life, apart from her heroic commitment to the ordinary. In using the Council and the contemporary experience of the Church, we are not being anachronistic, or reading into Thérèse's life what is not there; rather, we are helped by our own understanding of the work of the Holy Spirit to interpret Thérèse and see more deeply the extent and nature of God's grace in her life. Thérèse certainly knew the work of God in her, even though she did not have the language or training to express it with the clarity we can now employ.

The notion of charism
The Church rediscovered charism very gradually. Charism, the word and role, was the subject of a clash of viewpoints in the second session of Vatican II. Cardinal Ernesto Ruffini objected to the emphasis being given to charism in the Constitution on the Church. He held a view, termed 'dispensationalist', according to

which charism, though widespread in the early Church, after the first few centuries was only given in exceptional cases. The opposing view was expressed by Cardinal Léon-Joseph Suenens in a noteworthy speech on 22 October 1963.[1] His view that charism belonged to the nature of the Church reflected important writing in the 1950s; it eventually prevailed in the Council. The Council teaching demands careful rereading of the New Testament evidence.

The word 'charism' (Gk *charisma,* plur. *charismata*) is derived from the Greek word *charis* meaning grace. Its precise denotation must in each case be sought from its context.[2] In Paul it can mean the fundamental gift of redemption and eternal life (e.g. Rm 5:15-16), or particular gifts such as those given to the Israelite people (Rm 11:29). There are four lists of charisms in the NT. The Church in Corinth was particularly favoured (1 Cor 1:4-7; cf. 1 Cor 12:4-11; 1 Cor 12:27-30). Love is not enumerated among the gifts; it is 'a more excellent way' within which the charisms have their true scope (1 Cor 12:31-13:10).

The special Pauline usage is plural and is used mainly about gifts given in the Body or community. The first Letter of Peter gives guidance about charisms:

> Like good stewards of the manifold grace of God, serve one another with whatever gift [charisma] each of you has received. Whoever speaks must do so as one speaking the very words of God; whoever serves must do so with the strength that God supplies, so that God may be glorified in all things through Jesus Christ (1 P 4:10-11).

Here we have charisms divided into speaking gifts and serving gifts. These are to be used for the glory of God. It is also implied that each person has received a gift, which is Paul's presumption too (cf. 1 Cor 7:7; 12:7,11). Paul is extremely positive about the gifts, despite the confusion and disorder they occasioned at Corinth (1 Cor 12-14): 'strive for the spiritual gifts' (*pneumatika* – 1 Cor 14:1).

Vatican II

Vatican II has some general references to charism: the Holy Spirit instructs and directs the Church through a diversity of gifts, both hierarchical and charismatic (LG 4; cf. LG 7). The main treatment is in LG 12: there we find the Spirit's activity in sanctifying the Church apart from sacraments, ministries and virtues, for

> he also apportions his gifts 'to each individually as he wills' (1 Cor 12:11), and among the faithful of every rank he distributes special graces by which he renders them fit and ready to undertake the various tasks and offices which help the renewal and building up of the Church, according to that word: 'to each is given the manifestation of the Spirit for the common good' (*ad utilitatem* – 1 Cor 12:7).

These graces are called 'special' because of the way in which they are given – directly by the Spirit, and because of their *purpose* which is service of the Church and the world.[3] Whilst charism in the New Testament can be described as 'free gifts of the Spirit intended for the building up of the Church, the Body of Christ,'[4] in the council documents a charism can be more broadly described as 'a grace-given capacity and willingness for some kind of service that contributes to the renewal and upbuilding of the Church'.[5] Two other important texts speak of the wide distribution of gifts among the faithful and of the obligation and right of using them.[6]

A key distinction, one that must not however be over-used, is that charism is for others, for the Church, whereas special graces, including mystical ones, may be mainly for the benefit of the individual. In some cases these two kinds of divine gifting may in practice be somewhat blurred.

Thérèse and charism

This teaching of the New Testament and of Vatican II will naturally prompt us to be alert to charism in the life and writings of Thérèse. The experience of the Charismatic Renewal will lead us to see charism where others might only notice talent or coincidence. In Thérèse's case we need to make some important clarifications and distinctions. In one sense her whole life was charismatic. As Hans Urs von Balthasar pointed out in a major study in 1950 she had a special mission to teach the Church fundamental truths about its life and mission.[7] On the other hand there are gifts which confirm that mission, even though they may primarily be given for the sanctification of Thérèse. Finally, there are gifts which are clearly given for the benefit of others. The range of gifts which the Lord showered on Thérèse would certainly give the lie to any suggestion of the life of Thérèse being totally ordinary and banal. At the same time we find in her response to these gifts a profound exercise of love in the heart of the Church.

The beatification process

There are many special gifts attested in the beatification process. There were the usual questions about extraordinary graces, which would reflect, both in language and concepts, the current dispensationalist views. But with our deepened awareness of charism we can grasp more accurately the gifts which Thérèse received, and at the same time seek her guidance about such gifts.

In 1910 the promoter for the faith, the Sulpician theologian and canonist, Canon Pierre-Théophile Dubosq, drew up for the diocesan process a simple questionnaire covering thirty topics. The twenty-second read:

The witness is to be asked whether he or she knows or heard it said that the Servant of God was sometimes during her life enriched with heavenly gifts, such as apparitions, revelations, the gift of prophecy, reading hearts, rapture or ecstasy, etc. A witness answering in the affirmative is to tell what he or she knows, any necessary or appropriate circumstances and the nature of the knowledge.[8]

The questionnaire for the Apostolic Process seven years later was drawn up by Canon Alexander Verde. It is somewhat more specific:

The witness is to be asked whether he or she knew or heard it said that the Servant of God was ever given by God heavenly gifts or charisms, that is prophecy, the reading of hearts, ecstasy, visions, apparitions or similar favours. In so far as witnesses affirm such, they are to say: What were these, when and to what extent were they bestowed? Did the Servant of God ever speak of these gifts, and if so, when? Was such speaking necessary and how? Was it for the good of her neighbour and how? Was such speaking from some divine instinct and how, or from vainglory and why? All the circumstances are to be given and the source of such knowledge is to be given.

A new area investigated at this stage was that of miracles or healings.[9]

The language here is traditional, but it is clear that we are dealing both with what are striking graces for Thérèse herself, and with what are strictly speaking charisms. It will be helpful to follow the account of the process and supplement the accounts of its witnesses with statements from Thérèse.

Visions and other mystical graces

Some care is needed in speaking about special and mystical graces in the case of Thérèse. On the one hand, there is some evidence of remarkable graces; on the other, we have a suggestion from Thérèse herself, eagerly taken up by biographers and commentators, that there was little remarkable about her life. The truth is more subtle.

Visions

The best known of the extraordinary mystical graces received by Thérèse was the smile of the Virgin when she was at the point of death. This is attested by several witnesses at the process and by Thérèse herself in her autobiography. There is no doubt about the seriousness of the illness, even though elsewhere I indicated that it was probably in part psychosomatic. It was during a novena of Masses to Our Lady of Victories, on Pentecost Sunday 1883, that she seemed to get worse; then, as Marie and Léonie prayed intensely, turning to the large statue which had earlier spoken to their mother:

> All of a sudden the Blessed Virgin appeared *beautiful* to me, so *beautiful* that never had I seen anything so attractive; her face was suffused with an ineffable benevolence and tenderness, but what penetrated to the very depths of my soul was the *'ravishing smile of the Blessed Virgin'*. At that instant, all my pain disappeared.[10]

She had a deep instinct that she should keep silent about the vision, for if she did her happiness would disappear. But her sisters realised that she had been cured and cajoled the secret from her. Soon it would be out in the Carmel at Lisieux, where she was endlessly questioned. She retained, with complete honesty, the core truth without amplifying it, saying then and afterwards to herself, 'The Blessed Virgin had appeared *very beautiful,* and I had seen her *smile at me*. She would seem to have been made feel that she was lying about the vision. Though it was a profound cure, the memory of the incident became a very bitter one for Thérèse, so that she remarked, 'humiliation becoming my lot, I was unable to look upon myself without a feeling of *profound horror*. Ah! what I suffered I shall not be able to say except in heaven!'[11] In fact she recovered her peace only when she visited the shrine of Our Lady of Victories in Paris on her way to Rome:

> Ah! what I felt kneeling at her feet cannot be expressed. The graces she granted me so moved me that my happiness found expression only in tears, just as on the day of my First Communion. The Blessed Virgin made me feel *it was really herself who smiled on me and brought about my cure*.[12]

Mystical graces

Thérèse had a major mystical experience, probably on 14 June 1895, a week after she made her offering to merciful love. She explained it to her sister during her last illness:

> Well, I was beginning the Way of the Cross; suddenly, I was seized with such a violent love for God that I can't explain it except by saying it felt as though I were totally plunged into fire. Oh! What fire and what sweetness at one and the same time! I was on fire with love, and I felt that one minute more, one second more, and I wouldn't be able to sustain this ardour without dying. I understood, then, what the saints were saying about these states which they experienced so often. As for me, I experienced it only once and for one single instant, falling back immediately into my habitual state of dryness.[13]

Mother Agnes admitted that she appeared to pay no attention to

Thérèse when she told her about this incident. She apologised to Thérèse in July 1897 for this, but Thérèse significantly said: 'You did not distress me, I simply thought that the good God permitted that for my greater good.'[14]

In the same conversation Mother Agnes quotes Thérèse as saying about the incident:

> This is what the saints so often experienced. You know we read about it in their lives. As for me, I only experienced it once in my whole life, and the dryness quickly came to fill my heart. I lived in this dryness almost the whole of my religious life, as it were. It is very rarely that I have received any consolation. Moreover, I have never desired them. On the contrary I am proud that the good God is not bothered with me; extraordinary graces have never tempted me; I would prefer to repeat to God: my desire is not to see you below.[15]

Mother Agnes stated that Thérèse referred to this experience as 'a wound of love'.[16] But as she recalled the stations of the cross experience, she also mentioned other graces:

She later added:

> At the age of fourteen, I also experienced transports of love, Ah! how I loved God! But it wasn't at all as it was after my Oblation to Love; it wasn't a real flame that was burning me.[17]

She clearly distinguished this experience from earlier childhood transports of love (*assauts d'amour*).[18] It came as what is often called 'a consolation without previous cause', something that is quite unexpected, and she immediately returns to darkness. But she unhesitatingly equates it with the experiences of the saints, even though she sees hers as lesser than theirs.

These occurrences can be correctly interpreted only in the perspective of love. Looking back at that period Thérèse remarked:

> Above all, I was growing in love for God; I felt within my heart certain aspirations unknown until then, and at times I had veritable transports of love. One evening, not knowing how to tell Jesus that I loved Him and how much I desired that He be loved and glorified everywhere, I was thinking He would never receive a single act of love from hell; then I said to God that to please Him I would consent to see myself plunged into hell so that He would be loved eternally in that place of blasphemy. I realised this could not give Him glory since He desires only our happiness, but when we love, we experience the need of saying a thousand foolish things; if I talked in this way, it wasn't because heaven did not excite my desire, but because at this time my heaven was none other than Love.[19]

Her theological precision here is quite impressive; she can distinguish quite accurately her overwhelming desires and the foolish utterances of love from the truth of God's glory being seen in communicating his goodness, not his punishment to us.

There were also other experiences of love. During her last illness she recalled an experience in the hermitage of St Madeleine in the Carmel grounds which left her in some way suspended from her body for a week:

> It was as though a veil had been cast over all things of this earth for me...I was entirely hidden under the Blessed Virgin's veil. At this time, I was placed in charge of the refectory, and I recall doing things as though not doing them; it was as if someone had lent me a body. I remained that way for a whole week.[20]

She would seem to have referred to this as what St Teresa of Avila called 'flight of the spirit'. It seems surprising that Thérèse had this special grace so early in her spiritual journey, but, as we do not have enough evidence to be precise, we cannot assume that times and circumstances of particular mystical graces for one person are normative for others.[21] However, when Mother Agnes was pressed about this at the diocesan process she gave indications of other graces and of Thérèse's ability to distinguish these last from the more profound 'flight of the spirit'. When asked if this was different from moments of profound recollection, she replied:

> Certainly, for she was always very recollected, and if it had only been that she would not have spoken of it as a special state. When I asked her if during her religious life she had experiences of extraordinary movements of grace, she replied: 'In the garden, several times at the time of the evening 'great silence' I felt a great recollection and my heart seemed so united to God that I formed these aspirations of love with such ardour and without any effort that they seemed to be the graces called 'flights of the spirit' by Saint Teresa.[22]

Prophetic gifts

The investigations for Thérèse's beatification paid special attention to prophecy. There is quite an amount of evidence of the presence of the prophetic charism in Thérèse's life. Her first such experience was the vision at about the age of six or seven of her father bent with age, his face covered with a veil. Mother Agnes testified at the diocesan process: 'She was convinced, not only of the reality of the vision, but also that this vision had a significance that would be manifested later, that it foretold some trial or ill fortune.'

She saw it fulfilled in the five years of her father's trial.[23] In her autobiography she recalled that the impression of the vision remained:

> All this lasted but an instant but was engraved so deeply on my heart that today, after fifteen years, it is as present to me as though I were still seeing the vision before my eyes…. Very often my imagination presented again the mysterious scene I had witnessed. Very often, too, I tried to lift the veil which was hiding its meaning from me because I kept in the bottom of my heart the conviction that this vision had a meaning which one day would be revealed to me.[24]

Thérèse saw this prophetic warning fulfilled in her father's illness.[25]

There were other prophetic enlightenments especially during her last illness. She seems to have experienced some very clear intimation of her approaching death, even before she was at all ill. But we do not know what details about her death she communicated to Sister Thérèse of St Augustine, who felt that what Thérèse had foretold was fulfilled.[26] We know that she made the Novena of Grace in honour of St Francis Xavier for a very specific intention: that she would be able to spend her heaven doing good on earth. She prayed to St Joseph for the same intention on his feast which followed a few days later.[27]

She has a presentiment that her autobiography will be significant. Her sister Mother Agnes testified at the diocesan process:

> She said, 'The manuscript [the story of her life] must be published without delay after my death. If you delay, the devil will lay traps for you to prevent this publication, which is, however, important.' I said to her, 'Do you think then that you will do good to souls by means of this

manuscript.' 'Yes, it is a way that God will use to hear me. He will do good to all sorts of souls except for those who are in extraordinary ways.' 'But,' I added, 'if our mother throws it into the fire?' 'Well then, I would not care, nor have the least doubt about my mission. I would think that God will hear my desires by some other means.'[28]

A rose was given to Thérèse a fortnight before her death. She unpetalled it, touching each petal to the wounds on a crucifix, and when the petals were slipping off the bed onto the floor she said quite seriously: 'Gather up these petals, little sisters, they will help you to perform favours later on...Don't lose one of them.'[29] She felt too that people would be looking for relics and asked the sisters keep these carefully, even nail clippings.[30]

Another example of prophetic insight from her last illness concerned Mother Gonzague, who always had a fear of frequent Communion; Thérèse of course had a great desire to receive Holy Communion frequently and found the views of Mother Gongazue too narrow. Shortly before her death Thérèse said: 'Mother, when I go to heaven, I will change your mind for you.'[31]

These examples of prophetic gifting clearly fall within the Vatican II perspective of charism. They are given to Thérèse, but are really for the advantage of others, in fact of the wider Church.

Prayer gifts

From her childhood there were clearly special gifts of prayer. There were also quite special gifts of prayer apart from the more mystical ones described above. When she was eleven, she was able to spend long periods before the Blessed Sacrament.[32] But she recalled that several years earlier she would go alone to pray when her father was fishing:

> Sometimes I would try to fish with my little line, but I preferred to go alone and sit down on the grass bedecked

with flowers, and then my thoughts became very profound indeed! Without knowing what it was to meditate, my soul was absorbed in real prayer.... Earth then seemed to be a place of exile and I could dream only of heaven.[33]

Though her later life was marked predominantly by dryness, she did receive many insights at prayer, a number at least of which could rightly be called charismatic, and are perhaps best treated there. We noted in an earlier chapter that there was rather little evidence of Thérèse or her family praying for their father's recovery. There would seem to be some intuition given to Thérèse that he would not be cured, and she was to support him him by her intercession and especially by her suffering.[34]

Charisms

Here we take the word 'charism' in the strict sense of Vatican II as being a grace primarily for others. The Diocesan Process summarises such gifts, paying special attention to what are often called 'knowledge gifts' and to the visions noted above:

> Sister Thérèse of the Infant Jesus received many supernatural gifts during her life, first and foremost the gift of knowledge. God who loves to communicate himself to truly humble souls and to pure hearts instructed this young religious, as she said herself, about the mystery of her vocation, about the distribution of his grace in the world, about the direction of souls. She expressed in a very simple and agreeable way the most elevated theological ideas.[35]

As we shall see in the concluding chapter there is an exact parallel with St John of the Cross, who saw his friend, Mother Ana de Jesús, profoundly enlightened by God about theological truths.

The Diocesan Process focuses attention on the gifts Thérèse exercised in the direction of her novices. She herself describes as the 'goods of heaven' those 'inspirations of the mind and heart, profound thoughts' to which one can wrongly claim ownership, but which are 'lent' by God.[36] Mother Gonzague, who treated Thérèse with much severity, none the less recognised her qualities, even to having her function as novice mistress, albeit without the title. She also recognised her gifts; even though the word 'charism' is not used, it may well be included. Thérèse writes:

> You did not hesitate, dear Mother, to tell me one day that God was enlightening my soul and that he was giving me even the experience of years.... the Almighty has done great things in the soul of His divine Mother's child.[37]

Thérèse knows herself to have been given special knowledge: writing in the story of her life to Mother Gonzague, she said, 'Jesus granted your child, dear Mother, the grace of penetrating into the mysterious depths of charity.'[38] Further, she knew what is was to receive a grace for the benefit of another, what we would call charism. She speaks of the Lord being 'free to use me to give a good thought to a soul'.[39] She speaks too of the Lord 'using His creatures as instruments to carry on his work in souls.'[40] She also recognises gifts that are primarily for herself:

> I do not hold in contempt beautiful thoughts which nourish the soul and unite it with God; but for a long time I have understood that we must not depend on them and even make perfection consist in receiving many spiritual lights.[41]

A fine example of a very powerful charism operating in a most simple way is found in the account of how she firmly but delicately restored a relationship that had become rather unspiritual on the part of another sister. Thérèse recognised that a permission to have spiritual conferences with another was no longer fulfilling its purpose. She had a profound sense that she had to wait for the Lord's timing. When she sensed that a particular Sunday was the right day, she asked for the gift of right words. The results surpassed her expectations and the sister received great graces.[42]

Thérèse's apparently artless simplicity as she writes about her work as assistant novice mistress may hide from the reader a profound theology and practice of charism. A long passage shows how she acted and the spiritual intuitions that lay behind her practice:

> I saw immediately that the task was beyond my strength. I threw myself into the arms of God as a little child and, hiding my face in His hair, I said: 'Lord, I am too little to nourish Your children; if You wish to give through me what is suitable for each, fill my little hand and without leaving your arms or turning my head I shall give your treasures to the soul who will come and seek for nourishment.[43]

She realises that she needs some special grace and she is confident that if it is needed she will receive it. She is quite indifferent about whether people find her acceptable or not: she knows that if it is agreeable, it is from God; if people complain,

> my peace will not be disturbed, and I shall try to convince her that this nourishment comes from You and be very careful not to seek any other for her.[44]

Behind these few words is a profound spirituality of direction. She is confident that irrespective of how her guidance is received, she will be detached. She also recognises the danger of trying to please, and so depart from what she has received. This indicates great sureness; she does not think that she may be mistaken and needs to try something else. In the whole area of charism we find Thérèse very assured: she may boast of being little, but she is very, very confident. She concludes by giving the basis for this confidence:

> From the moment I understood that it was impossible for me to do anything by myself, the task you imposed on me no longer appeared difficult. I felt that the only thing necessary was to unite myself more and more to Jesus and that 'all these things will be given to you besides'.[45]

She then reflects on her experience of direction:

> In fact, never was my hope mistaken, for God saw fit to fill my little hand as many times as it was necessary for nourishing the soul of my Sisters. I admit, dear Mother, that if I had depended in the very least on my own strength, I would very soon have had to give up.[46]

Thérèse is careful to state that the parameter out of which direction properly works can only be love. She says that the novices know that she loves them, but then adds:

> I am prepared to lay down my life for them, but my affection is so pure that I don't want them to know it. With the grace of Jesus never have I tried to attract their hearts to me; I understood that my mission was to lead them to God.[47]

Just before that she noted the selflessness that is necessary in true direction:

> One feels it absolutely necessary to forget one's likings, one's personal conceptions, and to guide souls along the road that Jesus has traced for them without trying to make them walk one's own way.[48]

We know from various hints that Thérèse had to struggle against the desire to be the centre of attention, to be noticed, to receive affection or affirmation. She later saw herself in the fable of 'The Donkey and the Dog', trying to share the sympathy her cousin Marie was receiving for a headache; Thérèse sought to draw attention to her almost daily headaches but she was quite misunderstood.[49] Again in the convent she confessed to an almost intolerable urge as a postulant to receive a word of comfort or understanding from the prioress.[50] Now, however, we see her here, writing within four months of her death in serene detachment. She places herself at the service of his God and his charisms, and of her sisters; she has completely overcome any temptation to be manipulative with charism or in direction.

Two charisms in particular stand out in the latter part of her life: her ability to read the depths of scripture and a certain preternatural knowledge. In her autobiography she states:

> Often the novices say to me: 'You have an answer for everything; I believed I would embarrass you this time. Where do you get everything you say? There are those who are simple enough to believe I can read their soul because it has happened that I anticipated them by saying what they were thinking.[51]

Thérèse denies that she can 'read souls', which was a gift well-known in the lives of the saints. But she did in fact have something of that charism, nowadays called 'word of knowledge' in some circles, though not in the dramatic form in which a whole person's inner self is made known to another. She then gives an example of such a word of knowledge and concludes:

> If I had made the moon fall at her feet, she could not have looked at me with greater surprise. Her astonishment was so great that it even took hold of me, and for an instant I was seized with a supernatural fright. I was really sure that I didn't have the gift of reading souls, and this surprised me all the more because I had been so right. I felt that God was very close, and that, without realising it, I had spoken words, as does a child, which came not from me but from Him.[52]

This gift, here powerfully operative, belongs to the word or knowledge gifts, which themselves are part of the prophetic order of charism where one speaks for God.

The charism for reading the scriptures is very familiar today in the Church. It is not a contradiction of scholarly exegesis, but light from another source. When a person reads the text, the Holy Spirit may speak through the text in a way that does not run counter to scholarly exegesis, but goes beyond it. Thus Thérèse writes that sometimes she reads without comprehension, or

> If I do understand (something in a book), my mind comes to a standstill without the capacity of meditating. In this helplessness, Holy Scripture and the Imitation come to my aid; in them I discover a solid and very pure nourishment. But it is especially the Gospels which sustain me during my hours of prayer, for in them I find what is necessary for my poor little soul. I am constantly discovering in them new lights, hidden and mysterious meanings.[53]

She then expands this thought which is a commentary on her experience of charism:

> I understand and I know from experience that: 'The kingdom of God is within you.' Jesus has no need of books or preachers to instruct souls; He teaches without the noise of words. Never have I heard Him speak, but I feel that He is within me at each moment; He is guiding and inspiring me with what I must say and do. I find just when I need them certain lights which I had not seen until then, and it isn't often most frequently during my hours of prayer that these are most abundant but rather in the midst of my daily occupations.[54]

Here we find the intuitive quality of much of the prophetic-type charism: it is not logical, so much as 'given,' arriving when unexpected. This unforeseen quality of a charismatic insight is itself some guarantee or at least indication of its genuineness. We have earlier referred to the somewhat different but none the less helpful sense in which St Ignatius of Loyola speaks of 'consolation without previous cause'.[55] The element of surprise then is often a sign of genuineness.

A remarkable example of the charism of being able to read the scripture is of course Thérèse's discovery of being love in the heart of the Church. The passage is analysed elsewhere, but from our point of view here we notice that in what she described as a martyrdom of desires, her eyes fell on a critical passage in 1 Corinthians 12-13. But this was after she had already decided to look for a solution in Scripture; apparently she was used to obtaining light from the Word. We should note a progression. She moved from finding the passage helpful, to deeper prayer with humility, to some consolation, to the blinding insight in which she 'understood' – the word is repeated five times – her vocation in the Church.[56]

Surely another example of the charismatic reading of scripture is her discovery of her Little Way, based on two texts (Prov 9:4; Is 66:13.12). She found them in a notebook of Old Testament passages which Céline had brought into the convent when she entered. Nuns at the time did not have a bible, and they were discouraged from reading much of the Old Testament. The texts are remarkable in that what Thérèse discovers is already, we might think, much clearer in New Testament texts that she must have read dozens of times, e.g. texts about the Fatherhood of God and children (e.g. Mt 11:25-30). Another example is her rich discovery and incomplete commentary on 'Draw me, we shall run after you in the odour of your ointments' (Cant 1:3), with which her manuscript closes.[57]

Finally we might notice another apparent example of special gifting. There was also an incident of supernatural strength which impressed the sisters. The statue which had smiled on her for her cure was given to the Carmel. It was found to be too heavy for anyone to lift, but Thérèse, who was very slight, hoisted it up bodily and carried it to where it was to be erected, saying 'she's not too heavy for me'.[58]

Conclusion

It is clear from the Church's experience that one can have charisms, and even act with their help, without even knowing that there is such a thing as charism. Thérèse felt herself guided by God. Some of the charisms in her life were indeed quite remarkable, even though exercised in a quiet way. She trusted in the way she was led and found it bearing fruit in her own life and in the lives of others. She followed a wise rule about all religious experiences and charisms: 'proceed with caution'. If one does not respond to what may be divine light or inspiration, the work of the Lord may not be done. But there is also the possibility that the source of an impulse may not be God; hence the need for caution so that one does no harm to others or oneself.

We can see then that Thérèse was richly gifted with charismatic gifts, gifts given to her for the sake of others. The most remarkable charism is, however, the teaching charism. There are many saints, unknown mystics and holy people as well as those who are canonised as an example for the Church. There is a much smaller number who have been given the grace of being able to communicate for the sake of the Church the gifts they have received. Thérèse, who is being seriously proposed as a doctor of the Church, belongs to this restricted group of holy persons. The gift of writing, of clear communication, of accurate theology, of some exquisite poetry, are all charisms that have enriched the Church. Thérèse is charismatic in her personal gifts, in the gifts she shared with those immediately surrounding her through conversation and letters, and in her writings that the Church has taken to itself.

EPILOGUE

Chapter Twelve

A Theologian of the Church?

It is not easy to be neutral about Thérèse. Some people cannot get over the cultural accretions of late nineteenth-century France, her bourgeois culture or the tawdry piety that grew up around her. They remain blocked; Karl Rahner seems to have been one such. Others speak with approval about the probability of her being declared a doctor of the Church. They repeat with obvious relish the often-quoted pronouncement of Pius XI that Thérèse was 'the greatest saint of modern times', a statement that others, however, find off-putting. There is also the danger of centenary year hype. Exaggerations do no service to Thérèse whose whole life was marked by a passion for truth. A few weeks before her death she affirmed, 'I can nourish myself on nothing but the truth,' and on the very day she died she said, 'It seems to me that I have never sought anything but the truth.'[1] If we are to evaluate her contribution to theology, especially ecclesiology or the theology of the Church, it is, one could suggest, a time also for cool heads.

A theologian?

There is in the title of this chapter an ambiguity: it can mean a theologian who belongs to the Church or a theologian with a contribution to make about the Church. The word 'theologian' has various meanings. In the western Church it most commonly means a person who has obtained some higher degrees in theology and who is engaged professionally in explaining and exploring the sacred mysteries. But we have to remember that theology *(theos-logos)* is a word or discourse about God, especially an attempt to penetrate the meaning of the sacred mysteries. It is sometimes said that every believer is consequently a theologian, as all the followers of Christ must ask what these mysteries mean in their lives. Though there is some validity in this approach, the extension of the word 'theologian' to everybody can run the risk of emptying it of real meaning. One has to ask if Thérèse is a theologian in any but this most general sense.

Thérèse had a very limited education, which was rather spasmodic before and after her short attendance at the Abbey Benedictine school (October 1881-February 1885). Until she was about eighteen, she read a limited amount of devotional literature, especially the conferences of Abbé Charles Arminjon, *Fin du monde présent et mystères de la vie future,* about which she said, 'This reading was one of the greatest graces in my life.'[2] After that time she read little other than *The Imitation of Christ,* the works of St John of the Cross, and the Gospels, eventually reading mainly the scriptures.[3] It would appear that the classic of Dom Prosper Guéranger, *L'année liturgique,* was read both in her home and in the convent; it was the inspiration of two early poems.[4] She had, then, little formal education, and still less theological training.

A more helpful answer comes from considering the eastern Churches. In them theology is above all knowledge of the Blessed Trinity,[5] and theologians are those who communicate what they have themselves experienced of the divine mysteries. The east, therefore, considers three people to be theologians par excellence: John the Evangelist, Gregory of Nazianzus, and Simeon the New Theologian. Eastern theology is existential and even experiential to a degree which is not common in the west. In another chapter we saw a key text from St John of the Cross in which he contrasts scholastic theology and what he calls 'mystical theology.' The recipient, Mother Ana de Jésus did not have the former, but she was richly endowed with the latter, 'which is known through love and by which these truths are not only known but at the same time enjoyed'. Moreover, he described his work as 'composed in a love flowing from abundant mystical understanding'.[6] With John of the Cross and the eastern tradition we are able to grasp the sense in which Thérèse can truly be called a theologian. It is not through academic research, but through being taught directly by God in and through love. Thérèse teaches what it is to experience the divine mysteries.

Already by the turn of the century the quality and depth of Thérèse's writing was being recognised by competent persons. Fr Godefroid Madelaine,[7] a Premonstratensian, read her autobiographical writings at the request of the prioress and with a view to indicating the *nihil obstat* that would allow publication. At the process for beatification he attested:

> I had the occasion to read all her writings: not only do they not contain anything contrary to the faith and commandments, but they breathe forth a fragrance of the love of God and of the Church which is quite remarkable and which explains the immense diffusion of all her writings.[8]

Earlier he had spoken to the Diocesan Process:

> I have highlighted in the manuscript an elevation and a precision of doctrine which bear witness to lights which are clearly supernatural. Without entering into all the details, I would indicate in particular the opportune use she continually makes of scripture and the marvellous developments which she gives on fraternal charity.[9]

The Jesuit Fr Pichon, who was spiritual director of three Martin sisters, gave a similar testimony at the ordinary process:

> I read the 'Story of a Soul' or her biography written by

herself. I can attest that this account is the most candid and true expression of her moral countenance. In 1900 I met Father de Causans, superior of our house in Rouen, an excellent judge in spiritual matters. He said to me in so many words about this book: 'After the works of St Teresa and of St John of the Cross, I know nothing finer.' [...] It is a special feature of this biography that it is open to five, six or seven readings – always with fresh profit. What gives special charm to such reading is the fragrance of virtue which issues from this life and the influence it has on the soul to encourage it to advance in perfection by this 'little way of abandonment', which is so accessible to everyone of good will.[10]

Through studying Thérèse we can appreciate an important insight of two major twentieth-century theologians about the contribution of the saints to theology. For Karl Rahner and Hans Urs von Balthasar, the saints are another theological source, along with the writings of theologians and the Fathers, magisterial teaching, liturgy, etc., all of which feed theological reflection. The saints are, in Balthasar's phrase, 'a living commentary on the Gospel', and in an assertion of Rahner, 'creators of new styles of Christianity'.[11] Their love and prayer, their charisms and intuition, in addition to infused knowledge, give them profound insights into individual mysteries.

Contribution to theology

It is clear that Thérèse has made a major contribution to spirituality.[12] The Little Way and her Offering to Merciful Love have entered into the mainstream of Catholic spirituality.[13] Indeed Balthasar has pointed out a parallel between Thérèse and Martin Luther. Luther sought in scripture an answer to his tortured anxiety about grace and freedom and stressed 'trusting *fiducia* as opposed to ascetic practices and other good works, the clear-cut preference for New Testament mercy as against Old Testament justice'. Having carefully stated that all due reserves must be made, Balthasar states, 'the Little Way can be regarded as the Catholic answer to the demands and questions raised by Luther'.[14] Indeed Luther himself has never surpassed the starkness of two statements of Thérèse: 'Now, abandonment alone guides me. I have no other compass'[15] and 'everything is grace' (*tout est grâce*).[16]

Balthasar takes up the three phrases of Pius XI around the time of her canonisation: a 'new message', a 'new mission', a 'new model of sanctity'.[17] It is his contention that Thérèse received a mission in the Church to rescue the notion of holiness from an accountancy or pharisaic mentality[18] and to present in the Little Way an ideal of genuine holiness for our time.[19] He also helpfully outlines the characteristics of Thérèse's existential theology.[20]

Her autobiography has often been translated, and has never been out of print in any major language since its publication. Not everybody would be aware of her serious contribution to theology. Many writers have pointed out that Thérèse has something important to say to many of the issues of contemporary theology,[21] which became significant subsequent to Vatican II,[22] e.g. her stress on scripture,[23] on the Eucharist,[24] on the Holy Spirit,[25] on missions,[26] on Mary[27] and on the Communion of Saints[28] and, especially, on love.[29]

Doctor of the Church?

There is an expectation during the centenary year of Thérèse's death that she will be declared a doctor of the Church.[30] There have been many petitions to this effect, going right back to the 1930s. The possible implications of giving the title 'doctor' to Thérèse have not always been spelled out. At present there are thirty-two doctors of the Church.[31] The conditions for being declared a doctor of the Church were laid down by a canonist, who afterwards became Benedict XIV: a person must be a saint, renowned for learning and proclaimed 'doctor' by a pope of council. From the eighth century four great doctors of the western Church were acknowledged: Ambrose, Augustine, Jerome and Gregory the Great. In time four eastern doctors were recognised: John Chrysostom, Basil the Great, Gregory of Nazianzus and Athanasius. From the sixteenth century onwards others were added. Nine doctors were named in the present century: Ephrem, Peter Canisius, John of the Cross, Robert Bellarmine, Albert the Great, Anthony of Padua, Laurence of Brindisi and the only two women doctors, Teresa of Avila and Catherine of Siena, these last two in 1970. These names indicate the wide range of theological excellence that has been marked by the accolade of 'doctor'.

Clearly Thérèse does not have the range of such encyclopaedic geniuses as Augustine, Thomas Aquinas or Albert the Great. Nor does she deal with the spiritual life in a comprehensive way like Teresa of Avila and John of the Cross. Her writings in total comprise only 1173 smallish (less than A5) pages in the French *Oeuvres complètes*. It is an extremely sparse output when put alongside the writings of other doctors of the Church, or of others like Bernard of Clairvaux or Alphonsus Liguori. Nor is there a wide range of topics which have interested theologians. In many ways then Thérèse cannot be compared or put on a level with the existing doctors.

But if, as expected, the highest authority in the Church proclaims her to be a doctor of the Church, then what is involved is a new statement about the nature of theology and of the theologian's task. Thérèse could be named a doctor of the Church not for the breadth of her learning, but because she shows new possibilities of integrating doctrine into the life of faith. She drew out the implications of the merciful love of God and showed how people can respond by the way of littleness. Thérèse certainly developed powerfully and at great depth some intuitions about the spiritual life, especially love. But her greatness as a theologian lies not so much in the number of doctrines she enlightened with her wisdom as the methodology she offered to theology. After Thérèse theology should never again be an arid discipline pursued apart from the life of the Church; rather as Vatican II demanded, it should nourish the spiritual life.[32] Prayer and love have an indispensable contribution to theology, and, along with the rest of the Church, its clergy and other leaders included, the theologian in turn is invited to embrace the way of littleness. Since the Middle Ages or earlier, theologians have recognised the value of philosophy. In recent years the contribution of other disciplines such as the human sciences and art is being belatedly recognised. The proclamation of Thérèse as a doctor of the Church would be a decisive assertion that for the highest and purest theology holiness too must be cultivated.

Contribution to the Church

We come finally to delineate Thérèse's frequently studied[33] contribution to an understanding of the Church. Previous chapters looked at various aspects of the Church's life that have been enriched by Thérèse's contribution. But if we are to speak in Thérèse's case of an ecclesiology, or theology of the Church, we would need to point to some unifying principle, around which her insights would seem to cluster. An obvious one might appear to be her discovery of being love in the heart of the Church. But though love lies at the centre of all mysteries including the Trinity, by itself it does not offer an intellectual framework within which we can order the different aspects of the Church treated by Thérèse.

More promising is the Communion of Saints which exists from and through love. In chapter four we sketched Thérèse's sense of earth being joined with heaven. Each of the following chapters were further indications of the profound truths contained in the neglected dogma of the Communion of Saints. Her love and suffering were devoted to sinners, to priests, to missions and missionaries, to those being purified in purgatory, to those without faith. All these are different directions in which her limitless desires and practical love reached out. Finally, she was enriched not only with personal gifts but also charisms for the Church. In particular she had the charism, given only to relatively few, of being able to share with the Church the deep mysteries of divine love which she knew existentially and to draw others along this path. It would seem then that by placing the Communion of Saints at the centre of her concerns, we are in a position to develop a new kind of ecclesiology. We would then surely sense the profound appropriateness of her trial of faith being precisely a purification of her sensibility and attraction for this core mystery of the Communion of Saints.

We can turn again to Hans Urs von Balthasar for some conclusions that he did not himself draw. One of the most significant contributions he has made to ecclesiology is his identification of the Marian dimension of the Church. There are some difficulties in presenting his convictions here, not least because he never made an extensive presentation of his Marian vision of the Church in one place.[34] Again, though the main lines of his thought are clear and are perhaps broadly acceptable, some of his detailed applications and specifications would not receive a universal endorsement. The fullest expression of his vision is to see four New Testament principles: Peter (institutional), Paul (missionary and charismatic), John (contemplative), James (traditional and legal). The Marian principle is not alongside these, but is overarching, embracing all. In an earlier exposition he contrasted two principles, the Marian and the Petrine. The Petrine or institutional and hierarchical principle exists to serve the Marian dimension of the Church. The Eucharistic and Marian centre of the Church is revealed by taking the Annunciation and Calvary together with the love of Christ and the Church as developed in Ephesians 5:25-27.

It seems clear that though Thérèse respected the Petrine

principle of the Church, she was, however, most at home with everything suggested by the Marian principle. She supported the Petrine dimension of the Church by her suffering and prayer, but this contribution was precisely a Marian one, of receptivity, humility, offering and self-offering, of fruitfulness through the Holy Spirit, of spousal relationship with the Incarnate Word.

The Church faces a new century with much of the energy generated by Vatican II now dissipated in a hundred directions. There are many pessimistic voices around, just as there were before the Council itself. There are problems all around the Church, challenges and failures. There are many organisational areas in which renewal is needed. But if we have learned anything in the past forty years it is surely that structural changes themselves do not bring life. Thérèse's vision invites all the members of the Church to go to the heart of its concerns. It is from within the family of God, the Communion of Saints, that renewal will come. Without the values of Thérèse nothing worthwhile will be accomplished. Committees, councils and Church leaders must of course continue to meet; programmes, mission statements, academic research and pastoral planning must go on. But more is needed. Thérèse recognised this in her late discovery of the text of St John of the Cross:

> O my Jesus! I love you! I love the Church, my Mother! I recall that 'the smallest act of PURE LOVE is of more value to her than all other works together'.[35]

In her last illness she explained a parable of a tiny flame that could give rise to other flames to enlighten a wide area:

> It is the same with the Communion of Saints. Very often, without our knowing it, the graces and lights that we receive are due to a hidden soul, for God wills that the saints communicate grace to each other through prayer

with great love, with a love much greater than that of a family, and even the most perfect family on earth. How often have I thought that I may owe all the graces I've received to the prayers of a person who begged them from God for me, and whom I shall know only in heaven. Yes, a very little spark will be capable of giving birth to great lights in the Church, like the Doctors and Martyrs, who will undoubtedly be higher in heaven than the spark.[36]

On earth and in heaven Thérèse herself sought to be such a spark for the Church, especially through prayer and suffering, through the little things of daily life offered in love. Thérèse presented the Church with the gift of her Little Way and the Offering to Merciful Love. In her acute physical suffering and in her trial of faith she herself tested these two discoveries almost to the limits of human endurance. We have her assurance that even in the extremity of trials, we can rely on her Little Way and live in confidence and love. Knowing that all is grace, she patterned herself on Mary, Mother of the Church. Within the Communion of Saints it would be hard to think of anyone else who has so profoundly incarnated the Marian principle of the Church as St Thérèse of the Infant Jesus and of the Holy Face.

Notes

Chapter 1: The Many Faces of Thérèse

1. An extended version of this chapter with ample biography will be found as 'The Many faces of St Thérèse of Lisieux: A Centenary Overview,' *Milltown Studies* 39(1997), 96-111.
2. Jean de la Croix, 'La rose effeuillée: Notes sur l'iconographie de Thérèse de Lisieux,' *Carmelus* 20(1973) 212-245 (with 106 illustrations).
3. *Visage de Thérèse de Lisieux.* 2 vols. (Lisieux: Carmel, 1961).
4. LastConv 1,8,2/126 – OeuvC 1071; see testimony of Mother Agnes PO 176.
5. PO 147 and PA 201-202; see *Thérèse,* O'Mahony, 34, and OeuvC 60.
6. OeuvC 61.
7. PO 149 – OeuvC 61.
8. François de Sainte-Marie and Charles Bernard, 'Enfance spirituelle. IV – Du moyen-âge à nos jours,' *Dictionnaire de spiritualité* 4: 705-714 at 709.
9. London-Glasgow: Sands 1955. Also somewhat harsh is J.-F. Six, *Light of the Night. The Last Eighteen Months in the Life of Thérèse of Lisieux* (London: SCM, 1996) and his earlier *Thérèse de Lisieux au Carmel* (Paris: Seuil, 1973).
10. See S. Bianchi, 'Le basiliche minori nel mondo,' *Marianum Supplement* 38(1975), fasc. 3.
11. LastConv 9,6,3/62 and see 256 – OeuvC 1013, 1176.
12. LastConv 17,7, 1/102 – OeuvC 1050.
13. 17 July 1897, LT 257/Letters 2:1149 – OeuvC 613 with emphasis on last words from Thérèse.
14. M. Baudoin-Croix, *Léonie Martin: A Difficult Life* (Dublin: Veritas, 1993).
15. LastConv 14,9,1/190 – OeuvC 1128. See also testimony of Mother Agnes PO 175-176.

16. SSoul Ms A 2r/ch. 1, 13 – OeuvC 71.

17. *Derniers entretiens avec ses soeurs et témoignages divers* (Paris: Cerf-De Brouwer, 1971).

18. PO 471 – *Thérèse,* O'Mahony, 253.

19. PO 480 – *Thérèse,* O'Mahony, 264.

20. LastConv 18.

21. Ibid. 22.

22. *Therese von Lisieux: Eine mystagogische Deutung ihrer Biographie* (Würzburg: Echter, 1994), 75-99.

23. *Saint Teresa of Lisieux: A Spiritual Renascence* (London: Burns Oates and Washbourne, 1927, from French 1925).

24. *Sainte Thérèse de Lisieux: Une voie toute nouvelle* (Paris: Bonne Presse, 1946) and *The Message of Thérèse of Lisieux* (London: Burns Oates and Washbourne, 1950, from Paris 1946 edition).

25. *A Memoir of My Sister, St Thérèse* (New York: Kennedy, 1959) from *Conseils et Souvenirs* (Lisieux: Central Office, 1952 – Paris: Cerf, 1973).

26. From 1925-1992, becoming *Thérèse de Lisieux* in 1992.

27. From 1961.

28. See 'The Voice of Monsignor Vernon: Some Principles of the Little Way of Spiritual Childhood,' fifteen articles gathered from 49(1987) to 56(1994).

29. E.g. *Spiritual Childhood. A Study in St Teresa's Teaching* (London-New York: Sheed and Ward, 1953, with many reprints and editions).

30. E.g. J. Beevers, *Storm of Glory. St Thérèse of Lisieux* (London: Sheed and Ward, 1949); P. Liagre, *A Retreat with St Thérèse* (Dublin: Gill, 1947); F.J. Ripley, *All Love* (Glasgow: Burns, 1961).

31. See account by a doctoral student of Combes, G. Gennari, *Teresa di Lisieux: La verità è più bella – Analisi storico-critica: Traccia di sintesi dottrinale* (Milan: Àncora, 1974) 27-38; abbreviated in R. Laurentin, 'Thérèse de Lisieux: Bilan d'un centenaire,' *Carmel* 19(1974), 83-103 at 91-93.

32. See Philippe de la Trinité [Rambaud], *Thérèse de Lisieux, la sainte de l'enfance spirituelle: Une rélecture des textes d'André Combes* (Paris: Lethielleux, 1980) – bibliography of Combes' writings on Thérèse, 11-12.

33. *The Spirituality of St Thérèse: An Introduction* (Dublin: Gill, 1950) and *St Thérèse and Suffering: The Spirituality of St Thérèse in its Essence* (Dublin: Gill, 1951).

34. E.g. *The Heart of Saint Thérèse* (Dublin: Gill, 1952); *Saint Thérèse and Her Mission: The Basic Principles of Thérèsian Spirituality* (Dublin: Gill, 1956) and his collected articles *Theresiana* (Paris: Vrin, 1970).

35. *The Story of a Family: The Home of the Little Flower* (Dublin: Gill, 1947).

36. English *Therese of Lisieux* (London: Sheed and Ward, 1953).

37. German 1970, English *Two Sisters in the Spirit: Thérèse of Lisieux and Elizabeth of the Trinity* (San Francisco: Ignatius, 1992) with essays 'The Timeliness of Lisieux', *Carmelite Studies* 1(1980), 103-121 and 'Santità come esegesi', *Rivista di vita spirituale* 43(1989), 577-595. See critiques such as C. de Meester, *Dynamique de la confiance: Genèse et structure de la 'voie d'enfance spirituelle' de sainte Thérèse de Lisieux* (Paris: Cerf, 2nd ed. 1995), 389-392 n. 15; B.C. Butler, 'Some reflections on *Thérèse of Lisieux* by Hans Urs von Balthasar', *Sicut Parvuli* 17(1955), 41-47.

38. New York: Pantheon, 1959 from 8th German edition.

39. *Dynamique de la confiance* (n. 36).

40. *Thérèse and Lisieux.* Photographs by H. Nils Loose and text by P. Descouvemont (Dublin: Veritas – Grand Rapids: Eerdmans, 1996).

41. P. Descouvemont, 'Thérèse de l'Enfant Jésus', *Dictionnaire de spiritualité* 15: 576-611.

42. G. Gaucher, *The Story of a Life: St Thérèse of Lisieux* (New York: HarperCollins – London: Darton, Longman and Todd, reprint 1993).

43. *Les mots de sainte Thérèse de l'Enfant-Jésus et de la Sainte-Face: Concordance générale* (Paris: Cerf, 1996).
44. SSoul Ms B 3r-4r/ch. 9, 192-195 – OeuvC 224-227.

Chapter 2: The Church in the Time of Thérèse

1. B. Horaist, 'La dévotion populaire française rendue à Pie IX,' *Vie spirituelle* 141(1987), 438-447; C. Gerest, 'Le pape au XIXe siècle: Histoire d'une inflation', *Lumière et vie* 26/133(1977), 70-86;
2. L. M. Glendon, art. 'French School of Spirituality' in M. Downey, ed., *The New Dictionary of Catholic Spirituality* (Collegeville: Glazier-Liturgical Press, 1993), 420-423.
3. See M. Vilain, 'Influence de Jansénisme et Thérèse de Lisieux,' *Vie thérésienne* 19(1979), 189-210.
4. O. Köhler, 'Forms of Piety' in H. Jedin, ed. *History of the Church* (London: Burns and Oates, 1981), 9: 258-261.
5. Constitution on the Catholic Faith ch. 3/DS 3008 – trans. J. Neuner and J. Dupuis, eds. *The Christian Faith in the Doctrinal Documents of the Catholic Church* (London: HarperCollins, 5th ed. 1992) n. 118.
6. SSoul Ms A 55v/ch. 6, 121 – OeuvC 173.
7. SSoul Ms A 62r/ch. 6, 132 – OeuvC 173.
8. See E.D. Hirsh, Jn., *Validity in Interpretation* (New Haven: Yale University Press, 1967).
9. C. Journet, 'St Thérèse's Conception of the Church,' *Sicut Parvuli* 23(1961), 20-30 at p. 20.
10. A. Combes, 'L'Église pour sainte Thérèse de Lisieux,' *Divinitas* 13(1969), 581-622.
11. *The Spiritual Canticle Prol.* 1 and 3 in *The Collected Works of St John of the Cross.* Trans. K. Kavanaugh and O. Rodriguez (Washington: ICS, revised ed. 1991) 469, 470.
12. Ibid.
13. Congregation for the Doctrine of the Faith, 'The Church as

Communion' (1992), art. 1 – *Catholic International* 3/16 (September 1992), 761-767 at 761.

Chapter 3: Love in Thérèse's Final Years

1. See 'The Marian Principle' in *Elucidations* (London: SPCK, 1975), 70, 72.
2. Ibid.
3. 'L'Église pour sainte Thérèse de Lisieux,' *Divinitas* 13(1969), 581-622.
4. SSoul Ms A 71v-73r/ch. 152-157 – OeuvC 190-193.
5. SSoul Ms A 82r/ch. 8, 177 – OeuvC 209.
6. SSoul Ms A 82v/ch. 8, 177-178 – OeuvC 209
7. PN 8/61-63 – OeuvC 649-651.
8. SSoul Ms B 1r/ch. 9, 188-189 – OeuvC 220-221; Ms C 2v-3r/ch. 10, 207-208 – OeuvC 237-238.
9. PA 340/ *Thérèse,* O'Mahony, 192.
11. SSoul Ms A 84r/ch. 8, 180 – OeuvC 212.
11. G. Manzoni, 'Victimale (spiritualité),' *Dictionnaire de spiritualité* 16; 531-545.
12. SSoul Ms 84r/ch. 8, 181 – OeuvC 212.
13. Ibid.
14. SSoul Ms A 84v/ch. 9, 181 – OeuvC 213.
15. SSoul appendix 276 – OeuvC Pri 6, 962 (emphasis of Thérèse).
16. See LT 107 n. 8/Letters 1:623.
17. 'You know, Mother, I have always wanted to be a saint... Instead of being discouraged, I said to myself: God cannot inspire unrealisable desires.' SSoul Ms C 2v/ch. 10, 207 – OeuvC 237. See SSoul Ms A 71r/ch. 7, 152 – OeuvC 190; Ms C 22v/ch. 11, 238 – OeuvC 264.
18. SSoul Ms B 2v-3v/ch. 9, 192-195 esp. 193 – OeuvC 224-227, esp. 225.
19. SSoul Ms A 80r-80v/ch. 8, 173-174 – OeuvC 205-206.
20. Pri 6/SSoul 276 – OeuvC 963.

21. PN 16:1 – 1 OeuvC 666: 'I am coming to sing the unutterable grace of having suffered...of having carried the Cross.'

22. SSoul Ms A 73r/ch. 7, 157 – OeuvC 193.

23. Pri 6/SSoul 277 – OeuvC 963.

24. Pri 6/SSoul 276 – OeuvC 962.

25. SSoul Ms A 75v/ch. 8, 167 – OeuvC 199.

26. Pri 6/SSoul 277 – OeuvC 964 (emphases of Thérèse).

27. See her letter to Thérèse: Letters 2:997 – OeuvC 1330-1331.

28. 17 September 1896,LT 197/Letters 2:998-100 – OeuvC 552-553.

29. Recollection of Sister Marie of the Incarnation, Letters 2:1001, n.6.

30. LastConv 29,7,9/117 – OeuvC 1064.

31. LastConv 8,8,2/141 – OeuvC 1085.

32. LastConv 30,9, p. 205 – OeuvC 1144.

33. Pri 2/SSoul 275 – OeuvC 957.

34. See St John of the Cross, *Spiritual Canticle* 12:7-9.

35. SSoul Ms B 2v/ch. 9, 192 – OeuvC 224.

36. SSoul Ms C 2v/ch. 10, 207 – OeuvC 237.

37. SSoul Ms C 3r/ch. 9, 193 – OeuvC 225.

38. SSoul Ms C 3r/ch. 9, 192-193 – OeuvC 224.

39. SSoul Ms C 3r/ch. 9, 194 – OeuvC 225.

40. *Spiritual Canticle,* prologue 3, cf. 2.

41. Ibid.

42. SSoul Ms C 3v/ch. 9, 195 – OeuvC 226-227.

43. *Spiritual Canticle* 9:7. For coat of arms see SSoul Ms A 85v/OeuvC 214-215.

44. On love in Thérèse see *Thérèse de l'Enfant-Jésus docteur de l'amour.* Rencontre théologique et spirituelle 1990 (Venasque: Éd. du Carmel, 1990); H. Dalbet, 'La toute puissance de l'amour chez sainte Thérèse de Lisieux,' *Studies in Spirituality* 3(1993), 248-270; C. Frost, 'A Martyrdom of Love: The Carmelite Way,' *Spiritual Life* 40(1994), 74-81;

Marie-Eugène de l'Enfant-Jésus, *Ton amour a grandi avec moi: Un génie spirituel, Thérèse de Lisieux* (Venasque: Éd. du Carmel, 1987).

45. SSoul Ms B 4r/ch. 9, 195 – OeuvC 227.
46. SSoul Ms B 4r/ch. 9, 196 – OeuvC 227.
47. SSoul Ms C 4r-4v/ch. 9, 196-197 – OeuvC 227-228.
48. SSoul Ms B 5v/ch. 9, 200 – OeuvC 231-232.
49. SSoul Ms B 5v/ch. 9, 200 – OeuvC 232.
50. SSoul Ms B 4v/ch. 9, 197 – OeuvC 229.
51. *Spiritual Canticle* 29:3; see Pri 12 – OeuvC 969;
52. June 1897, LT 245/Letters 2:1129 – OeuvC 601.
53. 19 March 1897, LT 221/Letters 2:1069 – OeuvC 577.
54. See LastC 246n and Letters 2:1130, n. 4.
55. SSoul, Ms C 25v-35v/ch. 11, 242-257 – OeuvC 268-284.
56. SSoul Ms C 34v/ch. 11, 255 – OeuvC 281-282.
57. SSoul Ms C 34r-36v/ch. 11, 254-259 – OeuvC 281-285.
58. SSoul Ms C 34r/ch. 11, 254 – OeuvC 281.

Chapter 4: The Communion of Saints

1. See C. O'Donnell, *Ecclesia: A Theological Encyclopedia of the Church* (Collegeville: Glazier – Liturgical Press, 1996) 98-99.
2. OeuvC 786.
3. Constitution on the Liturgy, SC 111.
4. Art. 278.
5. LastConv 22,8,1/162 – OeuvC 1104.
6. PN 46/Poetry 188-189 – OeuvC 735-736.
7. M.-J. Nicolas, 'The Virgin Mary in the Gospel and in the Church according to St Teresa of Lisieux,' *Sicut Parvuli* 19(1957), 68-85, 116-125; *Revue thomiste* 52(1952), 508-527; M. Brieg, *Mehr Mutter als Königen: Die Marienverehrung des heiligen Theresia vom Kinde Jesus* (Leutesdorf: Johannes Verlag, 1979); R. Valabek, 'More Mother than Queen: Our Lady of Mount Carmel and St Teresa of Lisieux,' *Carmel in the World* 20(1981), 51-78.

8. SSoul Ms A 2r/ch. 1, 13 – OeuvC 71.
9. SSoul Ms A 16v/ch. 2, 40-41 – OeuvC 95.
10. SSoul Ms A 41r/ch. 4, 88 – OeuvC 135.
11. SSoul Ms A 29v-31r/ch. 3, 64-67 – OeuvC 116-118.
12. SSoul Ms A 56v-57r/ch. 6, 123 – OeuvC 164-165.
13. SSoul Ms A 31r/ch. 3, 67 – OeuvC 118.
14. LastConv 21,8,3/161 – OeuvC 1103.
15. Constitution on the Church, LG 54.
16. PN 54/Poetry 215-220 – OeuvC 750-756.
17. LastConv 21,8,2/162 – OeuvC 1104.
18. LastConv 21,8,3/161-162 – OeuvC 1103-1104.
19. Ibid.
20. Ibid.
21. LastConv 20,8,15 and 16/159-160 – OeuvC 1102-1103.
22. SSoul Ms C 25v/ch. 11, 242-243 – OeuvC 268-269.
23. Pr 21 – OeuvC 976.
24. To Léonie, January 1895, LT 174/Letters 2:896 - OeuvC 512
25. PN 8:1/Poetry 61 – OeuvC 649.
26. 20 August 1894/LT 170/Letters 2:884 – OeuvC 508 (italics and ellipsis points in original).
27. SSoul Ms A 35r-35v/ch. 4, 77-78 – OeuvC 125.
28. SSoul Ms A 32v/ch. IV, 73 – OuevC 120.
29. Letters 2:925; see 931-932, nn. 12, 21.
30. 23 February 1896, LT 182/Letters 2:925-930 – OeuvC 522-528.
31. 18 July 1894, LT 167/Letters 2:871 – OeuvC 503.
32. RP 8/OeuvC 944; see 1440, nn. 20-22.
33. Ibid.
34. 24 February 1897, LT 220/Letters 2:1060 – OeuvC 576.
35. See LT 221, nn. 11, 12/Letters 2:1074 – OeuvC 1498.
36. See Letters 2:1074, n. 11.
37. LastConv 17,7 and 18,7,1/102 – OeuvC 1050.
38. 14 July 1897, LT 254/Letters 2:1141-1142 – OeuvC 609-610.

39. 14 July 1897, LT 254/Letters 2:1142 – OeuvC 609-610; cf. Letters 1:589, n. 3.
40. LastConv 9,6,3/62, see 256 – OeuvC 1013, 1176.
41. 17 July 1897, LastConv 17,7/102 – OeuvC 1050.
42. SSoul Ms C 24v-25r/ch. XI, 241 – OeuvC 268.
43. SSoul Ms A 45v-46v/ch. 5, 99-100 – OeuvC 143-144.
44. SSoul Ms C 25r/ch. XI, 242 – OeuvC 268.
45. LastConv 12,7,3/91 – OeuvC 1038.

Chapter 5: Suffering

1. See M.A. Fatula, 'Suffering' in J.A. Komonchak, M. Collins and D. A. Lane, eds, *The New Dictionary of Theology* (Wilmington: Glazier – Dublin: Gill & Macmillan, 1987), pp. 990-992; R. Sparks, 'Suffering' in M. Downey, ed., *The New Dictionary of Catholic Spirituality* (Collegeville: Glazier – Liturgical Press, 1993), 950-953.
2. Constitution on the Church in the Modern World – GS 22.
3. LastConv 30,5,2,53 – OeuvC 1006.
4. The first major study was A. Combes, *St Thérèse and Suffering: The Spirituality of St Thérèse in its Essence* (Dublin: Gill, 1951) from French 1948. Extremely valuable is C. de Meester, *Dynamique de la confiance: Genèse et structure de la 'voie d'enfance spirituelle' de sainte Thérèse de Lisieux* (Paris: Cerf, 2nd ed. 1995) 124-145; See also E. Aresu, 'Un catechismo sulla sofferenza: Le lettere di S. Teresa di Lisieux a sua sorella Celine', series of articles in *La scala* 33-35(1979-1981); B. Laluque, 'Thérèse de Lisieux et la souffrance,' *Vie thérésienne* 26/101(1986) 5-20; Sr Marie-Paschale, 'Souffrir en aimant,' *Vie thérésienne* 27/105(1987) 19-38; N. Mariacher, 'Esperienza e sapienza della croce in s. Teresa di Lisieux,' *La sapienza della croce* 6(1991) 183-193; R. Zambelli, 'Thérèse et la souffrance,' *Vie thérésienne* 34(1994) 253-262. See below for studies of her final illness.

5. SSoul Ms A 3r/ch. 1, 15 – OeuvC 73; see Ms A 12r/ch. 1, 30 – OeuvC 87.

6. SSoul Ms A 4r/ch. 1, 16 – OeuvC 74.

7. SSoul Ms A 13r/ch. 2, 34 – OeuvC 89.

8. SSoul Ms A 25v/ch. 3, 58 – OeuvC 109.

9 . SSoul Ms A 26v-27r/ch. 3, 59-60 – OeuvC 110-111.

10. SSoul Ms A 27r/ch. 3, 60 – OeuvC 111. See testimony of Jeanne Guérin, a cousin married to Dr La Neele who visited Thérèse four times in her final illness. In the first process she gave it as family opinion that the illness was caused by Pauline's departure; they were not convinced by the medical diagnosis of St Guy's Dance and suspected another cause (PO 493). In the later apostolic process she cited her father's opinion, probably shared by the family, that the illness had a demonic cause (PA 515). This was also the view of Marie at the diocesan process (PO 240-241).

11. SSoul Ms A 28v/ch. 3, 62 – OeuvC 113.

12. SSoul Ms A 23r/ch. 3, 54 – OeuvC 105.

13. SSoul Ms A 34r/ch. 4, 75 – OeuvC 123.

14. SSoul Ms A 44v-45r/ch. 5, 97-98 – OeuvC 141-142.

15. SSoul Ms A 45v/ch. 5, 98 – OeuvC 142.

16. SSoul Ms A 49v/ch. 5, 106 – OeuvC 150.

17. 'I didn't want to speak to Céline about my desire to enter so young and this caused me much suffering, for it was difficult for me to hide anything from her. This suffering, however, didn't last long; soon my dear sister learned of my determination and, far from turning me away from it, she courageously accepted the sacrifice God was asking from her... Céline became, then, the confidante of my struggles and sufferings, taking the same part as though it were a question of her own vocation.' SSoul Ms A 49v/ch. 5, 106-107 – OeuvC 150.

18. SSoul Ms A 51r/ch. 5, 109 – OeuvC 153.

19. Ibid.

20. SSoul Ms A 64r-64v/ch. 6, 136 – OeuvC 177.
21. SSoul Ms A 65r/ch. 6, 137 – OeuvC 179.
22. SSoul Ms A 20r/ch. 1, 45-46 – OeuvC 100.
23. Letter of Céline to Pauline Romet, 18 February, LC 109/Letters 1:532-535 with notes.
24. SSoul Ms A 73r-73v/ch. 7, 156-157 – OeuvC 192-193.
25. The idea is found also in a letter to Céline, 5 March 1889/LT 83, Letters 1:542 – OeuvC 382. 'The Cherubim in heaven envy our joy.'
26. See letters LT 81/1:529-530; LT 82/1:536-537; LT 83/1:541542; LT 87/1:552-553; LT 89/1:556-558; LT 94/1:577-578; LT 96:587-588.
27. 26 April 1889, LT 89/Letters 1:557-558 – OeuvC 390.
28. Letter to Marie, perhaps end of May 1889, LT 91/ Letters 1:564 – OeuvC 392.
29. 23-25(?) January 1889, LT 81/ Letters 1:530 with n. 4 – OeuvC 380.
30. LastConv 29,7,12/117 – OeuvC 1064; see 29,7,2/117 – OeuvC 1063.
31. Autumn (?) 1889/LC 118 – Letters 1:586.
32. SSoul Ms A 69v/ch. 7, 149 – OeuvC 187.
33. SSoul Ms A 70v/ch. 7, 150 – OeuvC 188.
34. Ms C 29v-30r/ch. 11, 248-249 – OeuvC 274-275.
35. SSoul Ms A 44r/ch. 4, 92 – OeuvC 140.
36. SSoul Ms A 51r/ch. 5, 109 – OeuvC 153; Ms A 75v/ch 8, 165 – OeuvC 197; see letters 23 July 1893, LT 144/Letters 2:804 – OeuvC 468; 7 July 1894, LT 165/ Letters 2:862 – OeuvC 499.
37. 7 January 1897, LT 76/Letters 1:504 – OeuvC 372; see LT 74/Letters, 1:499 – OeuvC 370; the image of the little ball is developed in the context of her disappointment in Rome, SSoul 64r-v/ch. 6, 136 – OeuvC 177.
38. SSoul Ms A 42r/ch. 2,89 – OeuvC 137.
39. SSoul Ms C 4v-5r/ch. 10, 210 – OeuvC 240.

40. G. Gaucher, *The Passion of Thérèse of Lisieux: 4 April-30 September 1897* (Homebush UK: St Paul, 1989 from French 1973); with caution J.-F. Six, *Light of the Night: The Last Eighteen Months in the Life of Thérèse of Lisieux* (London: SCM, 1996).

41. See LastConv 29,5/52 – OeuvC 1005.

42. LastConv 27,7,17/115 – OeuvC 1062 with n. 92; see LT 208/Letters 2:1036 and n. 4 – OeuvC 566 and n. 5.

43. LastConv 27,5,2/50 – OeuvC 1003.

44. LastConv 15,8,6/149 – OeuvC 1092; earlier she had said: 'What does it matter! Suffering can attain extreme limits, but I'm sure God will never abandon me. LastConv 4,7,3/73 – OeuvC 1023; again, 'This saying of Job: 'Although he should kill me, I will trust in him,' has fascinated me from my childhood. But it took me a long time before I was established in this degree of abandonment. Now I am there; God has placed me there. He took me into His arms and placed me there.' LastConv 7,7,3/77 – OeuvC 1073.

45. LastConv 19,8,10/155 – OeuvC 1097. A similar statement is to be found in the notes of Marie: I myself suffer only at each present moment LastConv (Marie) 20,8/241 – OeuvC 1171; see also LastConv 23,7,3/106 – OeuvC 1054.

46. LastConv 18,5,1/45 – OeuvC 999.

47. LastConv 19,8,2/154 – OeuvC 1096.

48. LastConv 20,7,6/104 – OeuvC 1053.

49. LastConv 25,8,1/167 – OeuvC 1109 with n. 63.

50. LastConv 18,7,2/102 – OeuvC 1051.

51. LastConv 7,5,3/42 – OeuvC 996.

52. LastConv 8,7,17/82 – OeuvC 1031.

53. LastConv 6,6,6/59 – OeuvC 1011.

54. LastConv 31,7,3/122 – OeuvC 1068.

55. Above n. 4.

56. SSoul Ms A 10r/ch. 1, 27 – OeuvC 84.

57. Ms A 36r-36v/ch. 4, 79-80 – OeuvC 127.

58. Spiritual Exercises n. 330.
59. SSoul Ms A 36v-37r/ch. 4, 80 – OeuvC 128.
60. 'One would have to pass through this martyrdom to understand it well, and for me to express what I suffered for a year and a half would be impossible.' SSoul Ms A 39r/ch. 4, 84 – OeuvC 132.
61. LastConv 11,8,3/145 – OeuvC 1088.
62. LastConv 25,7,1/108 – OeuvC 1056. See a few weeks earlier: 'I wanted to suffer and I've been heard. I have suffered very much for several days now.' LastConv 4,6,2/56 – OeuvC 1008; later in September she said, 'Ah! I know what suffering really is!' LastConv 9,9,2/186 – OeuvC 1125.
63. SSoul Ms A 45v/ch. 5, 99 – OeuvC 142.
64. SSoul Ms A 45v/ch. 5, 98 – OeuvC 143.
65. 12 March 1889, LT 85/Letters 1:547 – OeuvC 385.
66. 14 July 1889, LT 94/Letters 1:577-578 – OeuvC 396-397; see also 15 October, LT 96/ Letters 1:587-588 – OeuvC 398-399.
67. 30 May 1889, LT 92/Letters 1:567-569 – OeuvC 392-394; the letter of Marie is found Letters 1:563-564.
68. LastConv 12,7,3/91 – OeuvC 1038.
69. LastConv 30,9/205 – OeuvC 1164.
70. SSoul Ms C 4v/ch. 10, 210 – OeuvC 239-240.
71. Poems PN 10:8/ 69 – OeuvC 654.
72. 4 April 1889, LT 87/Letters 1:552-553 – OeuvC 386-387.
73. LastConv 19,5/46 – OeuvC 999.
74. 14 July 1897, LT 254/Letters 2:1142 – OeuvC 610.
75. 18 July 1897, LT 258/Letters 2:1152 – OeuvC 614.
76. PN 54:16/218 – OeuvC 754 (italics of Thérèse).
77. See PN 20/110-111 – OeuvC 684-685; PN 31/150-151 – OeuvC 712-714.
78. PN 17:11/91 – OeuvC 669.
79. Pri 12 – OeuvC 969 with notes 1451-1452.
80. SSoul Ms A 81r/ch. 8, 174-175 – OeuvC 207.

81. SSoul Ms A 82v-83r/ch. 8, 178 – OeuvC 210.
82. SSoul Ms B 4r-4v/ch. 9, 196-197 – OeuvC 228.
83. LastConv 30,7,4/118 – OeuvC 1065.
84. LastConv 30,7,1/118 – OeuvC 1064.
85. LastConv 8,7,2/79 – OeuvC 1029.
86. LastConv 8,7,6/80 – OeuvC 1029.
87. LastConv 25,9,2/199-200 – LastConv 1137.
88. Letter to Céline for her twentieth birthday, 26 April 1889, LT 89/Letters 1:558 – OeuvC 390.

Chapter 6: Thérèse and the World

1. See standard reference works, e.g. P. Lamarche and P. Grelot, art. 'World' in X. Léon-Dufour, ed., *Dictionary of Biblical Theology* (London: Chapman, 2nd ed. 1973) 676-680; J.C. Haughey, art. 'World' in M. Downey, ed., *The New Dictionary of Catholic Spirituality* (Collegeville: Glazier – Liturgical Press, 1993) 1051-1062.
2. In addition to notes in chapter two see L. Glueckert, 'The World of Thérèse: France, Church and State in the Late Nineteenth Century' in J. Sullivan, ed., *Experiencing St Thérèse Today.* Carmelite Studies 5. (Washington DC: ICS, 1990) 10-27.
3. 20-21 July 1895, LT 178/Letters 2:908 – OeuvC 517.
4. SSoul Ms A 23r-v/ch. ch. 3, 54-55 – OeuvC 105-106.
5. SSoul Ms A 61r/ch. 3, 131 – OeuvC 172.
6. SSoul Ms A 3v/ch. 1, 16 – OeuvC 74.
7. SSoul Ms A 22r/ch. 1, 48 – OeuvC 103.
8. SSoul Ms A 32v/ch. 4, 73 – OeuvC 120-121.
9. Ibid.
10. SSoul Ms C 34r-v/ch. 11, 255 – OeuvC 281-282.
11. SSoul Ms A 40r/ch. 2, 86 – OeuvC 133-134.
12. E.g. SSoul Ms A 79v/ch. 8, 172 – OeuvC 204; see letters to Céline, 12 March 1889, LT 85/1:546 – OeuvC 384; 23 September 1890, LT 120/Letters 1:685 – OeuvC 425; 23

July 1891, LT 130/Letters 2:732 – OeuvC 441; RP 3, 'Joan of Arc Accomplishing her Mission' 23v – OeuvC 858.

13. See SSoul Ms A 51r in French text OeuvC 153; 8 October 1887, LT 27/Letters 1:289 – OeuvC 320.

14. SSoul Ms A 52v/ch. 3, 112 – OeuvC 156.

15. 22 October 1889, LT 98/Letters 1:590 – OeuvC 401.

16. 19 March 1897, LT 221/Letters 2:1070 – 578.

17. 26 April 1892, LT 134/Letters 2:747-749 – OeuvC 446-448; see 26 April 1891, LT 127/2:724-725 – OeuvC 436-437.

18. SSoul Ms A 82r/ch. 8, 176 – OeuvC 208.

19. See extended meditation on the life of the martyr Cecilia in a letter to Céline, in October 1893, LT 149/Letters 2:826-828 – OeuvC 476-478.

20. SSoul Ms A 82r/ch. 8, 176 – OeuvC 208; see letter to Céline 23 July 1891, LT 130/Letters 2:732 and n. 2 – OeuvC 441.

21. SSoul Ms A 82r/ch. 8, 176 – OeuvC 208.

22. SSoul Ms B 3v/ch. 9, 194 – OeuvC 226.

23. Letters 1:588 / LT 96 – OeuvC 399.

24. Pri 2/SSoul 275 – OeuvC, 957.

25. Letters 2:741 / LT 132 – OeuvC 444.

26. Letters 2:869 / LT 192 – OeuvC 545.

27. 10 May 1890, LT 106/Letters 1:620 – OeuvC 410.

28. SSoul Ms 76r-v/ch. 8, 166 – OeuvC 198.

29. SSoul Ms A 53v/ch. 5, 114 – OeuvC 158.

30. SSoul Ms A 30v/ch. 3, 66 – OeuvC 117.

31. E.g. 26 April 1891, LT 127/Letters 2:724 – OeuvC 436; 25 April 1897, LT 224/2:1085 – OeuvC 585.

32. SSoul Ms A 73v/ch. 7, 157 – OeuvC 193; 'Carmel's grilles are not made to separate hearts.' 26 March 1894/LT 159/Letters 2:846 – OeuvC 490; see 3 April 1894, LT 160/Letters 2:849 – OeuvC 492.

33. SSoul Ms C 33v/ch. 11, 253 – OeuvC 280.

34. SSoul Ms A 70r/ch. 7, 149 – OeuvC 187.

35. *Two Sisters in the Spirit: Thérèse of Lisieux and Elizabeth of the Trinity* (San Francisco: Ignatius, 1992) 104.

36. See detailed critique of C. de Meester, *Dynamique de la confiance: Genèse er structure de la 'voie d'enfance spirituelle' de sainte Thérèse de Lisieux* (Paris: Cerf, 2nd ed. 1995) 387-396 with important note 15. See also B.C. Butler, 'Some Reflections on *Thérèse of Lisieux* by Hans Urs von Balthasar,' *Sicut Parvuli* 17(1955) 41-47. For later presentation of his view, see H.U. von Balthasar, 'The Timeliness of Lisieux' in *Spiritual Direction – Carmelite Studies* 1(1980) 103-121.

37. SSoul Ms B 5r/ch. 9, 198-199 – OeuvC 230.

38. SSoul Ms C 6r/ch. 10, 212 – OeuvC 242.

39. PN 54:22/219 – OeuvC 755.

40. SSoul Ms A 38v/ch. 4, 83 – OeuvC 131.

41. SSoul Ms A 39r/ch. 4, 84 – OeuvC 131-132.

42. 'Living on Love' PN 17:11/91 – OeuvC 669.

43. Testimony of Mother Agnes, see OeuvC 1456.

44. SSoul Ms A 45v-46r/ch. 5, 99-100 – OeuvC 143-144.

45. SSoul Ms A 45v/ch. 5, 99 – OeuvC 143.

46. SSoul Ms A 56r/ch. 6, 122 – OeuvC 163; on her profession day she wanted 'to convert all sinners.' SSoul Ms A 76v/ch. 8, 167 – OeuvC 199.

47. 'Jesus, My Beloved Remember' PN 24:16/127, OeuvC 696.

48. LastConv 2,9,7/181 – OeuvC 1120.

49. See brief account G. Gaucher, *The Story of a Life: St Thérèse of Lisieux* (New York: HarperCollins, 1987) 166-167, 181-182.

50. 'The Triumph of Humility' 4r and 5r/OeuvC 922-923, 926

51. SSoul Ms C 5v/ch. 10, 211 – OeuvC 241.

52. See Gaucher (n. 49) 115-116; Letters 2:729-730, nn. 5, 6; M. Bécamel, 'Loyson (Charles)', *Catholicisme: hier, aujourd'hui, demain.* Vol. 7 (Paris: Letouzey et Ané, 1975) 1206-1208.

53. 8 July 1891, LT 129/Letters 2:728 – OeuvC 439.

54. LastConv note appended to 19,8,10/157 – OeuvC 1099, n.
55. Frequent in the letters, e.g. LT 95/1:580 – OeuvC 398; LT 96/1:588 – OeuvC 399; LT 104/1:615 – OeuvC 407; LT 109/1:641 – OeuvC 415.
56. SSoul Ms 45v/ch. 5, 99 – OeuvC 143.
57. February 1894, Pri 4/OeuvC 959.
58. OeuvC 1445; see 1894, Pri 5,6v: 'O mon Dieu, regardez la Face de Jésus, et des pauvres pêcheurs faites autant d'élus.'
59. 6 August 1896, Pri 12/OeuvC 970.
60. See L. van den Bosche, *The Message of Sister Mary of St Peter.* Trans. M.G. Durham (Carmel of Tours, ca. 1953).
61. 1896, Pri 15/OeuvC 971.

Chapter 7: Priests
1. PO 162.
2. G. Gaucher, 'Thérèse de Lisieux, les prêtres et les missions,' *Prêtres diocésains* 1241(1986), 97-102; F.J. Guimaraes, 'L' apôtre des apôtres: Thérèse de Lisieux et les prêtres,' *Vie thérésienne* 27/107(1987), 23-34; 28/109(1988), 5-20; J. Russell, 'The Image of the Priest in Thérèse of Lisieux' in P. Chandler and K.J. Egan, eds, *The Land of Carmel.* FS J. Smet (Rome: Institutum Carmelitanum, 1991), 439-450; C. Tricot, 'St Thérèse and the Priesthood,' *Sicut Parvuli* 56(1994), 40-46.
3. *Orat. 2 Apologeticus de fuga* – PG 35:407-514.
4. PG 47: 623-692, frequently translated.
5. PL 77:11-128 frequently translated.
6. *Church,* LG 28; *Priests,* PO 12.
7. SSoul Ms A 66v/ch. 6, 140 – OeuvC 181-182.
8. SSoul Ms A 16v/ch. 2, 40 – OeuvC 94.
9. SSoul Ms A 56r/ch. 6, 122 – OeuvC 163.
10. See G. Gaucher, *The Story of a Life* (New York: HarperCollins, 1993).
11. See G. Gaucher, *The Story of a Life: St Thérèse of Lisieux* (New

York: HarperCollins, 1993); P. Descouvemont and H.N. Loose, *Therese and Lisieux* (Toronto: Novalis – Dublin: Veritas – Grand Rapids: Eerdmans, 1996); see P. O'Connor, *In Search of Thérèse*. The Way of the Christian Mystics (London: Darton, Longman & Todd, 1987); still valuable, I.F. Görres, *The Hidden Face: A Study of St Thérèse of Lisieux* (New York: Pantheon, 1959).

12. OeuvC 50.

13. SSoul Ms A 16v/ch. 2, 40-41 – OeuvC 94-95.

14. SSoul Ms A 17v/ch. 2, 42 – OeuvC 96.

15. PO 587; complete testimony 585-588.

16. OeuvC 1447 n. 8.

17. Letter to Léonie, 5 November 1893, LT 151/Letters 2:831-832 – OeuvC 480-481.

18. PO 581-584; PA 100-106.

19. SSoul Ms A 60r/ch. 3, 129 – OeuvC 170.

20. SSoul Ms A 37v/ch. 2, 81-82 – OeuvC 129.

21. SSoul Ms A 36r/ch. 2, 79 – OeuvC 126.

22. SSoul Ms A 39r/ch. 4, 84 – OeuvC 132.

23. PO 531-534 at 532 and PA 395.

24. See Letters 2:623, n. 8.

25. Father Godefroid Madelaine recalled his praise of her, PO 516.

26. SSoul Ms A 65v/ch. 6, 138 – OeuvC 180. For Fr Révérony on the Rome trip see Ms A 63r-66r/ch. 6, 134-139 – OeuvC 175-180.

27. 16 December 1887, LT 39/Letters 1:388-389 – OeuvC 332.

28. LT 38 in three drafts, LT 40, 44/Letters 1:380-391, 405 – OeuvC 331-333, 336.

29. LastConv 27,8,2/171 – OeuvC 1112.

30. LastConv 4,7,4/73 – OeuvC 1023.

31. SSoul 80v/ch. 4, 173-174 – OeuvC 205-206.

32. See on Father Pichon a series of articles in *Vie thérésienne* 1967 and 1968.

33. 23 October 1887, LT 28/Letters 1:297-298 – OeuvC 321.

34. *Seeds of the Kingdom: Notes from Conferences, Spiritual Direction, Meditations* (London: Burns and Oates, 1961).

35. SSoul Ms A 28v/ch. 3, 62 – OeuvC 113-114.

36. SSoul Ms A 70r/Ch. 7, 149 – OeuvC 187-188.

37. SSoul Ms A 70r/ch. 7, 150 – OeuvC 188. St Teresa of Avila treats of these in *The Way of Perfection* ch. 6.

38. 4 October 1889, LC 117/Letters 1:584-585 and 20 January 1893, LC 151/Letters 2:767 – CG 502, 677.

39. PO 378-385; PA 112-119.

40. LastConv 25,10,1/199 – OeuvC 1136; see 6,7,1/74 – OeuvC 1024; on his sense of his own impending death LastConv 30,8,3/176 – OeuvC 1116-1117.

41. LastConv 6,6,2/58 – OeuvC 1010.

42. LastConv 22,7,2/106 – OeuvC 1054.

43. LastConv 8,7,1/79 – OeuvC 1028

44. PO 526-529 at 528; PA 398-401.

45. See Letters 2:986; OeuvC 1456.

46. PA 554-569 at 558; see PO 514-525.

47. 9 May 1897, LT 226/Letters 2:1092 – OeuvC 587; see LastConv 1,5,2/41 – OeuvC 995.

48. LastConv 6,9,2/185 – OeuvC 1123.

49. LastConv 21-26,1/46 and 27,5,10/52 – OeuvC 1000, 1005.

50. PN 47/Poems 190-192 – OeuvC 737-738.

51. LT 245/Letters 1128-1130 – OeuvC 601-602.

52. PN 40:8/Poems 171 – OeuvC 725.

53. E. Renault, 'Les aspirations sacerdotales des deux saintes Thérèses: Essai d'étude comparative,' *Vie thérésienne* 22/86(1982), 130-146.

54. SSoul Ms B 2v/ch. 9, 192 – OeuvC 224.

55. LastConv 4,8,5/132 – OeuvC 1076.

56. LastConv 6,8,6/137 – OeuvC 1081.

57. LastConv 21,8,3/161 – OeuvC 1102.

58. SSoul Ms A 45v/ch. 5, 99 – OeuvC 143; see also Ms B 1v/ch.

9, 189 – OeuvC 221; LT 141/Letters 2:785 – OeuvC 462-463; PN 24:10 and 25/Poems 125, 129 – OeuvC 694-695, 698-699; and coat of arms Ms A 85v/OeuvC 214.

59. SSoul Ms B 3r/ch. 9, 192-193 – OeuvC 224.

60. SSoul Ms A 79v/ch. 8, 172 – OeuvC 204.

61. Testimony of Mother Agnes PO 152 with n. 26. (Decree of S. Cong. of Bishops and Religious, 17 December 1891 (Acta of Leo XIII 10(1891) 353-357; see PO 152, n. 26 – those who obtained permission to communicate more frequently had to inform the superior.)

62. SSoul Ms B 3v/ch. 9, 194 – OeuvC 226.

63. 15 August 1892/LT 135, Letters 2:753 – OeuvC 449.

64. LastConv 7,8,2/139 – OeuvC 1083.

65. See J. Russell, 'The Image of the Priest in Thérèse of Lisieux' in P. Chandler and K.J. Egan, eds, *The Land of Carmel: Essays in Honor of Joachim Smet, O.Carm* (Rome: Institutum Carmelitanum, 1991), pp. 439-450.

66. *Way of Perfection* 1:2; see Letters 1:579, n.7.

67. SSoul Ms 69v/ch. 7, 149 – OeuvC 187.

68. SSoul Ms A 56r/ch. 6, 122 – OeuvC 163.

69. 14 July 1889/LT 94, Letters 1:578 – OeuvC 397 and 14 October, 1890 /LT 122, Letters 2:708 – -OeuvC 430.

70. Ibid.

71 15 October 1889, Letters 1:587-588/LT 96 – OeuvC 399. Ellipsis as in text.

72. LastConv 23,8,6/165 – OeuvC 1107.

73. SSoul Ms A 70r-71r, 74r/150-151, 158 – OeuvC 188-189, 194.

Chapter 8: Missions and Missionaries

1. SSoul Ms A 2v-3r/ch. 1, 14 – OeuvC 72.

2. Ibid.

3. A. Déclais, 'L'éveil missionnaire de Thérèse aux Buissonnets,' *Vie thérésienne* 17(1977), 87-96; E. Mura, 'Aux sources de

l'esprit missionnaire de sainte Thérèse,' *Vie thérésienne* 17(1977), 18-27; A. Picard, 'La vocation missionnaire de sainte Thérèse de Lisieux,' *Les annales de sainte Thérèse de Lisieux* 655(1987), 4-7.

4. SSoul Ms A 22v/ch. 3, 54 – OeuvC 104.
5. SSoul Ms A 34r/ch. 4, 76 – OeuvC 123.
6. Sr. Geneviève of the Holy Face (Céline Martin), *A Memoir of my Sister St Thérèse* (Dublin: Gill, 1959) 146-147 – *Conseils et souvenirs* (Lisieux: Carmel, 1959), ch. 5.
7. M. Jedin, 'St Thérèse and the Missionary Vocation,' *Sicut Parvuli* 54(1992), 34-45; F.-M. Lethel, 'La spiritualité missionnaire de sainte Thérèse de l'Enfant-Jésus,' *Vie thérésienne* 28(1988), 9-22; A. Picard, 'La vocation missionnaire de sainte Thérèse de Lisieux,' *Les annales de sainte Thérèse de Lisieux* 655(1987) 4-7; J.L. Ryan, 'St Thérèse of Lisieux and the Missions,' *Ensign* 1974/4, 1-5 – *Carmel in the World* 16(1977), 239-249; G.V. Tobón, *Santa Teresa de Lisieux: Apóstol y profeta en la corazón de la iglesia* (Bogotá: Ed. Paulinas, 2nd ed. 1986). See collected essays, *Therese von Lisieux 50 Jahre Missionspatronin* (Leutesdorf: Johannes-Verlag, 1977) and *Thérèse et les missions: Mission et contemplation*. Actes du troisième colloque international à l'occasion du premier centenaire du 4 au 4 février 1996 au centre Teresianum à Kintambo (Kinshasa: Éditions Carmel Afrique, 1996).
8. SSoul Ms B 3r/ch. 9, 192-193 – OeuvC 224.
9. SSoul 3v/ch. 9, 194 – OeuvC 226.
10. See letters to Geneviève, December 1896, LT 207/Letters 2:1035 – OeuvC 565-566; to Fr Roulland, 19 March 1897, LT 221/Letters 2:1071 – OeuvC 1071; LastConv 15,5,6/44 – OeuvC 998; PN 47:6/Poetry 192 – OeuvC 738.
11. SSoul Ms C 9r-9v/ch. 10, 216-217 – OeuvC 246.
12. SSoul Ms C 10r/ch. 10, 217 – OeuvC 247.
13. SSoul Ms C 9r-10r/ch. 10, 217-218 – OeuvC 247-248.

14. LastConv 2,9,5/180-181 – OeuvC 1119-1120.
15. LastConv 262 – OeuvC 1182.
16. LastConv 13,7,17/94-95 – OeuvC 1042.
17. LastConv 17,7,1/102 – OeuvC 1050.
18. LastConv with Marie 13,7,1/238 – OeuvC 1068.
19. Ibid.
20. LastConv 21-26,5,3/47 – OeuvC 1000.
21. LastConv 21-26,5,5/47 – OeuvC 1001.
22. SSoul Ms C 31v-32r/ch. ll, 250-251 – OeuvC 277-278.
23. S. Vrai, *Thérèse de Lisieux et ses frères missionnaires* (Paris: Médiaspaul – Montreal: Éditions Paulines, 1992); [D.C.L.], 'Maurice Bellière: Premier frère de Thérèse (1874-1907),' *Vie thérésienne* 17(1977) 283-317; 18(1978) 56-66.
24. LastConv 8,7,16/82 – OeuvC 1031.
25. Bellière LT 220/Letters 2:1061 – OeuvC 576; Roulland LT 193/Letters 2:978 – OeuvC 547.
26. LastConv 30,7,1/118 – OeuvC 1065.
27. SSoul Ms C 32r/ch. 11, 251 – OeuvC 277.
28. Vrai (n. 21) 23.
29. 21 July 1896, LD/Letters 2:971-972.
30. 21 October 1896, LT 198/Letters 2:1010-1011 – OeuvC 554-555. The reference to St Teresa is *Way of Perfection* 3:7.
31. LC 172/Letters 2:1023-1024.
32. Ibid.
33. 26 December, LT 213/Letters 1042-1043 – OeuvC 570.
34. 24 February 1897, LT 220/Letters 2:1060 – OeuvC 576.
35. 25 April 1897, LT 224/Letters 2:1084-1085 – OeuvC 583-585.
36. 9 June 1897, LT 244/Letters 2:1127-1128 – OeuvC 600-601.
37. 21 June 1897, LT 247/Letters 2:1132-1134 – OeuvC 603-604.
38. 13 July 1897, LT 253/Letters 2:1139-1140 – OeuvC 608; The last sentence is found in her conversation with Mother

Agnes on the very same day, LastConv 13,7,15/94 – OeuvC 1041.

39. Ibid.

40. 18 July 1897, LT 258/Letters 1152-1153 – OeuvC 614-616.

41. 17 July, LC 189/Letters 2:1150-1151.

42. 26 July 1897/LT 261, Letters 2:1163 – OeuvC 618.

43. 10 August 1897, LT 263/Letters 2:1173 – OeuvC 622.

44. 25 August 1897, LT 266/Letters 2:1181 – OeuvC 624.

45. SSoul Ms C 33v/ch. 11, 253-254 – OeuvC 279-280; see 9v/ch. 10, 216 – OeuvC 246.

46. Vrai (n. 21) 27-28; see on dates letter to Father Roulland, 30 July 1896/LT 193, Letters 2:978 – OeuvC 547.

47. 23 June 1896, LT 189/Letters 2:956 – OeuvC 537.

48. 30 July 1896, LT 193/Letters 978-979 – OeuvC 547-548.

49. 14 July, LT 254/letters 2:1142 – OeuvC 610.

50. Ibid.

51. 1 November 1896, LT 201/Letters 2:1014-1018 – OeuvC 557-561. For Moses text see Exodus 17:8-13.

52. 19 March 1897, LT 221/Letters 2:1069-1073 – OeuvC 577-581.

53. 9 May 1897, LT 226/Letters 2:1094 and 1095 – OeuvC 589 and 590.

54. Ibid.

55. 14 July 1897, LT 254/Letters 2:1141-1142 – OeuvC 609-610.

56. Ibid.

57. PN 35/Poems 161-162 – OeuvC 718-720. The capitalisation of He/Him for Father Roulland is from Thérèse, as are all the ellipsis points, including those after stanza ten.

Chapter 9: Purgatory

1. See C. O'Donnell, 'Purgatory' in *Ecclesia. A Theological Encyclopedia of the Church* (Collegeville: Liturgical Press – Glazier, 1996) 392-394; E. Lanne, 'The Teaching of the

Catholic Church on Purgatory,' *One in Christ* 28(1992) 13-30 – Irénikon 64(1991) 205-229; P. Miguel and C. de Sevssel, 'Purgatoire' in *Dictionnaire de spiritualité* 12:2652-2676.

2. *Catechism of the Catholic Church,* 1030-1032.
3. E.g. St Thomas Aquinas, *Summa theologiae,* Supplement aa. 2,3,8.
4. E.g. in English M. Canty, *Purgatory: Dogmatic and Scholastic* (Dublin: Gill, 1886); M. Jugie, *Purgatory and the Means to Avoid It* (Cork: Mercier, 1949); Father Hubert, The Mystery of Purgatory (Chicago: Franciscan Herald Press, 1975); Mary of St Austin, *The Divine Crucible of Purgatory* (London: Burns Oates and Washbourne, 1948); P. O'Sullivan [E.D.M.], *Read Me or Rue It* (privately published for the Association of the Holy Souls with approval of Cardinal Patriarch of Lisbon, 1936).
5. M. Viller, 'Acte héroique,' *Dictionnaire de spiritualité* 1:177-178.
6. See Philippe de la Trinité, *Il purgatorio? Che ne pensa S. Teresa di Lisieux* (Rome: Teresianum, 1972 = revision of *La doctrine de Sainte Thérèse de l'Enfant-Jésus sur le purgatoire.* Paris: Lib. du Carmel, 1950); L. Regnault, 'La pensée de sainte Thérèse de l'Enfant-Jésus sur le purgatoire,' *Vie thérèsienne* 26(1986), 21-29.
7. SSoul Ms A 84v/ch. 8, 181 – OeuvC 212.
8. SSoul 276 - OeuvC 962.
9. SSoul Ms A 76v/ch. 8, 167 – OeuvC 199.
10. PN 23:8/120 – OeuvC 691.
11. PN 17:6/90 – OeuvC 668.
12. 19 March 1897 / LT 221, Letters 2:1072 – OeuvC 580-581. The context of the saying of St Teresa of Avila is somewhat different from Thérèse's recollection of it; see *Way of Perfection* 3:6.
13. 9 May 1897, LT 226/Letters 2:1093 – OeuvC 588.

14. Ibid.
15. Ibid.
16. Ibid.
17. LastConv 4,6,1, p. 56 – OeuvC 1008. The reference to St Teresa of Avila is to *The Way of Perfection* 3:6, 'Do not think it is useless to have these petitions (for other religious and theologians) continually in your heart, for with some persons it seems a difficult thing for them not to be praying a great deal for their own soul. But what better prayer is there than these petitions I mentioned? If you are uneasy because you think your sufferings in purgatory will not be shortened, know that by this prayer they will be; and if you must pay some debts, so be it. What would it matter were I to remain in purgatory until judgment day if through prayer I could save even one soul?' *The Collected Works of St Teresa of Avila,* 3 vols., trans. O. Rodriguez and K. Kavanaugh (Washington: Institute of Carmelite Studies, 1976-1985), 2:50.
18. LastConv 8,7,15/81 – OeuvC 1030-1031.
19. LastConv 30,7,3/118 – OeuvC 1065.
20. Cited LastConv 273.
21. LastConv 29,7,8/117 – OeuvC 1063.
22. PA 286-287.
23. SSoul Ms A 45v-46r/ch. 5, 99-100 – OeuvC 143-144.
24. See SSoul Ms C 13v/ch. 10, 222 – OeuvC 252.
25. PA 334.
26. LastConv 11,9,5/188 – OeuvC 1126.
27. LastConv 6,8,4/137 – OeuvC 1080-1081.
28. SSoul Ms A 76v/ch. 8, 167 – OeuvC 199. She refers to this prayer in a letter, 6 January 1889, LT 74/Letters 1:500 – OeuvC 370.
29. Cited in SSoul 275 – OeuvC 958.
30. 23 February 1896, LT 182/Letters 2:925 – OeuvC 523.
31. SSoul Ms A 78v/ch. 8, 170 – OeuvC 202.

32. *Purgation and Purgatory.* Trans. and ed. by S. Hughes. Classics of Western Spirituality (New York: Paulist, 1979).

33. E.g. D. Lane, *Keeping Hope Alive: Stirrings in Christian Theology* (Dublin: Gill & Macmillan, 1996) 143-148; E. Fleischhak, *Fegfeuer: Die christlichen Vorstellungen vom Geschick der Verstorbenen geschichtlich dargestellt* (Tübingen: Katzmann, 1969); J. Le Goff, The Birth of Purgatory (Chicago: University Press, 1984); G.L. Müller, 'Fegfeuer: Zum Hermeneutik eines umstrittenen Lehrstüucks in der Eschatologie,' *Theologische Quartalschrift* 166(1986) 25-39 – *Theology Digest* 34(1987) 31-36; K. Rahner, 'Purgatory,' *Theological Investigations,* Vol. 19 (London: Darton, Longman and Todd, 1984) 181-193; K. Reinhardt, 'Das Verständnis des Fegfeurs in der neueren Theologie,' *Trierer theologische Zeitschrift* 96(1981) 111-122; J.R. Sachs, 'Resurrection or Reincarnation? The Christian Doctrine of Purgatory,' *Concilium* 1993/5, 81-87; R. J. Schreiter, 'Purgatory: In Quest of an Image,' *Chicago Studies* 24(1985) 167-179.

34. *'De quaestionibus actualibus circa eschatologiam,' n. 9 – Gregorianum* 73(1992) 395-435 at 424-426 – *Irish Theological Quarterly* 58(1992) 231-232. Texts of St John of the Cross cited: *Living Flame* 1:24; *Dark Night* 2:6,6 and 2:20,5.

Chapter 10: Living by Faith

1. See M.A. Fatula, 'Faith' in M. Downey, ed., *The New Dictionary of Catholic Spirituality* (Collegeville: Glazier – Liturgical Press, 1993) 379-390; J. O'Donnell, 'Faith' in J.A. Komonchak et al, *The New Dictionary of Theology* (Wilmington: Glazier – Dublin: Gill & Macmillan, 1987) 375-386.

2. J. O'Donnell (n. 1) 385.

3. See audiotape, M.P. Gallagher, 'Thérèse and the Crisis of

Faith Today.' Centenary Year Congress, Dublin (Dublin: Avila Carmelite Centre of Spirituality, 1997).

4. See for example M.P. Gallagher, *Help My Unbelief* (Dublin: Veritas, 1983); *Free to Believe: 10 Steps to Faith* (London: Darton, Longman & Todd, 1987); *Struggles of Faith* (Dublin: Columba, 1990); *Where Is Your God?* (London: Darton, Longman & Todd, 1991).

5. PA 557.

6. G. Gaucher, *The Passion of Thérèse of Lisieux: 4 April-30 September 1897* (Homebush NSW: St Paul, 1989); F.X. Durrwell, 'Une réflexion sur la mort chrétienne,' *Vie thérésienne* 16(1976), 252-258; L. Guillet, *Gethsémani: Sainte Thérèse, l'amour crucifié* (Lisieux: Office Central – Paris: Mame, 1980); P. Wroe, 'The Night of the Soul,' *Sicut Parvuli* 45(1983) 42-51. Doctoral dissertation, F.L. Miller, *The Trial of Faith in the Writings of St Thérèse of Lisieux* (Rome: Angelicum, 1991). With caution see the valuable J.F. Six, *Light of the Night: The Last Eighteen Months in the Life of Thérèse of Lisieux* (London: SCM, 1996).

7. SSoul Ms C 5r-5v/ch. 10, 211 – OeuvC 241.

8. SSoul Ms C 5v-6r/ch. 10, 211-212 – OeuvC 241-242.

9. Ibid.

10. SSoul Ms C 5v/ch. 10, 212 – OeuvC 241; 6v/ch. 10, 213 – OeuvC 242-243.

11. SSoul Ms C 5v, 6v, 7r-v/ch. 10, 213-214 – OeuvC 241-244.

12. SSoul Ms C 7v/ch. 10, 214 – OeuvC 244.

13. SSoul Ms C 5v/ch. 10, 212 – OeuvC 241..

14. LastConv – Additional Conversations ('Green Copybooks') August/257-258 – OeuvC 1177.

15. PO 179.

16. SSoul Ms A 80v/ch. 8, 173 – OeuvC 205.

17. LastConv 29,6,3/68 – OeuvC 1019.

18. LastConv 8,8,2/141 – OeuvC 1085.

19. LastConv 15,8,7/150 – OeuvC 1092.

20. LastConv 28,8,3/173 – OeuvC 1114.

21. 20 July 1895, LT 178/Letters 2:908 – OeuvC 517.

22. SSoul Ms C 7v/ch. 10, 214 – OeuvC 243-244.

23. SSoul Ms C 7v/ch. 10, 214 – OeuvC 244.

24. SSoul Ms B 2v/ch. 9, 191 – OeuvC 223.

25. LastConv 9,6,2/62 – OeuvC 1013.

26. LastConv 22,7,1/106 – OeuvC 1054.

27. LastConv – Additional Conversations ('Green Copybooks') August/258 – OeuvC 1178.

28. LastConv 22,9,6/196 – OeuvC 1133.

29. SSoul Ms C 7v/ch. 10, 214 – OeuvC 244.

30. From oral tradition of Carmel – OeuvC 1456.

31. LastConv - Additional Conversations ('Green Copybooks') August/258 – OeuvC 1177-1178.

32. SSoul Ms C 7r/ch. 10, 213 – OeuvC 243.

33. SSoul Ms C 6v/ch. 10, 213 – OeuvC 243.

34. *Summa theologiae* 2-2ae, q.3, a.2 ad 2.

35. See Letters 2:986 – OeuvC 51, 1456.

36. Pri 19 – OeuvC 974.

37. 13 September 1896, LT 196/Letters 2:994 – OeuvC 549 = SSoul Ms B 1r/ch. 9, 187 – OeuvC 219.

38 17 September 1896, LT 197/Letters 2:999-1000 – OeuvC 552-553.

39 LastConv 6,6,2/58 – OeuvC 1010.

40. LastConv 6,8,1/135 – OeuvC 1079.

41 SSoul Ms C 7r/ch. 10, 213-214 – OeuvC 243.

42. To Céline 3 April 1891, LT 126/Letters 2:722-723 with nn. 1 and 4 – OeuvC 435-436.

43 LastConv 2.9,7/181 – OeuvC 1120.

44. LastConv – Additional Conversations ('Green Copybooks') August/257 – OeuvC 1177.

45. LastConv - Additional Conversations ('Green Copybooks') August/258 – OeuvC 1178

46. See *The Letters and Diaries of John Henry Newman.* Edited by

C.S. Dessain and T. Gornall. (Oxford: Clarendon, 1973) vol. 25:235; see 26:120 and I. Ker, *John Henry Newman: A Biography* (New York: Oxford University Press, 1988), 633, 659.

47. PN 45:5/Poems 186 – OeuvC 734.
48. SSoul Ms A 83r/ch. 8, 179 – OeuvC 210.
49. SSoul Ms A 73r-73v/ch. 7, 157 – OeuvC 193. There are many references to aridity in these years, e.g. Ms A 75v/ch. 8, 165 – OeuvC 197; Ms A 83r-83v/ch.8, 179 – OeuvC 210-211.
50. *Ascent of Mount Carmel* 2:13-14; *The Dark Night of the Soul* 1:8,3-11:2; *The Living Flame* 3:32-33).
51. SSoul Ms C 7v/ch. 10, 214 – OeuvC 244.
52. *Ascent of Mount Carmel* 1:1,3 in K. Kavanaugh and O. Rodriguez, trans., *The Collected Works of St John of the Cross* (Washington DC: Institute of Carmelite Studies, 2nd ed. 1991) 119. [In subsequent citations from St John of the Cross the page number of this edition will be added.]
53. *Night* 1:14,1/393.
54. *Dark Night* 2:1,1/396.
55. *Dark Night* 2:3,3/399; 2:4,1/400.
56. *Dark Night* 1:14,2/393.
57. *Dark Night* 2:13,5/425 see further 2:16,14/435 and 2:6,2/404.
58. SSoul Ms B 2r-2v/ch. 9, 191 – OeuvC 223.
59. *Dark Night* 2:7,3/407.
60. SSoul Ms A 83r-83v/ch. 8, 179 – OeuvC 211.
61. *Dark Night* 2:7,4-6/408-409; 2:10,9/418-419.
62. SSoul Ms C 7v/ch. 10, 214 – OeuvC 244.
63. SSoul Ms C 5v/ch. 10, 211-212 – OeuvC 241.
64 *Dark Night* 2:7, 4 and 6/408-409.
65. 24:2/565.
66. LastConv 8,9/186 – OeuvC 1124.
67. LastConv 24,9,10/199 – OeuvC 1136.

68. *Dark Night* 2, chs. 11-13/419-428; see also the ten steps of the ladder of love in chs. 19-20/440-445.
69 See *Dark Night* 2:13/424-428.
70. See Letters 2:723, n. 4.
71. SSoul Ms C 6v/ch. 10, 213 – OeuvC 243. See audiotape, Cardinal Cahal Daly, 'A Saint for the Third Millennium,' Centenary Year Congress Dublin (Dublin: Avila Carmelite Centre of Spirituality, 1997).

Chapter 11: Charisms and Other Gifts

1. 'The Charismatic Dimension of the Church' in Y. Congar et al, eds, *Council Speeches at Vatican II* (London – New York, 1964), pp. 18-21 – L.J. Suenens, *Coresponsibility in the Church* (New York, 1968) 214-218.
2. R. Laurentin, 'Charisms: Terminological Precision,' *Concilium* 109(1978) 3-12; F.A. Sullivan, *Charisms and the Charismatic Renewal. A Biblical and Theological Study* (Ann Arbor: Servant – Dublin: Gill & Macmillan, 1982), 17-46; B.M. Wambacq, 'Le mot charisme,' *Nouvelle revue théologique* 97(1975), 345-355. See C. O'Donnell, art. 'Charism' in *Ecclesia: A Theological Encyclopedia of the Church* (Collegeville: Glazier-Liturgical Press, 1996), 87-91.
3. Sullivan (n.2) 11-14; P. Mullins, 'The Theology of Charisms: Vatican II and the New Catechism,' *Milltown Studies* 33(1994) 123-164.
4. Laurentin (n. 2) 8.
5. Sullivan (n. 2) 13.
6. Priests (P0) 9; Laity (AA) 3.
7. *Two Sisters in the Spirit: Thérèse of Lisieux and Elizabeth of the Trinity* (San Francisco: Ignatius, 1992 from revised 1970 German).
8. PO 127.
9. PA 91.

10. SSoul Ms A, 30r/ch. 3, 65-66 – OeuvC 116-117; see testimony of Mother Agnes PO 1:173-174.
11. SSoul Ms A 31r/ch. 3, 67 – OeuvC 118.
12. SSoul Ms A 56v/ch. 6, 123 – OeuvC 164.
13. LastConv 7,7, 2/77 – OeuvC 1027.
14. Testimony of Mother Agnes, PO 175.
15. PO 175.
16. PO 175.
17. LastConv 7,7,2/77 – OeuvC 1027.
18. SSoul Ms A 52r/ch. 5, 112 – OeuvC 155: 'Above all, I was growing in love for God; I felt within my heart certain aspirations unknown until then, and at times I had veritable transports of love.'
19. Ms A 52r-52v/ch. 5, 112 – OeuvC 155-156.
20. LastConv 11,7,2/88 – OeuvC 1036; Mother Agnes PO 174.
21. St Teresa of Avila, *Life* 18:7; 20:1; *Way of Perfection* 6:5; 32:12-13.
22. PO 175. The reference is to St Teresa of Avila, *The Interior Castle* 6:5.
23. PO 173.
24. SSoul Ms A 20r-v/ch. 2, 46 – OeuvC 101.
25. SSoul Ms A 71v-75v/ch. 7, 152-161 – OeuvC 190-197.
26. Summary of apostolic process PA 67.
27. Letters 2:1074, n. 11.
28. PO 176; cf. LastConv 11,7,3/88 – OeuvC 1036; 1, 8, 2/126 – OeuvC 1071.
29. LastConv 14, 9, 1/190 – OeuvC 1128; see Mother Agnes' testimony PO 175-176.
30. PO 175.
31. PA 66 about testimony of Céline PO 304; see summary of Apostolic Process PA 66.
32. SSoul Ms A 40v/ch. 4, 87 – OeuvC 134.
33. SSoul Ms A 14v/ch. 2, 37 – OeuvC 91.
34. LastConv 23,7,6/107 – OeuvC 1054-1055; see SSoul Ms A

73r/ch. 7, 156 – OeuvC 192-193.

35. PA 56.
36. SSoul Ms C 18v-19r/ch. 11, 233 – OeuvC 259.
37. SSoul Ms C 4r/ch. 10, 210 – OeuvC 239.
38. SSoul Ms C 18v/ch. 11, 233 – OeuvC 259.
39. SSoul Ms C 19v/ch. 11, 234 – OeuvC 260.
40. SSoul Ms C 20r/ch. 11, 235 – OeuvC 261.
41. SSoul Ms C 19v/ch. 11, 234 – OeuvC 260.
42. SSoul Ms C 21r-v/ch. 11, 236 – OeuvC 262-263.
43. Ibid.
44. Ibid.
45. SSoul Ms C 22r-v/ch. 11, 238 – OeuvC 264-265.
46. Ibid.
47. Ibid.
48. SSoul Ms C 22v-23v/ch. 11, 238-239 – OeuvC 265-266.
49. SSoul Ms A 42r/ch. 2, 89 – OeuvC 137.
50. SSoul Ms C 22r/ch 11, 237 – OeuvC 263-264.
51. SSoul Ms C 26r/ch. 11, 243 – OeuvC 269-270.
52. Ibid.
53. SSoul Ms A, 83r-v/ch. 8, 179 – OeuvC 210-211.
54. SSoul Ms A 83v/ch. 8, 179 – OeuvC 211; see similar ideas in SSoul Ms B 1r/ch. 9, 187 – OeuvC 219.
55. *Spiritual Exercises* 330.
56. SSoul Ms B 3r-3v/ch. 9, 193-194 – OeuvC 225-226.
57. SSoul Ms C 34r-37r/ch. 11, 254-259 – OeuvC 281-285.
58. Summary of apostolic process PA 66.

Chapter 12: Thérèse: A Theologian of the Church?

1. LastConv 5,8,4 and 30,9,15/134, 205 – OeuvC 1078, 1144.
2. SSoul Ms A 47r-47v/ch. 5, 102 – OeuvC 146. The book published in 1881, had been borrowed from the Carmel by her father; Thérèse read it in 1887, copying out several passages to be found in OeuvC 1210-1211.
3. SSoul Ms A 83r-83v/ch. 8, 179 – OeuvC 210-211. We

cannot take Thérèse too literally in saying, perhaps late in 1885, that all books left her cold. She later read with great interest lives of contemporary martyrs, e.g. Venerable Théophane Vénard, and the revelations given to Sister Marie de Saint-Pierre, the Carmelite nun of Tours (d. 1848).

4. See OeuvC 1250, n. 64. See further PN 1 and 3/35-37 – OeuvC 1353; 1355.

5. See T. Spidlík, *The Spirituality of the Christian East: A Systematic Handbook* (Kalamazoo MI: Cistercian Publications, 1986) 22, 338-339.

6. Prologue to Spiritual Canticle, *The Collected Works of Saint John of the Cross.* Trans. K. Kavanaugh and O. Rodriguez (Washington: Institute of Carmelite Studies, 2nd ed. 1991) 470.

7. See above ch. seven and G. Gaucher, 'Le père Godefroy Madelaine et sainte Thérèse de Lisieux,' *Vie thérésienne* 36/142(1996) 28-35.

8. PA 564.

9. PO 517.

10. PO 381, 382.

11. See C. O'Donnell, arts. 'Saints' and 'Theological Sources' in Ecclesia: *A Theological Encyclopedia of the Church* (Collegeville: Glazier – Liturgical Press, 1996) 416-418, 443-444.

12. T. Bierle, *Ein Weg für alle – Therese von Lisieux* (Munich: Kaffe, 1981); L. Bouyer, 'Thérèse of Lisieux' in *Women Mystics* (San Francisco: Ignatius, 1993), 131-154; L. Chiappetta, *Una storia d'amore: Vita e spiritualità di s. Teresa di Lisieux* (Naples: Ed. Dehoniane. 1982); B.-L. Gabriel, 'Le fondement théologique de la spiritualité de ste Thérèse de l'Enfant-Jésus', *Vie thérésienne* 20(1980), 102-115; J. Guitton, 'The Spiritual Genius of Therese of the Child Jesus,' *Spiritual Life* 20(1974), 163-178; J.-M. Martin, *Thérèse de Lisieux: Trajectoire de sanctification* (Paris:

Lethielleux, 1990); P. Vercoustre, 'La tradition vivante de l'Église en la spiritualité de ste Thérèse de l'E.-J,' *Vie thérésienne* 15(1975), 245-253. See works of A. Combes in notes to chapter one.

13. C. de Meester, *Dynamique de la confiance: Genèse et structure de la 'voie d'enfance spirituelle' de sainte Thérèse de Lisieux* (Paris: Cerf, 2nd ed. 1995); see further G. Emonnet, *L'offrande thérésienne aujourd'hui* (Paris: Apostolat des Éditions, 1976); E. Rideau, 'L'acte d'offrande de sainte Thérèse: Pour dissiper un malentendu,' *Vie thérésienne* 16(1976), 7-16; M. Périer, 'La grâce de Thérèse éclairée par le père Marie-Eugène de l'Enfant-Jésus', *Les annales de sainte Thérèse* 656(1987), 6-9; J.F. Russell, 'Thérèse of Lisieux and Spiritual Childhood,' *Spiritual Life* 40(1994), 7-12.

14. *Two Sisters in the Spirit: Thérèse of Lisieux and Elizabeth of the Trinity*. Revised 1970 (San Francisco: Ignatius, 1992), 95-96.

15. SSoul Ms A 83r/ch. 8, 178 – OeuvC 210.

16. LastConv 5,6,4/57 – OeuvC 1009.

17. See (n. 14) 32.

18. Ibid. 237-270.

19. Ibid. 270-301.

20. Ibid. 54-80.

21. *Experiencing Thérèse Today.* Carmelite Studies 5 (Washington: Institute of Carmelite Studies, 1990) especially W. Thompson, 'Thérèse of Lisieux: A Challenge for Doctrine and Theology – Forerunner of Vatican II', 176-190; see E. Rideau, 'Sainte Thérèse de Lisieux et le monde moderne', *Vie thérésienne* 20(1980), 85-93; P. Vercoustre, *Le grandi intuizioni di s. Teresa di Lisieux* (Turin: Gribaudi, 1986).

22. T. Lombard, 'Sainte Thérèse de l'Enfant-Jésus et l'Église de Vatican II,' *Vie thérésienne* 10(1970), 135-151.

23. T. Bird, 'The Use of Sacred Scripture in the "Autobiography",' *Sicut Parvuli* 40(1978), 68-74; J. Courtès, 'Les citations

bibliques dans la correspondance de Thérèse de Lisieux', *Revue d'ascétique et mystique* 44(1968), 63-85; id. 'Les citations scripturaires dans les Manuscrits autobiographiques de Thérèse de Lisieux', *Vie thérésienne* 8(1968), 183-195; P.-M. Jerumanis, 'Un maître pour pénétrer dans la parole de Dieu' in *Thérèse de l'Enfant-Jésus: Docteur de l'Amour. Rencontre théologique et spirituelle* 1990 (Venasque: Éditions du Carmel, 1990), 33-58; Román Llamas, 'La Biblia, fuente espiritual en la vida y el mensaje de s. Teresa di Lisieux', *Ephemerides carmeliticae* 32(1981), 125-153.

24. T. Bierle, *Das eucharistische Leben der heiligen Therese von Lisieux* (Leutesdorf: Johannes-Verlag, 1982); L. Guillet, 'Thérèse et l'Eucharistie', *Vie thérésienne* 21(1981), 87-196.

25. R.F. Valabek, 'The Holy Spirit in the Life of St Thérèse', *Carmelus* 20(1973), 44-93.

26. See works cited in notes to chapter eight above, 'Missions and Missionaries'. See also *Heilsverantwortung bei Therese von Lisieux* (Leutesdorf: Johannes-Verlag, 1976); L. Ferrigno, 'Dall'esperienza mistica all'esperienza missionaria', *Riflessioni* 29-30(1990), 23-36; 33(1991), 17-23; 37(1992), 30-48.

27. E. Carroll, 'Thérèse and the Mother of God', *Experiencing Saint Thérèse Today*. Carmelite Studies 5 (Washington: Institute of Carmelite Studies, 1990), pp. 82-96.

28. D. Barsotti, *Nella comunione dei santi* (Milan: Vita e Pensiero, 1970).

29. *Thérèse de l'Enfant-Jésus: Docteur de l'Amour*. Rencontre théologique et spirituelle 1990 (Venasque: Éditions du Carmel, 1990); P. Descouvemont, *Sainte Thérèse de l'Enfant-Jésus et son prochain* (Paris: Lethielleux, 2nd ed. 1970); C. Gennaro, 'La sofferenza, sacerdozio d'amore: Teresa di Gesù Bambino,' *Rivista di vita spirituale* 36(1982) 534-547; E. Gutting, *Nur die Liebe zählt: Die Mission der Theresia Martin, ein Weg für alle* (Leutesdorf: Johannes-Verlag, 1974); F.-M. Lethel, *Théologie de l'amour de Jésus: Écrits sur la théologie des*

saints (Venasque: Éditions du Carmel, 1996), 161-196, see also 139-158.

30. A. Dagnino, 'S. Teresa di Lisieux, dottore della Chiesa?', *Rivista di vita spirituale* 39(1985), 286-297; P. Droulers, 'Le doctorat de sainte Thérèse de Lisieux proposé en 1932', *Vie thérésienne* 33/132(1993), 243-279 – *Ephemerides carmeliticae* 24(1973), 86-129; G. Gaucher, 'Thérèse, Doctor of the Church?', *Sicut Parvuli* 54(1992), 55-56; B. Laluque, *Un docteur pour l'Église: Thérèse de Lisieux* (Paris: Nouvelle Cité, 1987); J. Likoudis, ed., *St Thérèse of Lisieux: Doctor of the Church?* (New Rochelle NY: Catholics United for the Faith Inc., 1992); L. Merklen, 'Le doctorat ecclésiastique de sainte Thérèse de Lisieux,' *Vie thérésienne* 34, 83-86; P. Poupard, 'Sainte Thérèse de l'Enfant-Jésus, docteur de l'amour et le monde de l'incroyance,' *Vie thérésienne* 31(1991), 69-83; see collected essays in *Thérèse de l'Enfant-Jésus: Docteur de l'amour* (Venasque: Éditions du Carmel, 1990).

31. O'Donnell, art. 'Doctors of the Church' (n. 11), pp. 136-137.

32. See Decree on the Training of Priests, *Optatam totius* 16.

33. K.H. Braun, *Ich habe meinen Platz in der Kirche gefunden: Therese von Lisieux und die nachkonziliare Krise der Kirche* (Leutesdorf: Johannes-Verlag, 1983); C. de Meester, 'Thérèse contemplative et son sens de l'Église,' *Vie thérésienne* 11(1971), 133-144; P. Descouvemont, 'Être utile à toute l'Église', *Vie thérésienne* 19(1979), 87-96; C. Gennaro, 'Una santa di oggi nel cuore della chiesa', *Ephemerides carmeliticae* 17-18(1966-1967), 417-440 – *Mysterium ecclesiae in conscientia sanctorum* (Rome: Ed. del Teresianum, 1967), 417-440; Louis de sainte Thérèse, *Ma vocation dans l'église* (Tarascon, Bouches du Rhône: Éditions du Carmel, 1965); G.V. Tobón, *Santa Teresa de Lisieux: Apóstol y profeta en la corazón de la iglesia* (Bogotá: Ed. Paulinas, 1986).

34. See B. Leahy, *The Marian Principle in the Church according to Hans Urs von Balthasar* (Frankfurt am Main – Berlin – New York: Peter Lang, 1996); C. O'Donnell, art. 'Mary and the Church' (n. 11) 291-294 for bibliography.
36. SSoul Ms B, 4v/ch. 9, 197 – OeuvC 229; the text of St John of the Cross is *Spiritual Canticle* 29:2.
36. LastConv 15,7,5/99-100 – OeuvC 1048.